CLAMOR
AT THE GATES

CLAMOR
AT THE GATES

THE NEW AMERICAN
IMMIGRATION

Edited by

NATHAN GLAZER

ICS PRESS

Institute for Contemporary Studies
San Francisco, California

Inquiries, book orders, and catalog requests should be addressed to ICS Press, Suite 750, 785 Market Street, San Francisco, CA 94103 (415) 543-6213.

Library of Congress Cataloging in Publication Data
Main entry under title:

Clamor at the gates.

     1. United States—Emigration and immigration—
Government policy—Addresses, essays, lectures.
2. United States—Emigration and immigration—Economic
aspects—Addresses, essays, lectures. 3. United States—
Emigration and immigration—Addresses, essays,
lectures. I. Glazer, Nathan.
JV6493.C57 1985   325.73   85–175
ISBN 0–917616–70–7
ISBN 0–917616–69–3 (pbk.)

CONTENTS

I
Introduction

II
Making an Immigration Policy

III

Immigrants and the Economy

V

Portents of the Future

VI

Conclusion

PREFACE

The subject of immigration, particularly for those of us living in the American Southwest, has an air of critical immediacy about it that removes it from the area of merely academic consideration. Nor is the Southwest the only region whose economy, mores, and politics are being rapidly changed by incursions of peoples whose backgrounds are far different from those of citizens of the nineteenth-century U.S.

In the past, ethnically and attitudinally, immigrants moved more or less easily into the American scene. They came here to "be Americans." Today some of the arriving groups are not agreed on this goal; they want top priority to be given to preservation of their own culture, and, in some cases, even language. The term "Quebecization" is being heard more and more in Southern California, and "bilingual education"—how it is taught, what it really means, and in what direction it is leading our society—is becoming a political as well as an educational issue. Former Senator Hayakawa's emphasis on English as a national language is no longer the subject of lighthearted banter, but is more and more regarded as an attempt to cope with a serious problem.

In this study, the authors confront this most important issue, its ramifications, and its consequences. To understand this difficult and extremely complex problem is the obligation of every thoughtful citizen, and how to relate the warm and noble invitation on the Statue of Liberty to what is actually happening will require the best thinking of all of us.

Glenn Dumke
President
Institute for Contemporary Studies

I

Introduction

1

NATHAN GLAZER

Introduction

The United States, it seems, remains the permanently unfinished country. Created by immigrants—though we call those who came before the United States was established "pioneers" or "settlers"—we have for a hundred years struggled with the question of "whom shall we welcome," to use the title of a major report on immigration policy, issued in 1953 by a commission appointed by President Truman. In 1985, it is clear we will be struggling with the question for many years to come. Our most substantial effort in recent years to forge a new immigration policy, one responsive to a variety of needs and appealing, it was hoped, to the largest possible consensus of American opinion, failed in 1984. In the wake of that failure, the broadest and largest stream of immigrants since the 1920s continues to flow into the United States. And opinion is confused and uncertain as to whether this adds to our strength or our weakness, as well as whether it demonstrates our openness and generosity, or our simple incapacity to forge a national policy on the key question of who shall be allowed to become an American, along with our helplessness before the decisions of cynical nations trying to rid themselves of unwanted people.

Twice before in the past sixty years we have succeeded, or so we thought, in settling this question, first in 1924, and then again in 1965. The United States was open to immigrants from all over the world without restriction for the first hundred years of its national existence. Admittedly, if those immigrants had not been primarily from the British Isles and Northwestern Europe, we would probably not have been so open. And, indeed, when Chinese immigration led to a xenophobic reaction in California, we introduced our first restriction on immigration by banning Chinese in 1882. When the same happened with Japanese immigration, we restricted it by a "Gentlemen's Agreement" in 1907. And in the aftermath of World War I, the decision was taken to freeze the ethnic and racial composition of the United States by restricting immigration almost entirely to the countries of Northwestern Europe. Immigrants would still be allowed to enter, but only a very few, compared to the million a year that had been entering before World War I, and the enormous numbers that wanted to enter in the wake of that war. Those who would be allowed to enter would be primarily the British, Germans, and Irish, and other peoples from Northwestern Europe. Those from Southern and Eastern Europe would be limited to tiny quotas. Asians would be banned entirely. Canada and Latin America were not to be restricted by quotas, but immigration from Canada did not bother the xenophobic America of the early 1920s much, and, while Latin America was excluded from the quota restrictions on Europe for reasons of international relations, one suspects that congressmen understood that immigration from Mexico and south of Mexico, if it threatened to become large, could be controlled by means other than legislated quotas.

The Immigration Act of 1924 was a remarkable document. It required a study of the ethnic sources of America's white population from the origins of settlement: quotas were finally set on the basis of the contribution of each nation to that national composition.

Between 1929 and 1968, quotas were determined by the 'national origins' formula which provided that the annual quota equal one-sixth of one percent of the number of white inhabitants in the continental United States, less Western Hemisphere immigrants and their descendants. The annual quota for each nationality was then determined by the same ratio to 150,000 as the number of inhabitants of each nationality living in the continental United States in 1920 to the total inhabitants, although a minimum quota for any nationality was 100.[1]

For forty years it appeared that the effort to freeze the growth of the United States through immigration and to limit the change in the sources of its population would work. In the latter half of the 1920s, as the United States prospered, immigration was off drastically. It remained low during the depression. In the 1930s and 1940s the consensus that the United States should have very few more immigrants was so firm that it tragically became impossible to bend the iron restrictions of the Immigration Act in any way to allow in Jewish refugees from Europe. How many more could have escaped is conjectural; but the tiny quotas rigidly adhered to for Poland, the Soviet Union, Hungary, Czechoslovakia, and Rumania, combined with the anti-Semitism of officials responsible for immigration, guaranteed that almost none of the hunted Jews of Europe could enter after 1939. Despite the fact that the Jewish community was growing in political influence, it could do nothing to budge the immovable consensus against more immigrants.

Even more surprisingly, the consensus survived the war against a racist enemy, and Congress set its face adamantly after 1945 against abandoning restriction by quotas, though it most harmed Hitler's victims. President Truman had to struggle continuously against a resistant Congress to make it possible for Displaced Persons to enter outside the quota system. He only succeeded in 1948, when Congress passed a bill that, unbelievably, discriminated against the Jewish survivors of the war and in favor of the ethnic Germans who had been expelled from Soviet Russia and the Baltic states.

The quotas stood firm even as the United States entered the period of postwar prosperity. And they stood firm when the Immigration Laws were revised after extensive study and hearings in 1952. It is startling to read in 1985 the Senate's justification, only five years after the end of World War II, for maintaining the quota system and the favoring of Britain, Germany, and Ireland as sources of immigrants:

Without giving credence to any theory of Nordic superiority, the subcommittee believes that the adoption of the national origins formula was a rational and logical method of numerically restricting immigration in such a manner as to best preserve the sociological and cultural balance in the population of the United States. There is no doubt that it favored the peoples of western Europe over those from southern and eastern Europe, but the subcommittee holds that the peoples who had made the greatest contribution to the development of this country were fully justified in determining that the country was no longer a field for further colonization, and henceforth further immigration would not only be restricted but directed to admit immigrants considered to be more readily assimilable because of the similarity of their cultural background to those of the principal components of our population.[2]

This was the thinking that made it possible in 1952 for the Mc-Carran-Walter Act to pass and become the keystone of American immigration policy. But it could not long survive changes at home and abroad. At home the immigrants of the great wave from Eastern and Southern Europe, and their children growing to maturity, were becoming more and more effective politically, developing greater resources economically, becoming bolder in asserting their wishes against a weakening nativism. Abroad, crises that produced waves of refugees from Communism—in Hungary in 1957, in Cuba in 1960 and later—were also changing public opinion about immigration. Perhaps more potent in changing these attitudes was the fading of fears of depression, as postwar prosperity continued, marred only by occasional recessions. Perhaps most potent was the radical change in American attitudes on race that accompanied the rise of the civil rights movement. The attempt to freeze the composition of the American people by favoring Northwestern Europe was increasingly seen as basically immoral and wrong.

Thus in the atmosphere of 1964 and 1965, when America's unfinished business in regard to race, poverty, and prejudice was attacked with determination, immigration was not left out. One could have imagined all kinds of replacements for the McCarran-Walter Act. A radically simple solution, though far from any sophisticated notion of fairness, was adopted. The total number of immigrants was still to be limited. Africa and Asia were to be treated the same as Europe. Every nation, regardless of size, would be allowed a maximum of 20,000 immigrants. Senator Sam Ervin, fighting the abandoning of national origins quotas said, with some justice, that he couldn't see why Ethiopia should have the same quota as England or Germany.[3] But these perfectly reasonable considerations were swept aside.

Once again the United States was to be finished, and the matter of immigration was to be settled, this time in the liberal and open spirit of 1965 rather than in the crabbed and xenophobic one of 1924. No one expected—or wanted—any great change in the volume of immigration as a result of the Act. The bill set a ceiling of 170,000 immigrants from the entire Eastern Hemisphere. Even though China and India were now on exactly the same footing as England, France, or Germany, it was in truth not expected that the sources of American immigration would change much, aside from demonstrating that the United States did not discriminate against Asians. Attorney General Robert Kennedy told a House subcommittee in 1964:

I would say [the number of immigrants to be expected] for the Asia-Pacific triangle . . . would be approximately 5,000, Mr. Chairman, after which immigration from that source would virtually disappear; 5,000 immigrants could come in the first year, but we do not expect that there would be any great influx after that.[4]

No one disputed the Attorney General.

The bill also, for the first time, set a limit on Western Hemisphere immigration, against the opposition of the administration, which wanted to maintain the exemption of the Western Hemisphere from numerical limits as part of the "Good Neighbor" policy. But no one expected any increase in Western Hemisphere immigration. Why should there be, when it was so low under the McCarran-Walter Act, which set no numerical restrictions at all? Attorney General Katzenbach testified to a House subcommittee that "if you look at the present immigration figures from the Western Hemisphere countries there is not much pressure to come to the United States from these countries. There are in a relative sense not many people who want to come."[5]

The United States was giving itself the moral satisfaction of passing a nondiscriminatory immigration act that it expected would in no substantial way change the sources or volume of American immigration. The people who were fighting for the bill were Jews, Italians, Greeks, Poles, who hoped their relatives, their fellow countrymen, and their co-religionists would have an easier time getting in, and the bill itself favored strongly the principle of family unification. But the prophets were wrong. It turned out the chief beneficiaries of the new immigration regime were Asians and Latin Americans.

Starting from a modest base, the numbers of Asian immigrants increased rapidly; and as they increased family reunification played a greater and greater role in enabling immigration and resulted in steadily larger numbers of immigrants from Hong Kong and Taiwan, the Philippines, Korea, and India. The disaster in Vietnam added Vietnamese, Cambodians, and Laotians. In the decade of the 1970s, astonishingly, the number of Asians in the United States doubled to three-and-a-half million. It will undoubtedly double again in the course of the 1980s. In 1984 six out of the first seven countries, by size of number of immigrants sent to the United States, were Asian.[6] But the first was Mexico. And that, too, was not foreseen by the reformers of 1965.

Thus a bill that had been expected to remove discrimination against the countries of Southern and Eastern Europe, that had been passed by the political weight of immigrants from those countries and their children and grandchildren who had become warp and woof of the United States, benefited others and was taken advantage of by others. For Europe, too, was benefiting from postwar prosperity. There was no longer any strong demand from Europe to enter the United States. Europe's standards of living approached and in some countries surpassed that of the United States, its social benefits certainly surpassed that of the United States, class boundaries there were increasingly a thing of the past, and educational opportunities expanded and abounded. What need for the United States?

Not so for the countries of Asia, Latin America, the West Indies, or, perhaps tomorrow, Africa. Immigration from Europe, as Figure 1 reproduced from the *Statistical Abstract* dramatically demonstrates, turned downward in the decade of the 1960s, and even more sharply down in the decade of the 1970s, while immigration from Asia and Latin America expanded dramatically.

Those who passed the Immigration Act of 1965 saw it as cleaning up some messy unfinished business of the past. But it remained unchallenged as the charter of American immigration policy for a very brief period. Of the two unexpected consequences, it was the immigration from Mexico and Latin America that put

Figure 1
Immigrants by Continent

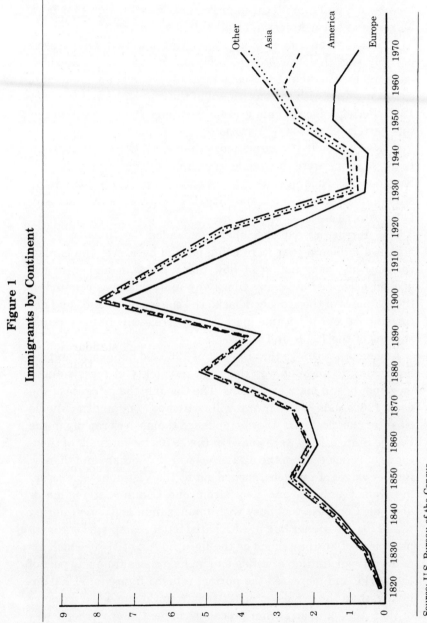

Source: U.S. Bureau of the Census.

the greatest strain on the consensus. The issue was not the substantial legal immigration. The United States had moved so far from prejudice that immigration again became an issue only because of the large illegal immigration. Why immigration from Mexico and Latin America, legal and illegal, expanded so rapidly in the 1970s and 1980s, is an interesting question. One reason possibly was that the *bracero* program for temporary Mexican laborers, instituted in 1942, coincidentally came to an end almost simultaneously with the enactment of the immigration reforms of 1965. Perhaps illegal immigration was only the continuation of this pattern of seasonal migration.

But very rapidly it became more than that. Other countries in Latin America were in trouble, economically and politically; and Salvadorans, Nicaraguans, Dominicans, and others joined the stream of migrants, legal and illegal. Nor were the illegals only Latin Americans.

The number of expelled aliens expanded: by the late 1970s almost a million a year were being pushed back over the border, without any clear notion of how many came in and were not pushed back, or how many times any individual was counted in the statistics of those pushed back. The consensus of 1965 had not come apart, but it became increasingly irrelevant to the circumstances of the 1970s and 1980s.

Among other things that the Act of 1965 did not expect and did not take into account was the grim possibility of mass refugee movements and mass expulsions. The Cubans, the refugees of the early 1960s, came of their own will, to escape Communism. Middle class for the most part, they established themselves rapidly in the United States. They were joined in the 1970s by hundreds of thousands of refugees from the disastrous war in Vietnam and then by further waves of refugees, pushed out by the Vietnamese or escaping from Cambodia and Laos, from one Communist regime or another. Congress was busy with immigration legislation during the 1970s. No sooner had it, with satisfaction, completed one complex piece of business, such as the Refugee Act of 1980, which expanded the definition of refugee to include those from any part of the world, and increased the normal refugee figure to 50,000 annually, than the expulsion of 120,000 from Cuba made a mockery of that Act—and any other procedure to deal in any orderly way with a refugee influx.

In 1981, as the Carter administration left office amidst a wave of immigrants, expellees, refugees, and undocumented aliens that seemed to be reducing American immigration policy to a shambles, the most distinguished of the various commissions and committees that have studied what to do about immigration reported.[7] The Select Commission had been set up by act of Congress in 1978. It was chaired by Father Theodore M. Hesburgh, president of the University of Notre Dame, and composed of members appointed by the President, the president of the Senate, and the Speaker of the House of Representatives. Its large and able staff was headed by professor Lawrence H. Fuchs of Brandeis University. The commission sponsored many volumes of research, conducted hearings, engaged in consultations, and its report and proposals have set the terms of debate over immigration policy in the years since it reported. But its proposals have not become law. The great effort to forge a bill based on the principles it proposed and that would satisfy a majority of Congress failed when the Simpson-Mazzoli Bill was finally abandoned in conference in 1984.

The issue of immigration will have to be addressed again, whether on the basis of the principles proposed by the Select Commission and Simpson-Mazzoli, or on some other basis. For it is hardly likely that the American people and its representatives will live indefinitely with the present situation in which no effective measures to control illegal immigration exist and we are divided on the question of what principles should govern our efforts to control immigration. No policy set by Congress, or the Executive, or even the courts—though their interventions have affected policy deeply—now truly control "whom we shall welcome." The country will not, I believe, allow the major lines of immigration policy to be set indefinitely by the individual decisions of the millions who would like to become part of the United States, or by the actions of nations, whether formally hostile or friendly, who drive out their own people or tolerate or create conditions that drive them to emigration. We will want to determine immigration policy on the basis of our interests. But what are those interests? Economic prosperity—what bearing does immigration have on that? Political unity—what bearing does immigration have on that? Are "interests" the sum of the decisions of an assemblage of individuals, citizen and noncitizen, businessman and worker, legal and illegal resident, each following his or her own interest—and is that the best we can do?

The first group of articles in this volume deals directly with the making and enforcing of immigration policy. Lawrence H. Fuchs considers the principles that should underlie our decisions, as formulated by the Select Commission and by the framers of the Simpson-Mazzoli bill, which was close to passage as he wrote. Harris N. Miller describes the problems of making a consensus in the Congress on immigration, problems overcome in the shaping of the Simpson-Mazzoli bill even though it finally failed to come out of a House-Senate conference. Edwin Harwood discusses problems of implementation of policy, which have in the last half dozen years loomed large in discussions of immigration, and raises the question of just how any policy we decide upon can be practically enforced. Rodolfo O. de la Garza brings up a key question that will continue to affect immigration legislation: what do Mexican Americans and their leaders think should be done, what shapes their thinking?

The next group of articles touches on a set of issues that immediately comes up in discussion of immigration, derived from the economic impact on other Americans. Thomas Muller discusses the impact of immigration on what has become the new chief "port of entry," Southern California. Vernon M. Briggs, Jr. asks about the potential economic impact of immigration on the present low-income and minority population. While immigration is generally discussed from the point of view of impact on labor markets, many immigrants become independent small businessmen or professionals. Ivan Light has long been concerned with the role of small business in immigrant and minority adjustment, and discusses here this phenomenon as it appears among Korean immigrants in Los Angeles.

The next group of articles deals with a disparate array of topics related to the social and political adaptation of immigrants. Peter I. Rose reviews the condition of the various groups of Asian immigrants. Nathan Glazer discusses the role of education in affecting the integration of immigrants and their economic opportunities. Peter Skerry takes up the topic of the political role of the Mexican Americans. Already our second largest minority group, and with growing political influence, the question inevitably comes up, is their political role to be similar to that of other immigrant and minority groups or different? All these articles deal basically with the question, how is the American melting pot now working? Better, worse, or just different?

The final two articles deal with the significance of borders, national sovereignty, and citizenship. Michael S. Teitelbaum considers the problem of mass expulsions, in which some people are stripped of their citizenship or their right to reside in a country—and other countries, the United States pre-eminently, must take them in. Peter H. Schuck asks how the impact of recent changes in law affect the status of illegal alien, alien, resident alien, citizen. The law plays an independent role in every American issue owing to the powerful role of an independent judiciary. It has extended the personal rights that had so expanded in the course of the 1960s to groups that were formerly not considered eligible for these rights. This expansion raises sharply the question of the boundaries of our political community. What should they be? It raises in the sharpest terms, "whom shall we welcome"—and why those and not others?

The articles in this volume attempt to provide the information and analysis that can help us in these determinations. No effort has been made to come to a common conclusion, or to propose policy. Rather it is the hope of the editor and authors of this volume that information and analysis can guide us to some kind of conclusion better than the policies that now prevail, policies set by law but in large part by drift and evasion of difficult issues.

II

Making an Immigration Policy

2

LAWRENCE H. FUCHS

The Search for a Sound Immigration Policy: A Personal View

In October 1978 the United States Congress established the Select Commission on Immigration and Refugee Policy, charging it with a review and analysis of all aspects of U.S. immigration policy. By the spring of 1979 all sixteen members of the commission had been appointed (four from the Senate; four from the House; four cabinet officers; and four appointed by President Carter, including Chairman Reubin O. H. Askew, later succeeded by Fr. Theodore M. Hesburgh). On May 22 I was appointed by the full commission as its executive director. After nearly two years of thoroughly bipartisan work, the commission made its report to Congress and President Reagan as specified by law. Subsequently, the Simpson-Mazzoli Immigration Reform Act of 1981 was introduced, embodying many of the most important recommendations of the Select

Commission. As former director of the staff of the commission, I often have been involved in defending its recommendations and supporting the Simpson-Mazzoli bill. Rarely have I been asked how I would disagree with or improve either, and I welcome this opportunity to do so.

Immigration is such an emotional issue, involving deep personal feelings and values as well as interests, that no one can be totally free of bias in approaching it. My own bias is and has always been clear. My father was an immigrant, as were my four grand-parents. I am clearly sympathetic to the view of the vast majority of immigrant historians that immigration is one way for the United States to do well by doing good. When the Swedish Academy of Sciences announced its Nobel Prize winners in 1984, three of the four American winners were immigrants.[1] This kept with the pattern that finds more than 30 percent of all living American Nobel Prize winners to be immigrants, as are 25 per-cent of the members of the American National Academy of Sci-ences. In addition to intellectual and cultural distinction, immi-grants contribute to economic growth, strengthen the cultural and linguistic resources of the U.S., and have children who actually outperform those of the native-born in school and workplace.[2]

These conclusions led the Select Commission on Immigration and Refugee Policy to recommend an increase in the admission of immigrants, the clearing of existing backlogs of immigrant ap-plications, and a substantial legalization of foreign nationals who are in the country illegally.[3] Yet, the commission was perceived by some as anti-immigration because of its recommendations for a more efficient enforcement of immigration limits to deter the future flow of illegal aliens. In fact, the commission's recom-mendations were pro-immigration and anti-illegal immigration, fundamental positions with which I agree.

The subject of immigration lends itself to a consideration of principles because it addresses fundamental questions of Ameri-can identity, and I urged the commissioners to think historically and in terms of principles. To address immigration policy is to ask: What kind of a country are we? What kind of a country do we wish to be, and why?

In debates on immigration narrow interests often masquerade as principle, as when U.S. Senators debating Simpson-Mazzoli and also representing agricultural employers took an uncharacteristically strong civil libertarian position that would have required the Immigration and Naturalization Service (INS) to obtain a search warrant before entering an open field where illegal aliens were believed to be working. But principles are critical to a discussion about the meaning of the country's past and future, and in the discussions of more than one hundred policy recommendations made by the Select Commission, three principles came up repeatedly: international cooperation, the open society, and the rule of law.

International Cooperation

The moderation of transnational migration pressures will require a sustained, long-term, and cooperative effort by many nations in order to reduce the tremendous disparities in opportunity that exist among nations. The poorest nations will continue to need substantial foreign aid and technical assistance to establish the basic elements of productive societies: educated, healthy populations, and minimal capital infrastructures. Better-off developing nations need to be able to sell their goods more freely in richer countries so that they can earn their way in the world economy. They also need foreign financing for their development programs. Certain essential actions such as land reform, population programs, and the extension of freedom must be taken by the poorer nations themselves. Others, like the establishment of international food reserves, will depend on regional or global agreements.

Unfortunately, the precise relationships of aid, investment, and trade strategies to the reduction of migration pressures are not clear.[4] One important benefit for the United States from a large-scale legalization or amnesty program should be the precise information it would give on the sources and characteristics of undocumented/illegal aliens now in the U.S. Such information would enable this country to target its aid and investment policies more precisely in order to reduce migration pressures in towns and villages that have sent many persons illegally across our borders in recent decades.

As difficult as it is to know what to do to reduce migration pressures, the Select Commission made a series of recommendations for the United States to take the initiative in promoting international cooperation on migration questions. Migration—like food, energy, and arms control—is an international problem, but that does not mean nations will respond to it through international action. Even though we live in a world of nation states, many of which in recent years have responded to international migration pressures simply by becoming more restrictive, the effort toward international cooperation must be made.

The U.S. perspective on migration pressures must also be regional, and the Select Commission made several recommendations to facilitate regional cooperation in its final report. Eventually, the United States, Canada, and Mexico may sign agreements that provide for free-trade zones and the free movement of persons across borders, but that time has not yet come. The question is how to get there. The U.S. must make its immigration policy clear and enforce it consistently and firmly while it also works toward strengthening international cooperation to alleviate migration pressures.

Unfortunately, the Reagan administration, while accepting many of the Select Commission's recommendations for legislative action, has virtually ignored recommendations for executive action leading toward international cooperation. Perhaps the problems blocking consultation are too formidable, but at the very least the U.S. should initiate discussion to promote regional cooperation on the following: economic strategies to help reduce migration pressures at the source; methods for enforcing the immigration laws of various countries effectively and humanely; ways to promote the human rights of aliens; and methods—probably through a regional convention—of preventing forced migration and arranging for the permanent and productive resettlement of asylees who cannot be repatriated to their countries of origin.

Even as we recognize the limits of international cooperation, we must recognize the long-term limits of a nation-state world in dealing with migration problems.

The Open Society

Since we do live in a nation-state world, we must decide what kind of a nation we want to be. To say that the United States is an open society is to repeat a cliche that needs specific definition. In terms of immigration to the U.S., the open society has come to mean that:

- Non-immigrant aliens—whether tourists, business persons, students, or others—will be welcome to this country as long as they do it no injury;

- Immigrants and refugees will be admitted to the United States in substantial numbers without regard to color, nationality, or religion;

- Once admitted to this country as resident aliens, such persons will be covered by the fundamental rights of the Constitution and the vast majority of entitlements afforded U.S. citizens; and

- Resident aliens, if they choose, may place themselves on a fast track to citizenship, becoming eligible for naturalization in the relatively short period of five years.

To say that immigrants and refugees will be admitted in substantial numbers is to imply that the open society does not mean limitless immigration. The application of both qualitative and quantitative limits is a function of national sovereignty. But those limits must never be imposed by reason of color, nationality, or religion; and once admitted to the United States, aliens should be welcomed and encouraged to take part in it and to contribute to its well-being.

While there is widespread public consensus in support of this definition of the open society, fundamental policy questions remain concerning the number of immigrants to be admitted and the criteria for choosing them, issues addressed below.

The Rule of Law

Like the open society, the rule of law has come to be another cliche in American public discourse. Everyone is for it, even though there is strong disagreement as to what it means. To the Select Commission it meant essentially two things: that the United States should not permit the buildup of an underclass society living outside of the protection of the law; and that measures to

enforce the immigration law should be effective without themselves engendering lawlessness or promoting an abridgment of
due process.

Unfortuntately, immigration lends itself to lawlessness. The
benefits are great; the tickets are scarce; administrative discretion is wide; political interference is commonplace; and the judicial
system governing immigration is slow and often lacking in cred-
ibility. At various points the commission addressed all of these
problems, although no recommendations can get around the facts
that there always will be wide administrative discretion and that
the possibility for political intervention and pressure with respect
to the allocation of extremely scarce and significant benefits will
continue under our system of government.

Principles do not make a policy, but they help. Even given agreement on these general principles, members of the commission did
not agree on all details of policy. What is remarkable is the extent
of the agreement that they did achieve. Consider, for the first
example, the question of how many immigrants should be admitted lawfully to the U.S. each year.

How Many?

In addressing the question, the Select Commission bumped into
the question of illegal immigration. How many illegal aliens are
there in the United States? What is the annual rate of illegal
entrants? How long do they stay?

Before the commission undertook its work in 1979, newspapers
frequently carried wild speculations by government officials as to
the number of illegal aliens in the U.S. A commonly repeated
guess was that there were as many as twelve million. One of the
first actions I took was to request the assignment of three top
demographers at the Census Bureau to review all of the studies on
counting illegal aliens. Concluding that "there are currently no
reliable estimates of the number of illegal aliens in the country or
of the net volume of illegal net migration to the United States in
any recent past period," they inferred from the available studies
that "the total number of illegal residents in the United States for
. . . 1978, is almost certainly below 6.0 million and may be substantially less, possibly only 3.5 to 5.0 million."[5]

The acceptance of those "guestimates" enabled the Select Commission to focus on the question of whether or not the U.S. should expand or reduce lawful immigration. Secretary of Labor F. Ray Marshall maintained that it was not sensible to recommend a change in the number of immigrants until it became clear that efforts to curtail illegal immigration would work, a position eventually adopted in the Simpson-Mazzoli bill. Still, a majority of twelve commissioners supported a recommendation made by Representative Hamilton Fish (R.-N.Y.) to increase numerically restricted immigration from 270,000 to 350,000 a year (exclusive of the immediate relatives of U.S. citizens and refugees). Representative Fish also recommended accepting an additional 100,000 resident aliens a year for five years to phase in backlogged applicants and the derivatives of newly legalized aliens, a recommendation that I believe is sound, in order to accommodate other Select Commission proposals to change the immigrant admissions system.

The backlog clearance plan recognized that the immediate family members of recent refugees (more than 200,000 in 1980) and the family members of newly-made resident aliens (and citizens in five or six years) would under the legalization program put some additional pressure on the immigrant admissions system. Finally, and most important, it was the overwhelming view of the commission that since lawful immigration is good for the country, a marginal increase in numbers would serve the United States well.

Keeping in mind that unemployment in the United States had reached double digits at the time of the commission's recommendation; the widespread public misperception that all immigrants take jobs away from Americans; the outrage of the American people when Fidel Castro pushed his own citizens out of Cuba in 1980; and the growing anger about visa abuse and illegal border crossings, recommendations for an increase in immigration may have seemed unusually bold at the time (1981).

But the recommendation was modest—assuming a growing capacity to curtail illegal migration. Although many journalists mistakenly suggest that immigration is now at an all time high, the proportion of foreign-born in the United States in 1970 was at an all time low since 1850 when the government began to keep those statistics and is still much lower than it was earlier in the century. Since the U.S. has the lowest population density of any wealthy industrial nation in the world, with the exceptions of Canada and Australia, and since the U.S. with only 6 percent of the world's population accounts for one-quarter of its gross national product, the recommendation to increase numerically limited immigration from 270,000 to 350,000 annually seems modest enough, particularly when one considers the enormous amount of evidence presented to the commission that we will want more skilled and unskilled labor by the year 1990, when there will be 7.1 million fewer persons between the ages of fifteen and twenty-four than there were in 1980. When one combines these factors and adds the recommendations for the effective curtailment of illegal migration—as distinguished from the Simpson-Mazzoli bill, which contained loopholes for the continued flow of illegal immigration—the commission's position that the front door could be opened a little more widely was not bold.

There is no magic or precision to the number 350,000. I certainly would support a larger number, as would have several commissioners; but the political opposition to even such a modest increase would be formidable in the face of continuing illegal migration. Opposition to the expansion of legal migration comes from organized labor, environmentalists, and xenophobes. Organized labor worries about the protection of the U.S. labor market, but as John Kenneth Galbraith testified before the commission, "one of the oldest errors in economics" is that "the job supply is limited."[6] Environmentalists argue that since Americans use non-renewable resources so voraciously, it is a mistake to add to our numbers. But I believe the argument of several ecologists who testified before the Select Commission that immigration to the United States probably has a positive effect on world ecology, since the populations in places such as Haiti, other Caribbean islands, parts of Latin America, most of India, Pakistan, and sub-Saharan Africa are abusing their natural resources at a far greater rate than is the United States. In addition, immigration to the U.S. actually may help to slow world population growth slightly, since the children of immigrants adapt to American fertility patterns rather quickly, and because the proportion of the world's population concerned about population control and environmental quality will be increased as a result of the transfer of ideas and appropriate technologies concerning resource conservation. The commission's recommendations for an increase from 270,000 numerically limited immigrants to 350,000 and for an additional 100,000 for five years starting in 1980 would yield an annual average of permanent net migration of about 500,000. This would bring the U.S. to a population of only 274 million by the year 2050, with a negative growth rate (population going down) of −0.08 in a world of perhaps as many as ten billion people, based on the following assumptions:

- Numerically restricted immigration would be 350,000 annually, with the rate of emigration at 30 percent;

- Numerically unrestricted immigration for the close relatives of U.S. citizens would average 170,000 annually, with the rate of emigration at 30 percent;

- Refugees would yield an annual average addition of 100,000 for sixty of the seventy years projected and 50,000 for ten of these years, with emigration at a rate of 5 percent.

- An additional 100,000 numerically restricted immigrants would be included to clear the backlogs for each of the first five years after the initiation of the new preference system, with approximately 30 percent emigration;

- The net permanent migration of undocumented aliens would be reduced to an average of 50,000 annually under *effective employer sanctions*, with emigration at about 30 percent;

- The legalization program would not significantly increase the number of permanent entrants to the United States; and

- National fertility would continue at a rate of 1.8.

Each of these assumptions is reasonable (but obviously subject to change) as explained in detail in the staff report of the commission.[7] With more economical living habits and appropriate technologies, the quality of life in the United States could be improved vastly even with a population of well over 274 million. Given the advantages of immigration to the United States—the reunification of families, the strengthening of linguistic and cultural resources, enhanced productivity and economic growth, a short-term strengthening of the Social Security base, and a validation of the American ideals of opportunity and freedom—we should be ready to increase lawful immigration just as soon as we make progress in controlling illegal migration. As for fears that an increase in immigration would negatively alter the composition of the population (the fear of foreignness so common in human experience) there are no objective facts to support them as long as the U.S. civic culture remains strong and we begin to get control over illegal migration.

What to do About Illegal Migration

The number of immigrants admitted lawfully to the United States for purposes of work through the third and sixth preferences may be no more than 54,000 a year (close to 40,000 one admitted) including children and spouses, who make up about one half of the total. The real labor recruitment immigration policy comes through illegal immigration, a condition that satisfies a great many interests: their employers; some ethnic group mobilization leaders and service providers; the governments of Mexico and other sending countries; and even American consumers. It is no wonder that it is so difficult to achieve a fundamental reform that might deter the flow of illegal or undocumented workers. Those interests are rationalized in terms of six basic perspectives, which would lead one to conclude that since nothing is broken there is nothing to fix. Despite the appeal of several of them, it is an argument I find unpersuasive.

The first perspective is the romantic immigration perspective. It holds that since most of us came from immigrant stock we ought to welcome those who seek opportunity, even if they come illegally. The second perspective focuses particularly on our relationships with Mexico. It holds that we cannot afford to turn off the safety valve of illegal migration from Mexico, even though it may constitute only about half of all illegal migration, because the future stability of that country will be adversely affected if we do. Third is the human rights perspective, holding that since there is a universal right to emigrate there must also be a human right to immigrate. This perspective involves a religious and/or humanistic view which puts the human needs of migrants above the sovereign authority of nations to limit immigration. A fourth outlook is the economic growth perspective, which holds that since undocumented labor actually increases the quality as well as the size of labor in the U.S. and in the aggregate contributes to economic growth, it would be biting off our nose to spite our face to attempt to defeat it.

There are two other more narrowly based perspectives. The first is the employers' perspective, held by those who benefit most directly from the availability of inexpensive labor (although many consumers also have an interest in the lowered cost of items produced by undocumented workers). There also is the perspective of Mexican American leaders, which stems in part from their desire for more constituents to lead and also from brotherly and sisterly feelings toward those who share ancestral culture and language, and who, like their own forebears, seek opportunity in the United States. That perspective is also shaped by some apprehension that new measures to curtail the flow of undocumented aliens will be harmful to Mexican Americans.

There are four other perspectives on illegal migration that would lead one to conclude that strong measures should be taken to prevent it. The xenophobic perspective applies to immigrants generally. The labor standards and labor displacement perspective emphasizes that docile workers lower standards and wages and even cause displacement. The environmental perspective maintains that unbridled illegal immigration will lead to a voracious consumption of resources in this country. The perspective of law and order and national sovereignty emphasizes that our borders are out of control and that the U.S. cannot exercise a basic right of sovereignty unless it regains control of them.

This last view shaped some of the deliberations of the Select Commission, although it seems to me that still other perspectives are the most compelling: fairness and national unity. The fairness perspective holds that it is unfair to have an immigration law that establishes limits and preferences in which a great many people find themselves waiting in line while others abuse their visas or cross the borders without valid documents. The national unity perspective holds that the growth of an underclass identified by ethnicity will undermine the civic culture, which holds American society together, by leading to rigid ethnic stratification, vitiating equal opportunity and protection of the laws.

Out of this melange of perspectives comes six basic approaches to the problem: leave it alone; regularize the flow through a guest-worker program; step up conventional enforcement, mainly at the border and through the enforcement of labor standards; pass an employer sanctions law combined with a secure system of employee eligibility and a legalization program for a substantial portion of the undocumented aliens already here; focus on the economic development of the sending countries; and develop a North American common market.

The last four approaches are not incompatible, and the Select Commission emphasized the third, fourth, and fifth. Its main legislative recommendations—employer sanctions and legalization—were adopted by the Reagan administration and made the centerpieces of the Simpson-Mazzoli bill. But important modifications were made in the recommendations of the commission during debate in Congress. The most important was the weakening of employer sanctions, largely at the behest of the Chamber of Commerce and the growers of perishable fruits and vegetables. Although Mexican American leaders were most noticeable in their opposition to employer sanctions, it was the pressure of the growers and business interests that succeeded in imposing changes intended to weaken and/or postpone employer sanctions. Thus Simpson-Mazzoli included: a transitional program for employers of illegal aliens to keep them for up to three years; a prohibition for the INS on making raids in open fields without a search warrant; and most important of all, a postponement on the development of a secure (counterfeit- and transfer-resistant) system of employee eligibility.

Much was made in the debate over Simpson-Mazzoli about the potential dangers of discrimination against foreign-sounding or foreign-looking persons as a result of employer sanctions. Opponents of the bill often charged that employers would choose not to hire such persons as a way of protecting themselves against potential prosecution. The same opponents usually decried the introduction of a national identification card as a part of the employee eligibility system. Actually, such a card is specifically repudiated in Simpson-Mazzoli, as it was by the commission. Of course, the identifier would have to be universal for the system to be secure and to protect aliens and others against discrimination, a point somehow obscured in much of the debate, but it would be a work-eligibility identifier to be used only when applying for a new job, and not a national ID that had to be carried everywhere or that could be requested by police and other authorities.

Also ignored by the opponents of employer sanctions is the fact that a tremendous amount of discrimination already exists, but mainly against young native-born Americans, particularly young unskilled blacks, and also against lawful resident aliens. The commission heard from many such persons, including one from Oakland, California:

I knew of many instances where my two younger brothers and other blacks would apply for jobs at the local factories only to be turned away. The pattern soon became very obvious to them. The majority of the workers in unskilled labor positions were Mexicans . . . the Mexican workers were cheaper and easier to have around. Many of the employers saw blacks as asking for too many things, such as equal wages, benefits, improved safety conditions, and unions.[8]

The fear that a system of employer sanctions would lead to discrimination is understandable, given the history of discrimination against Mexicans and Asians, particularly in the West and Southwest. It is a valid fear to the extent that the system is insecure and employers bear a burden of responsibility for deciding who is illegal and who is not. Under Simpson-Mazzoli, the system would have been unreliable for at least three years, but having seen and noted the identification requested, the employer would have a complete legal defense against sanctions, inhibiting an increase in discrimination. Since the appetite of employers for efficient, hardworking, and uncomplaining laborers is enormous, and since illegal aliens would be able to produce documentation providing presumption of legality when they apply for jobs (given the criterion of identification established in Simpson-Mazzoli), the problem would not be an increase in discrimination as much as a fundamental weakness in enforcement. My own view is that both the Congress and the commission failed by not specifying a reliable system of employee eligibility.

It was easy for the commission to agree on the principles that should underlie such a system of employee eligibility—reliability, uniformity and nondiscriminatory application, minimal disruption of existing employer practices, protection of civil liberties, and cost-effectiveness—but only eight of the commissioners favored the development of a more secure method of identification beyond existing forms. Most commissioners—including some who voted for a more secure method of identification and some who voted for an existing form of identification—preferred an updated, counterfeit- and transfer-resistant Social Security card. In my opinion, the Congress should move toward strengthening the reliability of the Social Security card and use it as the identifier in the employee eligibility system under a new employer sanctions law. That is the best way to prevent discrimination and enhance enforcement.

Simpson-Mazzoli attempted to deal with the concern many have about discrimination. It called for periodic reports by the President to the Congress as to whether or not employer sanctions seemed to be leading to discrimination against citizens and permanent resident aliens who are members of minority groups. It also required a report by the Controller General to determine if a pattern of discrimination was resulting from employer sanctions, and required the Judiciary and Labor Committees of both Houses to hold hearings on those reports annually. The conferees appointed to resolve differences between the Senate and House versions of Simpson-Mazzoli agreed on a modified version of an unusual amendment that passed the House, which created an Office of Special Counsel in a new U.S. Immigration Board within the Justice Department. Resident aliens who had expressed an intention to become citizens could complain to the new office if they believed they had been the victims of employment discrimination. A private complaint would trigger an investigation, strong remedies for the alien, and penalties for the employer, if found to be true. This procedure would have added an extraordinary measure of protection to aliens (in businesses employing four to fifteen persons) not available even to citizens under the Equal Employment Opportunity Commission (EEOC).

The principle of adding a specific measure of protection against alienage discrimination is highly controversial. I believe it is a sound one that should allay the fears many Mexican American leaders have expressed that employer sanctions will engender discrimination against Hispanics by employers who use the excuse of their anxiety about violating the law as a disguise for not hiring lawful resident aliens or citizens with a foreign accent. However such fears may be exaggerated—and I believe they are—the responsibility to protect against new expressions of discrimination is considerable for those of us who support the principle of employer sanctions.

There are alternative strategies to the one agreed to by the congressional conferees in October 1984, only forty-eight hours before Congress adjourned. I would find at least as attractive an extension of coverage for the EEOC or an amendment that would explicate that the Civil Rights Act passed after the Civil War (42 US Code 1981) to protect aliens against employment discrimination in businesses employing from four to fifteen persons. There are several advantages to amending Section 1981: citizens as well as aliens would be covered, the remedies would be more extensive, the statute of limitations would be longer, and there already is a body of judicial interpretation on the statute. The disadvantage would be that the courts are slow: the administrative remedies provided in the abortive Simpson-Mazzoli conference report would provide remedies more quickly. Either approach, or extending the coverage of EEOC, would recognize that as long as a large number of persons have a reasonable fear of discrimination because of the introduction of employer sanctions, there should be remedies provided in the event that those fears prove justified.

While the proponents of employer sanctions would have recognized that principle in the conference report, the opponents of sanctions never budged from their adamant opposition. They failed to acknowledge five basic facts supporting the view that employer sanctions would be a much more humane way of enforcing immigration limits and more protective of civil rights than the situation under the status quo. First of all, they ignored the injustice and ambiguity of an immigration law that specifically exempts employers from penalties for hiring illegal aliens. Second, they relied on conventional enforcement methods—an endless game of cops and robbers with frequent, terrible cases of exploitation, torture, rape, and murder of illegal aliens by smugglers and others—which are much less humane than employer sanctions as a means of deterring illegal migration. Third, the absence of a satisfactory identification for employment eligibility has led to discrimination against young citizens and resident aliens seeking employment. The fourth fact is that without employer sanctions

there is the real possibility of the growth of an underclass population well beyond the three-and-a-half to six million estimated by
the Select Commission, perhaps fifteen to twenty million by the
year 2000. Then it will be too late to act without either extremely
harsh measures (or a mass amnesty), and any attempt at their
implementation could tear the country apart. Finally, the opponents of sanctions never acknowledged the considerable good that
could have been accomplished by the legalization programs envi-
sioned by Simpson-Mazzoli as a part of the overall enforcement
strategy.

Legalization

The companion recommendation of employer sanctions—the
legalization of a substantial number of illegal aliens already in the
country—was not recommended by the Select Commission as a
trade-off to employer sanctions, as was frequently stated during
the Congressional debates on Simpson-Mazzoli, but because the
existence of such a large underclass is harmful for several reasons. It is an invitation to further illegality, since illegal aliens are
often afraid to report crimes committed against them. It invites
the breaking of laws regulating wages and work standards. It
takes enforcement resources away from the border and ports of
entry to the interior where they are less effective and more likely
to result in violations of civil rights and civil liberties. It also identifies certain kinds of work as fit only for foreigners and even certain nationalities.

Legalization was seen by all sixteen commissioners as a part of
the overall enforcement strategy and as a way to improve the
health of American democracy. Simpson-Mazzoli followed the
basic commission recommendations on legalization: to make it
relatively simple and comprehensive. Following these criteria, its
legalization provisions constituted a substantial improvement
over those recommended by Presidents Jimmy Carter and Ronald
Reagan. Whereas the conferees on Simpson-Mazzoli stipulated a
cutoff date of January 1, 1981, for legalization eligibility, the
cutoff date for participation in the program, in my view, should be
no longer than two years prior to legislation. Even then, no more
than 60 percent of the illegal aliens would be likely to qualify. The

unpopularity of the legalization idea—called "amnesty" by many—is understandable, and it is a tribute to Simpson-Mazzoli that it provided for a substantial legalization program against popular sentiment.

Guestworkers

Probably the most difficult issue faced by the Select Commission was the question of the desirability of a large-scale temporary worker program. Agricultural employers particularly stressed that even a substantial legalization program would not meet their need for seasonal employees. They acknowledged freely that they had become dependent upon illegal aliens. The Executive Vice President of the National Council of Agricultural Employers told the commission:

We're very concerned . . . that there may be legislation which would prohibit the employment of undocumented workers. And if such legislation is passed, then we feel with great alarm the problem of where we will get enough U.S. workers to do the jobs that have to be done.[9]

While recognizing the problems of agricultural employers, the commission recommended by a vote of 14 to 2 that the H-2 visa program, which requires an individual labor market test for temporary workers, should not be turned into a guestworker program, but only be streamlined to improve the timeliness of decisions regarding the admission of foreign workers.

My own view, after studying the history of contract labor in the United States and guestworker programs in Europe, is that the commission recommendation was exactly right.[10] The H-2 program, which permits employers to petition for the entry of foreign workers to perform temporary services or labor when U.S. workers capable of performing such services or labor cannot be found (including cane growers, sheep herders, musicians, dancers, and athletes) has averaged a little under 20,000 workers annually in recent years. About 12,000 of those workers have been agricultural workers, and no harm would come if it were expanded to about 50,000 or 75,000, as long as employers were obliged to upgrade standards for them as suggested below.

I favor the same changes in H-2 as incorporated in Simpson-Mazzoli before it was amended in the House into a guestworker program, an amendment that was eliminated in the conference. The Simpson-Mazzoli bill, as it passed the Senate, would have strengthened the program to shorten the period by which employers must request needed workers by obliging the Secretary of Labor to give a relatively prompt decision. In the event of a negative decision, the Secretary of Labor would have had to make a decision on an appeal within seventy-two hours after it had been requested, meaning that employers would not have had to wait until it was too late to get workers for some crops. But not enough was done in Simpson-Mazzoli to balance the interests of American workers against those of the employers. Because many H-2 workers do not participate in Social Security and unemployment compensation programs, a payroll tax gap exists between American and H-2 workers of 12 to 30 percent, placing a sharp disincentive on the recruitment and hiring of American workers. The disincentive could be bridged by requiring employers to pay FICA and unemployment insurance for foreign workers, some of whom could even collect sums owed to them after they returned to their own countries.

In general, immigration policy should not be used as a labor subsidy on a large scale for any sector of the economy. It is one thing to bring in a relatively small number of sheep herders who are expert in their tasks when American workers cannot be found to do the job. It is quite another to subsidize an entire industry with foreign labor, making it more difficult for workers to organize to improve wages and standards, and discouraging employers from developing innovative techniques of production. Employers have an insatiable appetite for inexpensive labor that should not be stimulated by a large guestworker program at the expense of American workers and innovative management.

Refugees

The basic provisions of the Refugee Act of 1980 should be left alone. I personally wish the United States and other receiving countries accepted more refugees than they have in the last two years, although I recognize that the up-front costs for refugees are substantial. I believe we can do much more than we have done to reduce the welfare dependency of refugees and that in the long run refugees and their children pay back considerably more than the initial costs to the rest of society.

I accept the Refugee Act's definition of a refugee as a person with "a well founded fear of persecution on account of race, religion, nationality, membership in a particular social group, or political opinion . . ." excluding only those who "ordered, incited, assisted, or otherwise participated in the persecution of any person . . ." The act thus provides a universal standard not bound by the specific ideological or geographic criteria that had been used in earlier definitions. However, in the actual allocations process, geographic and ideological considerations still are more important than they should be. That process begins in the State Department, and is refined in the White House before presentation to the Congress. As the Select Commission recognized, a lingering presumption exists in favor of allocating the bulk of numbers to refugees from Communist countries or who have fled past Communist persecutions. The act itself does not have to be changed, but in the allocations process specific numbers should be provided for political prisoners, victims of torture, and persons under threat of death, regardless of their geographic origin. Such an additional allocation based on refugee characteristics would increase flexibility and institute greater equity in allocations, as intended by the Congress in 1980.

Asylees

This aspect of our immigration policy needs change badly. Although the number of asylum claimants is not likely to be great in any given year, there are presently more than 160,000 whose claims have not yet been decided because of the large number of Iranian students claiming asylum, the flight of Salvadorans from their war-torn country, and the unusual number of Cubans (due to the Mariel exodus) and, to a lesser extent, Haitians, who have come to the United States in the last few years.

In contrast to refugees, asylum applicants must bear an individualized burden of proof in establishing their claim, giving tremendous discretion to INS examiners who sometimes require the applicant to produce documentary evidence and eye witnesses to substantiate it. Asylum admissions officers, now located in the

INS and carrying other duties, should get special training to deal with cultural distinctions in applicants' situations, a good grounding in interviewing techniques, and an understanding of the legal and ethical principles on which the definition of asylee is based. Placing the responsibility for the initial asylum determination in more expert hands would be an important step toward developing consistency and fairness in asylum policy. That is why I recommend that such responsibility be lodged in one unit of a highly prestigious Immigration Advisory Council.

Under the present system, applications require an advisory opinion from the Bureau of Human Rights and Humanitarian Affairs of the State Department before a final INS decision is made. That advisory opinion, understandably governed to some extent by foreign policy, is invariably conclusive, with the most flagrant example of the politicization of asylum policy having taken place in recent years in the routine denials of asylum to Haitians and Salvadoran applicants. In my view, asylum decisions should be taken out of the INS and the State Department altogether. I would give special responsibility for asylum decisions to the Immigration Advisory Council, which will be discussed subsequently. I would have group profiles developed by its research unit for use by asylum admissions officers, who would be specially trained in another operating unit. I also would create an Article I Immigration Court independent of the Justice Department, to hear appeals on decisions made by the asylum admissions officers. Simpson-Mazzoli went part way in attempting to improve the efficiency of the asylum decision-making process. It would have required asylum cases to be heard by specially trained immigration judges whose negative decisions could be appealed to a nine person U.S. Immigration Board within the Justice Department with one further appeal possible on specified grounds to a Federal Court of Appeals. The process would be insufficiently independent of the political system, and the State Department advisory opinions would continue to carry tremendous weight. Finally, I would create a new category of persons temporarily admissable to the United States, those who did not meet the well-founded fear of persecution test but who were fleeing from civil war and a strong possibility of death. For such persons the law should create the temporary status of safe haven, an issue not addressed in Simpson-Mazzoli.

By What Criteria Should Immigrants be Admitted?

The criteria for the admission of immigrants revolves around four issues. What proportion of the total number should be family related to citizens and resident aliens? What is meant by family? How should non-family immigrants—independents—be chosen? Should special consideration be given to geography or nationality?

Simpson-Mazzoli would not have changed U.S. policy with respect to any of these issues. My view is that an expansion of the total number of immigrants admitted would provide the flexibility to alter the balance between family and independents slightly, and that, in any case, greater emphasis should be put on expediting the reunification of *immediate* family members.

The Select Commission wisely recommended to separate independent, or non-family related immigrants, from those who come to reunify families. The best way to structure immigration policy to meet the goals of family reunification and for workers with needed skills would be to establish separate immigration channels, reducing competition between the two kinds of immigrants and providing for more flexibility than is possible under the present single-channel system.

Only two slight changes should be made in the admission of immediate family members of U.S. citizens *without* numerical restriction. Spouses and only *minor* children have long been admitted to the United States without limit. I believe it is advisable to allow all unmarried children of U.S. citizens to immigrate without limit regardless of their age. The distinction based on age makes little sense to me, and the change would not result in a significant increase in immigration since the existing first preference demand, a restricted category that now accommodates the adult unmarried children of U.S. citizens, has been for about 5,000 visas annually in recent years.

Parents of adult U.S. citizens also have been admitted as numerically exempt immigrants since 1965, and that should continue. I do not agree with the often made recommendation to admit the parents of minor U.S. citizens without limitation, or even under a numerically restricted preference, since that would be likely to encourage circumvention of the law, with even more women entering the U.S. illegally to have babies. But I would add the category of grandparents of adult U.S. citizens to the

numerically unlimited category. The number would be small, taking care of those few grandparents who, in many cultures, are
among the closest of relatives, and who might be left alone in their
homelands during their later years as a result of the emigration of
their families.

A great deal of thought has been given in recent years to expediting the immigration of second-preference applicants—the
spouses and minor children of U.S. resident aliens. Presently, they
are restricted numerically on a world basis (26 percent of 270,000)
and also fall under equal per-country ceilings (20,000). Many have
argued that the spouses and unmarried sons and daughters of permanent resident aliens should have the same numerically exempt
immigration status as those of U.S. citizens. That the exemption of
this group from numerical limitations would increase substantially the number of immigrant admissions does not trouble
me as much as the fact that it would weaken the significance of
citizenship in relationship to the allocation of immigration visas. I
think it is extremely important that the concept of membership in
the United States be made more robust than it is. But I would provide a substantial increase in the allocation of visa numbers for
this category—what is now second preference—in a new family
reunification system. If as many as 250,000 of 350,000 total
numerically limited visas were made available for family
reunification, up to 175,000 (70 percent) of these should be allocated to the spouses and unmarried sons and daughters of permanent resident aliens in order to expedite their immigration.

Presently, the backlogs for second preference are great in
several countries, separating spouses from each other and children from parents for many years. Expediting the reunification of
immediate families is extremely important as a matter of
domestic public policy, since resident aliens separated from
immediate family are much more likely to risk health and other
problems than those who have their spouses and/or children with
them. To further expedite the admission of such persons, I would
lift country ceilings for the spouses and unmarried children of permanent resident aliens and permit them to come on a first come,
first served basis within a worldwide ceiling set for that preference, a position adopted by the commission. While a reasonably
good argument can be made for the maintenance of equal per-

country ceiling in all other categories, the reunification of husbands with wives and parents with unmarried children should not be delayed for several years because of the nationality of the potential immigrant as it is under the present system for applicants from Mexico, Hong Kong, and other countries.

Another important change I would make in the law would be to provide for the numerically limited immigration of *unmarried* brothers and sisters of adult U.S. citizens rather than all brothers and sisters. The political resistance to such a change is strong, but its desirability is based on two considerations. First, the exponential growth in visa demand, particularly among married brothers and sisters (a sister-in-law emigrates with her husband and several children and in five years proceeds to petition for her brother and sister-in-law and children and so on). Second, the large number of visas that are currently allocated for all brothers and sisters of U.S. citizens (24 percent of the 270,000 numerically restricted immigrants) means that there are fewer visas for the spouses and minor children of resident aliens.

Independents. At the present time, no more than 20 percent of the 270,000 visas assigned annually under our world ceiling go to third-preference (members of professions, scientists, and artists) and sixth-preference (needed skilled or unskilled workers) immigrants—non-family immigrants and their spouses and children—called "independents" by the Select Commission. To actually qualify for third or sixth preference, immigrants must generally have special skills and have a job offer. The prospective employer must obtain labor certification from the Secretary of Labor showing that U.S. workers are not available and that the employment of aliens will not adversely affect the wages and working conditions of similarly employed workers in the United States.

I would assign approximately 100,000 visas to independent immigrants, including a small, numerically limited preference for those with exceptional qualifications in the arts, sciences, or the professions. It is important to expand the independent category because many persons who would like to immigrate live in newly-created countries in Africa and Asia that have not had recent immigrants and refugees to the United States, so there is no real base to reunify families. Others live in European countries such as the Netherlands or Ireland, whose migration patterns have been broken significantly in recent decades. Expansion of the independent category might also help to speed access for persons from countries such as the Philippines or India, where family reunification is an important method of immigration, but where the backlogs for third and sixth preference are particularly long.

Expansion of the independent category would encourage a continued diversity of immigration from many countries and counterbalance somewhat the heavy concentration and domination by three or four, something that would be enhanced if we lifted country ceilings for the immediate relatives of resident aliens as I recommended above. Independents still would have to qualify for entry. An increased proportion of entrants screened for labor market impact presumably would add some additional measure of protection to the U.S. labor market, while enhancing the pool of immigrants seeking opportunities to apply their skills. My own preference would be that such immigrants should be admitted unless the Secretary of Labor ruled that their immigration would be harmful to the U.S. labor market, a simple test that would facilitate the entry of ambitious hard-working immigrants, some of whom might be less skilled than those who qualify under the present third and sixth preferences.

Simpson-Mazzoli did not touch the per-country ceilings system, with the exception of providing an additional 20,000 visas for Mexico and for Canada. This was done primarily as a gesture to Mexico in recognition that until 1965 immigration from that country and from all over this hemisphere was subject only to qualitative exclusion and not to numerical limitation. It was also a gesture to both countries in recognition that Mexicans and Canadians have an affinity to the U.S. not shared by other nations. Presidents Ford, Carter, and Reagan all advocated extra visas for Mexico, along with Senator Kennedy and other congressional leaders on immigration. My own view is that extra visas should not be granted unless there is *at least* a commensurate increase in the overall world ceiling, something Simpson-Mazzoli failed to do. Otherwise, the practical effect is to take visas away from other high-application countries such as the Philippines, India, China, Korea, and Jamaica each year in favor of Mexicans and possibly Canadians. One should never forget that immigration basically deals with human beings and not with countries. Although there may be a good argument for equal per-country ceilings for a portion of the immigration flow to promote ethnic diversity, any system of equal per-country ceilings puts people in line according to nationality. Any system that allocates a larger number of visas to two countries makes it more difficult for persons from other countries to immigrate.

Exclusions. No analysis of the criteria for admitting immigrants should ignore the system that has evolved for excluding immigrants from entry into the United States. Here is a major policy issue that the Select Commission, and especially Simpson-Mazzoli, ducked. Although the commission voted 13 to 3 that "the present exclusionary grounds should not be retained," and recommended that Congress "re-examine the grounds for exclusion presently set forth in the INA," the issue was too much of a political hot potato, at least in the views of Senator Simpson and Representative Mazzoli.

Over 100,000 aliens each year are refused visas on the basis of one or more of the existing thirty-three exclusions, and in recent years from 350,000 to more than 400,000 aliens have been refused visas as non-immigrants on one or more of those grounds. There is no question that the United States has the right and obligation to bar the entry of aliens whose presence is likely to be harmful. But exclusions have not always been rational or fair. Often they have been racist, as in 1882 with the beginning of the Chinese exclusion laws, and in 1917 when the U.S. barred the entrance of Asians. In 1952 widespread fear of the Soviet Union led to legislation which excluded individuals for beliefs rather than actual or likely behavior. As a result, many distinguished scientists and philosophers have been excluded even from visits to lecture or attend conferences. Homosexuals are kept out, too, on the absurd ground of "psychopathic personality," and the legislative history of that term makes it clear that their exclusion was intended by Congress, no matter how much one might disagree with that intent. The results are extraordinarily harsh, as the commission heard repeatedly in public hearings. One man testified that his sister could not visit him, even temporarily, because she had previously stated she was a lesbian. The commission heard a story about the harassment of a group of women, traveling from Canada to a music festival in Michigan, by an inspector curious about their sexual preference. The exclusion that perpetually bars the entry of all drug offenders—even lawful permanent residents with long periods of residency—makes no distinction between a narcotics trafficker and a person guilty of possessing one marijuana cigarette. One U.S. citizen told the commission of his French Canadian wife who was permanently ineligible for a visa because of a conviction for possession of less than half an ounce of marijuana.[11] The time is long overdue for making fundamental changes in our system of exclusions. The key to rational change is to get rid of exclusions based on an individual's presumed beliefs or lifestyle, and to retain only those exclusions that bar persons whose presence in the United States would constitute harm to national security, public safety, public health, or public welfare (the public-charge exclusion should be retained to keep out those likely to go on welfare).

One other desirable change not touched in Simpson-Mazzoli has to do with the re-entry doctrine, which subjects resident aliens returning to the U.S. from a temporary trip abroad to scrutiny under all thirty-three exclusions. It is disgraceful that persons who have lived here for decades should be subject to a public-charge exclusion if they once received welfare payments. The only exclusions that should be maintained for returning resident aliens are for those who have committed crimes, engaged in persecution, or entered the country unlawfully.

Through What Process: The Administration of Immigration Policy

The problems of administering grounds for exclusion concerning belief and lifestyle speak to a critical issue in the administration of immigration policy generally: administrative discretion. It is not possible to avoid giving wide latitude to administrators of immigration laws and regulations even though in an asylum and refugee hearing the stakes may be life or death. The INS adjudications officer reviewing a petition to adjust an applicant's status from visitor to immigrant, and the State Department consular official reviewing an application for admission as an immigrant, have the power to decide the future of a human being. Yet, someone must do these things. The questions are who, within what structure, by what guidelines, with what supervision, and providing what protections for the individuals being affected?

The INS often has been treated as a pariah by Congress. Congressmen who frequently put pressure on INS officials to handle special cases in a certain way have routinely refused to vote funds to upgrade INS service and enforcement functions.[12] The service function has been neglected because of insufficient personnel and antiquated record keeping, and also because of the development of an enforcement culture, an *I gotcha* mentality in an agency in which border patrolmen are frequently advanced to the position of District Director. In answer to the question, What should we do about the INS, one commissioner, a member of Congress, told me: "Abolish it and start all over." In the end, the commission decided that the problems were not structural so much as attitudinal. Unlike the Truman Commission in 1952, which recommended the creation of an entirely new commission to administer immigration laws, the Select Commission recommended that the present structure be retained, with visa issuance in the Department of State and domestic operations in the INS of the Department of Justice. To change the structure might only cosmetize what is a fundamental problem of will. Does the country, through the Congress, care sufficiently about immigration policy to provide for a well staffed agency with proper resources to carry out its responsibilities?

One recommendation that should be made into law but that is unattended in Simpson-Mazzoli, is that the head of the INS should be upgraded to Director, at a level similar to that of other major agencies within the Department of Justice, such as the FBI, and he or she should report directly to the Attorney General. Another important change would be to have a clear budgetary and organizational separation of the service and enforcement functions of INS, to keep the enforcement mentality from penetrating the service responsibilities. The Select Commission also made important recommendations—although not a matter of law—to upgrade the professionalism of INS employees, along with recommendations for increased funding levels, so that INS could better carry out its job.

An immigration advisory council. There are certain important functions now not being performed or being performed inappropriately by the INS and the State Department that should be lodged in an Immigration Advisory Council. Made up of prestigious Americans given overlapping terms, the council, which might have appointees including ex-Presidents or ex-Secretaries of State, would have a small central administrative staff and three functional sections: research, asylum admissions, and general inspection. The research unit would be responsible for coordinating all research in the federal government on immigration and its impacts, and for developing group profiles for use by the second unit. The Asylum Admissions Office would make the initial determinations in asylum cases, as already mentioned. The third unit would be an Inspector General's Office, whose small staff of ombudsmen would investigate complaints and initiate inspections to improve rationality and equity in the various agencies responsible for the administration of immigration policy (the Department of Justice, the Department of Labor, and the Department of State). The Advisory Council would be responsible for making annual reports to the Congress, and every five years it would make recommendations on immigration policy changes. It would be authorized every other year to modify the total world ceiling on immigration within set limits of no more than 15 percent up or down, depending upon global and domestic factors affecting immigration.

In its reports the council would highlight problems in the administration and coordination of immigration policy, something that is rarely done presently from within the Departments of Justice, State, and Labor. Because of the prestige of the council members, it might be influential in helping to reduce conflict and ambiguity in the administration of policy (at one point, the INS did not exclude homosexuals but the State Department did). With its independent, prestigious status, the council also might serve as a check on unwarranted congressional interference in the administration of immigration laws.

Another major structural change—recommended by the Select Commission but not a part of Simpson-Mazzoli—that should be adopted by Congress would be the creation of an Immigration Court under Article I of the United States Constitution to replace the existing Board of Immigration Appeals. As noted above, the U.S. Immigration Board created under Simpson-Mazzoli would also be in the Justice Department, which means that it would not be as significant or as resistant to political influence as an independent Article I court. The advantage of the new system under Simpson-Mazzoli is that the new board would hear decisions made by immigration judges appointed by the chairman of the board instead of by the Attorney General. The change is a slight step forward, but an Article I Immigration Court would be more likely to attract outstanding jurists than the Immigration Board created by Simpson-Mazzoli. A majority of the Select Commission was converted to this view including the Attorney General, Benjamin Civiletti, even though the power of the Justice Department and the Attorney General would have been reduced. An improvement in the caliber of personnel would enhance the quality of decisions and generally eliminate the need for further review except in rare cases. The Immigration Court should include a trial division to hear and decide exclusion and deportation cases, and an appellate division to correct hearings and permit definitive, national, binding resolutions of such cases. An Article I court would promote judicial uniformity in the review of denials of applications and petitions, matters that now occupy the attention of district courts around the country. Although the remedy of Supreme Court review by petition for *certioari* would remain available for the rare immigration case of great national importance, time consuming reviews of immigration decisions by the U.S. Supreme Court of Appeals would be eliminated.

Simpson-Mazzoli—for all of its many merits—also failed to address several of the recommendations made by the Select Commission for enhancing both enforcement effectiveness and the due process of those who are the principals in asylum, exclusion, and deportation proceedings. Three major issues should be covered in new legislation beyond measures taken in Simpson-Mazzoli: the powers of INS officers, the right of aliens to legal counsel, and limits on the deportation of aliens. As pointed out above, the Immigration and Nationality Act allows INS officers great latitude to arrest, interrogate, and search. Because the statute is silent on several matters, the U.S. Supreme Court and lower federal courts frequently have issued opinions limiting INS enforcement practices in order to bring them within the purview of the Fourth Amendment, resulting in the curtailment of INS enforcement activities. In Simpson-Mazzoli, a major step is taken to go beyond the courts in restricting the INS. By amendments that were passed in both houses and strongly supported by employers as well as the Civil Liberties Union, the INS would have been prohibited from conducting a search on open farms without a search warrant, even though a recent Supreme Court decision permits a warrantless search in a factory under certain conditions.

The Select Commission, while greatly concerned about the due process rights of all individuals within the United States, took the view that the INS should not be hampered unreasonably in its enforcement activity. I would permit arrests in open fields without the authority of a warrant, but such arrests should be supported by probable cause to believe that the alien to be arrested is a person unlawfully present in the United States. Moreover, warrantless arrests should only be made when an INS officer reasonably believes that the person is likely to flee before an arrest warrant can be obtained. The law also should provide that arrest warrants may be issued by the INS District Directors or Deputy District Directors, the heads of sub-offices, and Assistant District Directors for investigations, acting for the Attorney General. This would make it possible to obtain warrants without undue delay. When persons are arrested outside of the border area without a warrant, they should be taken immediately to the INS District Director, the Deputy District Director, or before an immigration judge to determine whether sufficient evidence exists to support the initiation of deportation proceedings. As for arrests at the border, persons arrested without a warrant should be taken without delay before an immigration judge or a supervisory INS official to determine if the evidence is sufficient.

The key to fair process here is a uniform standard known to all enforcement officers and formulated in a manner that is consistent with the Fourth Amendment. The statute should authorize INS enforcement officers to detain temporarily a person for interrogation or a brief investigation upon reasonable cause (based upon articulable facts) that the person is unlawfully present in the United States. The INS must be permitted to do its job, but individuals must be protected against the arbitrary abuse of authority. Hence the need for a probable cause standard and for strong penalities written into the statute against officers who use illegal means to obtain evidence (instead of existing mild administrative remedies), even though such evidence probably should not be excluded in deportation cases.

Also important is that the right to counsel and notification of that right should be mandated at the time of exclusion and deportation hearings, and when petitions for benefits under the INA are adjudicated. Existing provisions of the INA limit the right to counsel to exclusion and deportation hearings under court rulings, something that should be corrected in the statute itself. As a matter of practice, INS already advises persons of their right to counsel at the time of arrest, but such a practice should be established in law.

Another improvement in due process would be to provide counsel at government expense to legal permanent resident aliens in deportation or exclusion hearings when they cannot afford legal counsel or obtain free legal services. With about one thousand such cases annually, the number is too small to impose a great cost. The matter is too important not to give maximum protection to permanent resident aliens involved in deportation proceedings. Finally, one change not made in Simpson-Mazzoli that is desirable has to do with the provision called "suspension of deportation." Suspension of deportation refers to a section of the Immigration and Nationality Act providing that persons who are in the U.S. unlawfully, have been here for seven years, and are not otherwise excludable should be allowed to stay in the country if they can show that their removal through deportation would result in extreme hardship. The word "extreme" has led to a variety of interpretations that often seem to be punitive to the alien involved, and it should be eliminated from the act.

Conclusion

Simpson-Mazzoli went a considerable distance toward fulfilling the requirements of an optimum Immigration and Nationality Act. It reaffirmed that this country will continue to remain a nation of immigration at substantial levels. It endorsed the Refugee Act of 1980, keeping the admission of refugees separate from and not in competition with the admission of immigrants. It provided for a more efficient system for adjudicating asylum claims, although it did nothing to deal with the troublesome question of

the politicization of those determinations. It struck a balance between the needs of enforcement authorities and the right of
aliens, although I do not agree with some of the details of the
change. It would have introduced a national policy of deterring
illegal aliens through employer sanctions, in full recognition of the
fact that it will take at least seven to ten years for that system to
become substantially effective. It attempted to upgrade the
resources of the INS, although it did not make fundamental structural changes such as I have recommended to take certain functions away from the INS and the State Department and to place
them in an Immigration Advisory Council.

In all, Simpson-Mazzoli kept the front door open and made a
strong attempt to close the back door. I would open the front door
more widely and strengthen both the definition of family and independent immigrants; make much more explicit what must be done
to close the back door; and take greater care to protect the rights
of aliens in the processes of admission, exclusion, and deportation.
At the same time I would strengthen and upgrade the INS and
provide for much more coherent and prestigious oversight of our
immigration policy through the Immigration Advisory Council
and an Article I independent immigration court appointed by the
President of the United States. Finally, I would recognize that no
nation should try to deal with the issue of international migration
by itself. I would take several initiatives to strengthen international arrangements to manage the problems that accrue as a
result of transnational migration, and to inhibit the flows that
cause those problems, remembering always that immigration is
not just a source of problems but also of creativity and strength,
especially in the United States.

3

HARRIS N. MILLER

"The Right Thing to Do": A History of Simpson-Mazzoli

Conventional wisdom has it that Congress should not deal with immigration. Members of Congress, and Congress as an institution, are not considered well-suited to provide leadership on difficult issues, especially leadership requiring serious legislative effort as opposed to one-day headlines in the hometown newspaper. Further, Congress and its members are believed to be particularly ill-suited to deal with immigration, as it is a "no-win" issue for most candidates.[1]

Immigration legislation, by and large, is restrictive. Interest groups most concerned about immigration are generally against restrictions, while that part of the American public more inclined to be in favor of restrictions is not organized. When organized groups support restrictionist legislation, they usually do so only within very limited terms (e.g., no legalization, no guestworkers).

Yet against these assumptions, Congress has demonstrated leadership over the past four years by systematically dealing with legislation designed to restructure our nation's approach to immigration, especially illegal immigration. While many strongly object to the legislation, congressional consideration has not been rancorous. It also has been without resort to the xenophobia and racism that often characterized similar debates in the U.S. and many other countries, recently surfacing again in places such as France and West Germany.

The legislative action could not have begun without the groundwork of previous Congresses (especially by House Judiciary Committee Chairman Peter W. Rodino, Jr., who promoted employer sanctions and legalization in the 1970s), without the support of four successive administrations, including the Reagan administration, and without the work of the Select Commission on Immigration and Refugee Policy—chaired by former head of the U.S. Civil Rights Commission and president of Notre Dame University, Father Theodore Hesburgh—which helped fashion a consensus on the issue.[2] But the 97th (1981–82) and 98th (1983–84) Congresses, with the leadership of two previously relatively unknown legislators, Republican Senator Alan Simpson of Wyoming and Democratic Congressman Romano Mazzoli of Kentucky, have faced the most difficult aspects of immigration reform and have fashioned legislation that attained widespread support.

As this article was written, it was yet to be determined whether the Immigration Reform and Control Act, the legislation crafted by Simpson and Mazzoli, would become law. The bill had passed both Houses of Congress, but differences between the two versions had to be reconciled in conference and each House then had to vote on the conference version—or the Senate had to accept the House-passed bill exactly as it stood. Also, President Reagan would have had to sign the legislation, which he had indicated in general terms that he was willing to do. Of course, even if it were to have been enacted, we do not know whether it would have achieved its objectives.[3]

Because the bill did not become law, others will have to judge whether or not the nation's best interests were served. However, that the legislation had come so far merits the attention of students of immigration, congressional scholars, and the American people who might be interested to know that the legislative process does work, sometimes.

It is often said, incorrectly, that our nation does not have an immigration policy. The large number of illegal immigrants already in our nation and the large numbers who continue to enter illegally are seen as proof that we do not have a policy.[4] But the absence of serious attempts to deal with illegal immigrants is itself a policy, as are the decisions guiding the legal admission of further immigrants. Just as tolerance of certain tax loopholes is a policy on taxation, so a choice not to enforce seriously rules on entry into our country is a decision on immigration. To understand our present policy better, it is necessary to examine the historical background of Simpson-Mazzoli.

The immigration laws of our country, like those of most nations, do not always make for proud chapters in our history. Starting with the Alien and Sedition Acts of 1798, through the 1882 Chinese Exclusion Act, the quota systems established just after World War I, and the McCarran-Walter Act of 1952—passed over President Harry Truman's veto—our country frequently enacted immigration legislation rooted in xenophobia and racism. Though the Statue of Liberty in New York Harbor and Emma Lazarus's famous quotation inscribed thereon, "Give me your tired, your poor . . ." are held up as the symbols of America's attitude toward immigration, most of the products of the legislative process have been restrictionist, at least toward those who attempt to enter the country legally.

Restricting the entry of foreigners is the sovereign right of any nation, but the restrictions in our laws have been directed at particular nationalities. Politicians have often acted on claims that one group or another would not mix well in America, the "great melting pot." Many academics argue that immigration, especially the large-scale immigration that occurred in our country around the turn of the century, is vital to our country's growth and economic development,[5] but that has not deterred many nationally elected officials from taking a dim view of newcomers.

Perhaps the brightest spot to date in immigration laws was the 1965 reform that removed, to a large extent, the country-based quotas established in the 1920s. While still far from perfect, the 1965 legislation removed the racially and ethnically biased national origins program, which permitted admissions based on the percentage of people native to a certain country and their descendants already residing in the U.S. This concept, meant to limit admissions to Northern and Western Europeans, was replaced by a more neutral, though not entirely open-ended, admissions program based on family reunification and allowing people with special skills to fill gaps in our labor market. These new policies allowed large numbers of legal immigrants to enter from Southern Europe, Asia, and Central and South America.

These policies focused on legal immigration: the admission of people, under process of law, to reside in the U.S. There had been discussion about the need to stop illegal immigration—involving both surreptitious entry and legal entry in which people overstayed their temporary welcome, thus becoming illegal—and there are laws on the books against illegal entrants. But Congress and the nation demonstrated ambivalence about illegal immigrants.

On the one hand, there was the general anti-foreigner perspective heightened by the status of illegal immigrants as lawbreakers by definition, which led some to argue for strict attitudes toward illegal immigrants. On the other hand, there was a curious mix of generous-hearted people, ethnic groups, and employers who used illegal immigrants as cheap labor, all of whom wanted government to ignore illegal immigration. The result was a laxness toward illegal immigration with intermittent breaks for a show of toughness, such as the 1954 Operation Wetback, which led to the apprehension of over *one million* people, including some U.S. citizens.[6]

One of the most telling signs of Washington's refusal to deal systematically with illegal immigration was the failure to impose penalties on employers of illegal immigrants, though many believed such sanctions would discourage much of the illegal immigration. The policy of our nation was and continues to be that while those who are in the country without authorization are illegal immigrants, subject to deportation, those who hire illegal immigrants are not penalized.

In 1952 Washington made this policy explicit when it passed the so-called "Texas proviso" stating that the employment of illegal aliens was *not* "harboring," an offense under McCarran-Walter, passed the same year. The anti-harboring provision was meant to discourage the smuggling of illegal immigrants, a big business grown even bigger in recent years.[7] With the Texas proviso on the books, no employer could be found to have violated a federal law for hiring an illegal alien. The proviso, developed with the support of the southwestern growers, emphasized that Congress was not about to tackle what many felt was one of the major issues of illegal immigration—penalizing employers.

Various forces, especially organized labor, were unhappy with the Texas proviso's attitude toward cheap foreign labor. In the early 1960s, after twenty years of effort, labor was able to convince Congress to end the "bracero" program. This was a legal temporary work program bringing Mexicans into the U.S., which had been developed during the Second World War to deal with labor shortages. Still, the Texas proviso held. And to make enforcement even more difficult, the Immigration and Naturalization Service, the arm of the Justice Department charged with enforcing immigration laws, was systematically ignored and underfunded.

In the early 1970s, Congress decided to focus on employers. Congressman Rodino (D.-N.J.) introduced, and the House twice passed by overwhelming margins, legislation against hiring illegal aliens—the so-called "employer sanctions." With backing from President Richard Nixon's administration as well as organized labor, Rodino was able to convince a majority of his colleagues that illegal immigration was a serious problem and that it could only be controlled by making employers liable for hiring illegals.

Two groups Rodino could not convince were the employers themselves (especially in agriculture) and some leaders of the Hispanic American community. The latter group saw the legislation as potentially discriminatory against people with Spanish surnames. Hispanic spokesmen argued that if penalties were established against employers for hiring illegal aliens, the employers would refuse to hire people who "looked foreign," such as Hispanics.

While Hispanics did not have the political strength to stop employer sanctions, the agricultural industry did, particularly in the person of Senator James O. Eastland (D.-Miss.), Chairman of the Senate Judiciary Committee. Eastland bottled up the employer sanctions legislation in his committee after the House passed the bill. The numbers of illegal immigrants apprehended continued to grow, but Eastland would not budge.

By the mid-1970s Rodino, with support from the Ford administration, decided to tie employer sanctions to a limited form of legalization (or amnesty as it is more commonly known)[8] for some of the illegal aliens who had already been in this country for some time. One major argument for legalization was that it was the only practical way to deal with the hundreds of thousands, and perhaps millions, of illegal immigrants residing in the U.S. No one sought massive deportations such as occurred in the mid-1950s, even assuming the resources could be found for such actions. Also, deportations would seriously affect employers with illegal immigrants as long-term employees. Finally, legalization was humane. Chairman Rodino was able to get the employer sanctions/legalization proposal through his own Judiciary Committee in 1975, no further action was taken on the legislation.

The Carter administration tried to tackle the issue with a proposal in August 1977 for a new employer sanctions/legalization package. By this time, however, Rodino and other supporters of immigration reform had been disappointed so many times that this proposal also languished. To avoid accusations of doing nothing, Congress in 1978 established a Select Commission on Immigration and Refugee Policy to produce legislative recommendations.

Under the experienced hand of Father Hesburgh, the Select Commission—composed of members of Congress, members of the Carter cabinet, and public figures—conducted hearings throughout the country, developing policy positions that were drafted in December 1980. During the last few months of the commission's tenure, public interest in immigration was heightened by many things: by the Cuban boatlift, which brought more than 125,000 Cubans, some of them considered undesirable, to U.S. shores; by increases in admissions of legal refugees, mostly Southeast Asian "boat people"; and by growing press attention to the numbers of illegal entrants, past and present.

Laying the Groundwork

The Hesburgh Commission's voluminous report, issued in March 1981, made hundreds of recommendations on immigration and refugee reforms, most of them agreed to by the sixteen commissioners. The central recommendations were for employer sanctions and a legalization program. The commission also recommended revisions in the existing temporary worker program— called H-2, indicating its designation in the law—to help the agricultural growers, who would lose their large illegal immigrant labor force if employer sanctions were imposed.

Father Hesburgh put forth the central theme of the report when he wrote, in essence, that to keep the front door open, we must close the back door.[9] In other words, to maintain legal admissions, we must reduce illegal immigration. Hesburgh and the commission emphasized that in the minds of most Americans, and ultimately in the minds of their elected representatives, distinctions between illegal and legal immigrants were unimportant compared to how many foreigners entered the country. If the illegal flow could not be stemmed, the legal flow would face severe restrictions.

The commission's report was received graciously by congressional leaders and by Vice President Bush on behalf of the administration, though many believed it would meet the fate of most commission reports and be consigned to a shelf for study by scholars. Many factors stood against implementing its recommendations. Immigration was still a tough issue, and became even more controversial during the commission's existence, as noted above. In addition, the new Reagan administration played no part in preparing the report and there was no reason to think that this matter would be an administrative priority. Finally, the members of Congress chiefly responsible for handling immigration legislation in the 97th Congress, Alan Simpson and Romano Mazzoli, were new to their jobs as committee chairs and had not yet been tested.

Alan K. Simpson, a freshman Republican Senator from Wyoming, was no typical newcomer to Capital Hill when he was elected in 1978. His father, Millard Simpson, had represented Wyoming in the Senate, and the younger Simpson had a distinguished record in the Wyoming state legislature. Simpson was well liked and had served as a member of the Select Commission, supporting most of its recommendations. Still, when the Republicans became the majority party in the Senate after the November 1980 elections, few thought Simpson, who because of the new Republican majority became the chairman of the Senate Subcommittee on Immigration and Refugee Policy, was ready for a major legislative battle.

Democratic Congressman Romano L. Mazzoli, from Louisville, Kentucky, was first elected narrowly in 1970 and had a workmanlike reputation in the House. Also well-liked and respected, he was not known as a front-line legislator prepared to develop and pass controversial bills. He had never chaired a major subcommittee until he took over the House Judiciary Committee's Subcommittee on Immigration, Refugees, and International Law in 1981 and did not serve on the Select Commission, although he did sit in on their final deliberations. A Notre Dame graduate, Mazzoli had close personal ties to Father Hesburgh, who helped convince him to chair the Immigration Subcommittee.

Despite their comparative obscurity, Simpson and Mazzoli had several assets, perhaps the most important being that they liked and respected each other. Neither had overbearing career ambitions; both were known as workhorses rather than showhorses in the congressional corral. They realized early on that, to succeed in their project, they must hang together or hang separately; neither could proceed without the other.

Geographically the two congressmen represented areas where immigration was not a major concern and so they had no large interest groups from their districts closely monitoring their actions. While both had a personal interest in immigration (Mazzoli is the son of an Italian immigrant, and Simpson had been touched by the sight of World War II Japanese internment camps in Wyoming when he was growing up), they did not feel the electoral pressures experienced by legislators from California, Florida, and major industrial cities with large ethnic populations. To the extent that any legislator can rise above instincts for electoral survival on a tough issue, Mazzoli and Simpson were situated to do so on immigration reform.

To the surprise of many, Simpson and Mazzoli received important backing from the Reagan administration, particularly from

Attorney General William French Smith, although this took several months to develop. When the Hesburgh Commission report was issued, President Reagan appointed a task force, headed by Smith, to examine the recommendations and issue its own report. Skeptics believed the task force would be a graveyard. After all, President Reagan, Smith, and most of the White House inner circle were Californians, and California opposition to immigration reform, with the combined forces of growers and Hispanics, was well-known. Also, Commissioner Hesburgh and other Carter appointees were not favorites of the Reagan forces.

In July 1981 the Smith task force also proposed an immigration reform package, again with employer sanctions linked to legalization. The proposed legalization was much more limited than that recommended by the Hesburgh Commission, but was still tied to sanctions. The Reagan administration also proposed a 50,000-per-year guestworker program to help agriculture.

Attorney General Smith, a personal friend of President Reagan, came to believe strongly in the legislation—even if it meant a (to them) "generous" legalization program. His support was crucial, especially when certain Texas and California factions within the White House began to work against the bill and when the Office of Management and Budget began to throw around large cost figures associated with the legalization program.

A final positive element was the support of the newspapers. To an unusual degree, editorial boards from Maine to California adopted the central concepts of the immigration reform package as their own. With a few exceptions (the *Wall Street Journal* attacked employer sanctions regularly as an unworkable intrusion on business), liberal and conservative papers alike gave the issue of immigration reform a sense of urgency. Jack Rosenthal of the *New York Times* was awarded a Pulitzer Prize for his editorials on Simpson-Mazzoli.

Putting It Together

After extensive discussions, Simpson and Mazzoli had decided in the spring of 1981 to push their reform package, as quixotic as it seemed to most observers. They had no support as yet from the Reagan administration, many interest groups were against them, the House and Senate leadership had not made their positions known, and few of their colleagues were interested in voting on immigration matters.

Legislation, especially controversial legislation, needs to be ground through the congressional mill. Even though the fundamentals of immigration reform had been through extensive public hearings when Rodino promoted his bills in the 1970s, and when the Hesburgh Commission convened, Simpson and Mazzoli knew they would again have to conduct extensive congressional hearings. They had several objectives.

First, they had to educate themselves. As noted above, Senator Simpson was a member of the Select Commission and Congressman Mazzoli sat in on its final deliberations. But the Immigration and Nationality Act (INA), the basic statutory incorporation of immigration law, is one of the most complex and confusing on the books, even for those familiar with the subject. Initially the two did not know how much of the act they wanted to change. The Hesburgh Commission recommended significant changes throughout—changes that would have required a basic rewriting of the statute. Simpson and Mazzoli decided that hearings would have to cover many issues already studied by the commission.

They also needed to educate and ultimately gain support from their fellow subcommittee members. Though eventually some opposed the bill, in general Simpson and Mazzoli developed with their colleagues a rapport that aided the bill. Subcommittee members who supported the legislation strongly, particularly Congressmen Dan Lungren (R.-Ca.), Hamilton Fish (R.-N.Y.), Bill McCollum (R.-Fla.), Barney Frank (D.-Mass.), and Senator Charles Grassley (R.-Iowa), were important allies for Simpson and Mazzoli. That the very conservative Lungren and the very liberal Frank together developed a consensus in the House for the legislation indicated that it created strange ideological bedfellows, and that it could pass.

A third purpose of the hearings was to build a record for the House and Senate members. Hearings are often a "show and tell" exercise, in which the predilections of the members are reconfirmed by lining up supportive witnesses. This is especially true with respect to relatively uncontested legislation.

Immigration reform, controversial and initially lacking support in the committees and the bodies, required thorough and sub-stantive hearings. Further, extensive hearings provided a forum for opponents, especially Hispanic groups and business interests. Senator Simpson and Congressman Mazzoli very much wanted to develop a consensus on the bill, and hoped that the hearings would elicit ideas and approaches to immigration problems that would overcome the objections raised by groups initially opposed to the bill. In setting up their hearings schedules, both chairmen made special efforts to encourage those opposed to the bill to testify.

Counterbalancing the desire for extensive hearings was the realization that the two-year lifespan of Congress is indeed short. Unless the legislation was enacted during the First Session of the 97th Congress—during the calendar year of 1981—it was, in effect, doomed. No one would deal with immigration reform legis-lation in 1982, an election year. The two legislators decided to move quickly with initial hearings in the spring and summer of 1981 in the hope of introducing a bill and passing it late in 1981 or early 1982. This timetable proved unfortunately optimistic.

Simpson and Mazzoli began early on to try to maintain a bipar-tisan and nonideological approach. If issues became partisan or broke down along traditional liberal-conservative lines, chances for passing a bill would substantially diminish. They believed—correctly—that their most liberal and most conservative colleagues would be unlikely to support their bill because of employer sanc-tions and legalization, respectively. They needed a bill appealing to the ideological center.

Their first step was to schedule joint hearings of their two sub-committees, something unknown between the House and Senate Judiciary Committees since the hearings for the McCarran-Walter Act thirty years earlier. They could not hold all their hear-ings jointly, but wanted the initial testimony to be in front of their two panels. They held four days of hearings together, with wit-nesses such as Father Hesburgh, AFL-CIO head Lane Kirkland, leaders of business, religious, Hispanic, black, and agricultural groups, and, in mid-July, Attorney General Smith, who offered the administration's recommendations.

After the joint hearings Simpson and Mazzoli began more detailed hearings in their subcommittees. The Hesburgh Commis-sion report was never introduced in Congress in bill form, and although the Reagan administration bill was introduced, it was not considered an important vehicle for legislative action. Lacking a specific bill, both subcommittees held topical hearings that covered employer sanctions, legalization, temporary worker programs, and claims for asylum. While many groups could complain that their ideas were not adopted, few could say they were not heard.

Working and Waiting

Simpson and Mazzoli spent some four months in 1981–82 making decisions on legislative strategy. Most of those decisions were sustained through the next two years of Congressional consideration. One of their first agreements was to introduce a relatively simple bill of their own—that is, they were not going to rewrite the entire Immigration and Nationality Act. Most importantly, they were to introduce the same bill, at the same time, to each of their respective chambers. They knew their bills would change as they proceeded through the House and Senate, but they hoped that by introducing one bill they could focus the debate on basic concepts and more easily reconcile differences emerging in a conference of the two Houses should the bills pass.

On March 17, 1982, Senator Simpson and Congressman Mazzoli introduced the Immigration Reform and Control Act of 1982 (S. 2222, H.R. 5872) at a press conference. They had few cosponsors, but neither expected otherwise, since it would take time to develop support. At the time of introduction, those inside and outside of Washington who were interested in immigration had decided that Simpson and Mazzoli must be taken seriously. The hearings had been extensive and fair. They were not grandstanding, but had taken on a serious legislative task. Editorial writers, the Reagan administration, and various business, labor, ethnic, religious, and political elites around the country were supporting them and demanding action—though there were major disagreements on what that action should be.

Most thought (correctly, as it turned out) that there was not enough time left in the 97th Congress for passage of the bill. Senator Simpson and Congressman Mazzoli, with time as their enemy, moved quickly to hold hearings in their subcommittees on specific legislation known as Simpson-Mazzoli.

The legislation was pared down to what the authors considered to be the essentials. They emphasized a balance between ending the flow of new illegal immigrants and showing generosity to those already here. Primary were the sanctions and penalties against employers who knowingly hired undocumented aliens. They took as their own the argument that the flow of undocumented aliens would continue until the job lure ended, and that only by penalizing the employers could this be accomplished.

Coupled with this was a legalization provision, arrived at after intense discussion, allowing those who arrived prior to 1980 to apply for legal status. Neither Simpson nor Mazzoli was initially comfortable with legalization, but through their hearings and discussions both came to believe it was necessary and right. The legislation included a temporary status for the more recent arrivals. Some saw this addition as unfair, but in light of the very restrictive proposals floated in the past, it was considered generous.

Reflecting the concerns of agricultural interests who feared that employer sanctions would undermine their ability to find labor, the bill offered major revisions in the H-2 temporary worker program, a thirty-year-old provision of the Immigration and Naturalization Act used to admit very limited numbers of temporary workers. Simpson and Mazzoli decided it would be more efficient, and probably less controversial, to update and streamline an existing program rather than to establish a large, new guestworker program.

Their bill also made changes in the admission of legal immigrants, in response to the Hesburgh Commission's recommendations that 1965 reforms were too open-ended and not in line with the demand for entrance visas. They proposed a flexible limit on legal admissions (not including refugees who are admitted under separate provisions of the INA, under the 1980 Refugee Act) and future limitations on admission of certain relative categories, especially the so-called "fifth preference," brothers and sisters of U.S. citizens. With the number of people from around the world who were awaiting legal admissions reaching one million and escalating rapidly, Simpson and Mazzoli believed it was time for change.

The subcommittee hearings produced no startling results, and each chairman moved rapidly through the subcommittee mark-

ups. By early May, Simpson had guided the bill through subcommittee consideration, and Senate Judiciary Committee Chairman Strom Thurmond, supportive of Simpson's efforts (though he
had doubts about legalization), quickly scheduled the bill for consideration by the full committee. Senator Edward Kennedy (D.-
Mass.), ranking Democrat on Simpson's subcommittee and an expert on immigration who served on the Select Commission, had
major concerns about employer sanctions. However, he worked
constructively with Simpson to try to improve the bill. Full committee consideration ran smoothly. After some short delays,
Majority Leader Howard Baker (R.-Tenn.) moved the bill to the
Senate floor where it passed overwhelmingly, 80 to 19, on August
17, 1982.

Alan Simpson had convinced the U.S. Senate to pass an immigration reform bill. Perhaps what was most remarkable was his
ability to get a basically conservative, Republican-controlled body
to pass a generous legalization program.

Congressman Mazzoli's subcommittee also reported out a bill
with the major elements intact, on May 19, 1982. The fragile coalition he had started to build during the subcommittee hearings was
solidified during the markups. Chances for enactment during the
remainder of 1982 lessened considerably when full committee
chairman Rodino surprisingly announced that the House Judiciary Committee would not have its markup until after the Senate
passed its bill. Rodino's stated reason for his concern that the Senate might not pass a bill was that he did not want his committee to
go through a protracted markup, as it had three times in the
1970s, only to have the Senate fail to act again.

So Mazzoli and the growing number of House proponents had to
wait through the summer of 1982, until Senate passage, before the
bill went before the House Judiciary Committee in mid-September. The markup was lengthy but the bill emerged with its major
provisions intact, save for the removal of changes in the legal
immigration admissions. Rodino was able to convince a majority of
the members of the committee that those changes should not be
made—that the bill's focus should be restricted to problems of illegal immigration, not legal immigration. On September 22 the bill
passed the committee by a voice vote, but only after a motion to
send the legislation back to subcommittee narrowly failed. Oppo-

nents of employer sanctions and opponents of legalization had joined forces and almost ended consideration of the bill.

With only a few weeks until Congress was scheduled to adjourn for the year, and with four other committees wanting to look at the bill, Mazzoli might have been expected to give up. But he pushed forward with Rodino's help and encouragement from Republican Congressmen, and was given a reprieve when the congressional leadership decided a postelection session was necessary, mainly to handle appropriations legislation bogged down in preelection maneuvering.

The postelection House floor debate seemed anticlimactic because the House leadership, unsympathetic to the bill, allowed it to come to the House floor with almost unlimited amendments. The bill could only have been enacted in the last days of the session, with strong House leadership backing. Speaker Thomas P. O'Neill, Jr. (D.-Mass.), concerned about divisions within the Democratic party—especially between the Hispanics and liberals on one side and the more moderate Democrats on the other—had no intention of forcing the legislation through. Over three hundred amendments were filed—many by members of the Hispanic caucus opposed to the bill—and when last minute negotiations failed to yield any compromises, the House ended three days of debate with no resolution on the legislation. The 97th Congress ended, and so did the life of the first version of Simpson-Mazzoli.

Mazzoli had one consolation. As debate ended, he received a standing ovation from his House colleagues—a rare occurrence for any member. Whether they were for or against the legislation, the members of the House of Representatives knew they had seen an effort by Mazzoli that brought credit to the entire institution.

The Second Time Around

Simpson-Mazzoli did not pass the 97th Congress, but the stage was set to try again. For the first time, the Senate had passed a bill to deal with illegal immigration. The administration was generally supportive. The House came close to passage, and in its last few hours, the 97th Congress conducted a principled debate on an issue that had often generated bitterness. Broad support for immigration reform was now evident. Much opposition to the bill from business and agricultural interests had been tempered, with only Hispanic leaders remaining adamant.

Early in the 98th Congress, Simpson and Mazzoli decided to try again. Rather than introduce identical bills, as they had in 1982, they took up the legislation as it stood before adjournment of the 97th Congress. Simpson's bill, S. 529, was what had passed the Senate the previous August, and Mazzoli's, H.R. 1510, had passed the Judiciary Committee in September.

Each Congress begins with a clean slate, so hearings had to be held again. Both houses held hearings expeditiously. While the testimony was similar to what the legislators heard earlier, there were two differences. The agricultural interests developed a proposal, the "transition program," to adjust more slowly to the H-2 program. Some of the Hispanic opponents of the bill, especially Congressman Ed Roybal (D.-Ca.), the senior member of the Congressional Hispanic Caucus, advocated an alternative bill. Roybal proposed dropping employer sanctions and focusing on tougher enforcement of existing labor laws to clamp down on the hiring of undocumented aliens to work under conditions that violated those laws. Roybal argued that if employers could be forced to pay minimum wages and provide adequate working conditions, the incentive to hire the undocumented would be lessened.

Simpson and Mazzoli pushed their new subcommittee markups quickly, with both adopting as amendments a version of the "transition program." The Senate Judiciary Committee passed S. 529 on April 19, 1983, and after four days of debate the full Senate repeated its 1982 action by passing Simpson-Mazzoli by a vote of 76 to 18 on May 18, 1983.

Congressman Rodino again decided to wait for Senate action, but Senate passage was so quick that he scheduled House Judiciary Committee consideration for early May. The bill passed on May 5, 1983, by a 20 to 9 vote. The major amendment adopted, on a 15–14 tally, moved forward the cutoff for legalization to people who illegally entered the U.S. before January 1, 1982. The 1980 legalization cutoff date had been moved forward by Mazzoli's subcommittee to 1981, with the argument that another year had passed since Simpson-Mazzoli was first introduced; moving the cutoff date to 1982 was an even more dramatic change, because it greatly increased the number of individuals eligible for legalization.

The House committee consideration did not end there. As in 1982, four other committees—Education and Labor, Agriculture, Ways and Means, and Energy and Commerce—had some interest in the bill, and were allowed six weeks to offer amendments. The Education and Labor Committee, one of the more liberal House bodies, chose to study employer sanctions and the H-2 program. They agreed to amendments closer to the Hispanic caucus position, by calling for a weakening of the sanctions and the creation of a new procedure for complaints to be filed against alleged job discrimination produced by the sanctions. They also suggested limitations, as called for by unions, on the H-2 temporary worker program.

The Agriculture Committee proposed amendments to weaken employer sanctions in order to please the agricultural interests. They also adopted an amendment creating a new temporary worker program to allow foreign workers to harvest perishable commodities. Proponents of the amendment argued that the H-2 program, even with the Judiciary Committee improvements, still was not flexible enough to permit the entry of workers into the highly volatile perishable-commodity sectors of agriculture.

Mazzoli and Rodino, with the backing of the administration and the Republican Party leadership, pressed the House leadership for quick floor action, but nothing was scheduled. As the summer of 1983 passed into fall, the proponents had doubts about whether the bill would ever go the House floor. With a presidential election in 1984, Mazzoli was interested in getting rapid floor consideration.

Mazzoli's worst fears were confirmed in October, when Speaker Thomas P. O'Neill announced that the bill would *not* be considered on the House floor. The day the bill was introduced, Speaker O'Neill expressed concern about divisions within the Democratic party, particularly those setting the Hispanic caucus and liberal, big city members against Congressmen Mazzoli and Rodino. The Hispanic caucus, and particularly senior member Roybal, argued that Simpson-Mazzoli was a bad, Republican bill, and that its consideration would harm the Democratic party.

The event that influenced Speaker O'Neill was a report from Roybal that the White House planned to veto the bill when it passed Congress so that President Reagan would appear attractive to Hispanics, a major voting bloc believed to be up for grabs in 1984. Roybal informed the Speaker that the President's political strategists were convinced a veto would be a major political plus for him among the growing Hispanic voting population.

Although Simpson and Mazzoli were disappointed, they withheld comment. Not so the nation's newspapers and magazines, which launched a personal attack on the Speaker, the likes of which he had rarely suffered. From one end of the country to the other, editorials and ostensible news stories questioned his judgment. Few believed the President intended to veto the bill. Most saw the Speaker putting short-term partisanship above the national interest on a bipartisan issue. After weeks of persuasion, including a conversation in which Simpson was able to convince the Speaker that the President had no intention of a veto, Speaker O'Neill announced he would allow the bill to proceed to floor. Although he had no great love for the legislation, he would no longer stand in its way.

The next issue was how the bill could get reasonable consideration on the floor, offering sufficient opportunity for important changes, without the amending process becoming a filibuster. The complexity of the bill and its amendments, many of which referred to the same sections and were contingent on yet another amendment, only made matters worse.

In the end the House Rules Committee developed a strategem to allow sixty-nine amendments to be considered. These amendments, including all those proposed by the four other committees, and also key amendments by opponents of specific provisions (e.g., to strike employer sanctions) were placed in a pyramid when they dealt with the same provision of the bill. For instance, on legalization, members were given the chance to vote either for any or all of three amendments to limit the generous Judiciary Committee legalization program, or for an amendment that would strike the legalization program altogether.

After more delay, including avoidance of a vote on the bill prior to the June 5 California presidential and congressional primaries, debate began on June 11. It took seven days, but on June 20, in a vote closer than expected, the House adopted H.R. 1510, 216 to 211. The vote reflected many factors but the most fundamental one was that conservatives could not swallow the legalization provision and liberals could not accept employer sanctions. This situation, coupled with heavy votes by the large Texas and California delegations against the bill, gave Mazzoli only a small margin of victory—but victory it was.

Most amendments to the bill were defeated, including those to eliminate employer sanctions and the legalization program. However, the new temporary worker program, proposed by the Agricultural Committee, was adopted with lobbying from the agricultural groups and in spite of opposition by the AFL-CIO. Also, Majority Leader Jim Wright (D.-Texas), and heir-apparent to Speaker O'Neill, cool on Simpson-Mazzoli for the three years it had been before the House, offered and had adopted an amendment that retained the 1982 legalization cutoff date but added limitations, including a requirement that applicants study English. With his amendment included in the bill, Wright supported it, a vital addition given the narrow margin of passage.

How It Was Done

A majority of the U.S. Senate and a majority of the U.S. House of Representatives had been convinced that there is an immigration problem requiring legislation, and that the best possible solution would be any of the slightly differing versions of Simpson-Mazzoli. The President of the United States and the Attorney General were also behind the substance of the bill. Whatever the final outcome, the fact that the legislation had come this far—that the U.S. Congress, in particular, was willing to deal seriously with immigration reform—appeared to many to be a miracle.

There were the various agricultural interests, which, with a few exceptions, wanted to maintain the constant flow of illegal immigrants. Many business people, too, especially the Chamber of Commerce, were against the bill because of the employer sanctions, which they argued would force employers to become immigration officers, judging who is or is not in our country legally.[10]

Our neighbors in Mexico have not been supportive, seeing any attempts to close the border as a threat to a safety valve that allows many of their unemployed and underemployed to come to the U.S. and repatriate large sums of money. Also against the bill were civil libertarians who believed employer sanctions would mandate a national identity card (contrary to what the House bill explictly states); this was a threat to individual liberties in their eyes.

Many conservatives were against the bill because it would mean the legalization of large numbers of people who would, among other things, swell the U.S. population and tax the social benefits systems of many states. They could not accept that under any circumstances lawbreakers should be rewarded, even if those lawbreakers—the illegal immigrants—had entered mainly because the U.S. allowed them and even unintentionally encouraged them to do so by refusing to enforce seriously the integrity of our borders.

Organized labor was against the House bill because the House adopted the temporary worker program pushed by agriculture. Labor is for sanctions, border enforcement, and legalization—not the admission of temporary foreign workers to take jobs that they believe would go to American workers in the absence of the temporary worker program.

Finally, Hispanic political groups were strongly against the bill, though some public opinion polls showed a majority of Hispanic citizens supportive of employer sanctions. It seemed that no matter how generous the conditions for legalization or how extensive the protections against discrimination, Hispanic groups opposed the bill.

Who was for it? The *initial* support of organized labor was helpful, but they opposed the final version because of the new temporary worker program. Environmentalists concerned about population growth supported the bill, though they were uneasy with a generous legalization program.

Weighing the interest groups for the bill against those who opposed it, one certainly would have concluded that the bill should never have seen the light of day, let alone have passed the Senate and House. Also working against the bill, especially in the 1984 presidential election year, were presidential politics. The concern about trying to pass the bill in a presidential election year was one reason Simpson and Mazzoli moved so early in 1983. As noted earlier, agricultural and business groups, opposed to sanctions, tried to convince the Republican White House that President Reagan should not support Simpson-Mazzoli. Conservatives, opposed to en masse legalization, took the same position.

The Hispanic groups best exploited their weight as a voting bloc in the upcoming election by convincing all three major Democratic presidential candidates—Gary Hart, Jesse Jackson, and party nominee Walter Mondale—to oppose the bill. Hispanics did make up significant voting blocs in many primary and caucus states during the protracted Democratic nominating process, and advisors to all the candidates believed that support for the bill would be foolish. Gary Hart, with a large Hispanic population in his home state of Colorado, voted against the bill on both occasions when it came before the Senate. Jesse Jackson, forming his "rainbow coalition" in which Hispanics were to play a prominent role, argued strongly against the bill. Former Vice President Mondale, whose administration had proposed a forerunner to Simpson-Mazzoli, nevertheless also came out against the legislation. The Hispanics also tried to convince President Reagan that he had a shot at their support if he opposed the bill. Congressman Roybal had convinced Speaker O'Neill at one point that Republican strategists wanted the President to veto the bill to appeal to Hispanic voters.

Congress and the President, in tackling immigration reform legislation, demonstrated an ability to see a long-term issue and deal with it constructively. While it is difficult to distinguish all of the elements that contribute to a decision to face up to a given issue, examining the way immigration reform proceeded sheds some light. It takes a belief among opinion leaders that there is a problem, and that there is a viable solution. Newspaper editorialists, Father Hesburgh and his Select Commission, Chairman Rodino with his long look at the issue, and four successive Presidents and their Attorney Generals all helped foster the belief that illegal immigration was a real problem and that the basic elements of Simpson-Mazzoli were an appropriate remedy. No supporter believed the bill was perfect, but no one had developed a better alternative.

People on Capitol Hill and in the administration must be willing to operate against traditional political constraints because they believe in the issue. Simpson and Mazzoli were the keys to this bill, but many other Congressmen with dramatically different approaches to most issues also were willing to work together to help the legislation to emerge. Attorney General Smith refused to allow the administration to be diverted from its goal of seeing a bill enacted.

A compromise position, in "the public interest," was needed. Officials had to stand against the pull and push of special interests that want no legislation or only legislation on their own terms. The finely balanced compromise of employer sanctions on one side and amnesty on the other gave a majority of the members of the House and the Senate and the administration a position to support what arguably is best for the nation, if not best for each particular interest group.

It is said that Congress and the President have only dealt with immigration once in any generation: the post–World War I quotas, the post–World War II McCarran-Walter Act, and now Simpson-Mazzoli. Setting aside the question of whether immigration as a topic of legislation is in fact cyclical, and whether or not Simpson-Mazzoli was to be enacted and work as intended, it is unlikely legislation designed to deal with people coming to our shores will disappear from the political screen for another thirty years. Economists can debate how many immigrants we can afford to absorb and whether they help or hurt our nation. Demographers can debate population growth and the "push" and "pull" factors which send people from other nations to our country, but the issue will not go away. We can only hope that when future congressional and executive bodies are faced with immigration issues, they will deal with them constructively, as they have on Simpson-Mazzoli, so that we will never again see the day when nativism and racism become the basis of immigration policy.

Afterword

The 98th Congress did not take final action on Simpson-Mazzoli. The conference committee appointed by the House and Senate to work out the differences between the two bills reached agreement on most of the major issues in mid-September, but became deadlocked initially on an amendment to provide protections against possible discrimination against legal aliens, a murky area of the law. Congressman Charles Schumer (D.-N.Y.), who had not been active previously in the legislation, brokered an agreement on that matter, but it took a crucial two weeks near the end of the session for the agreement to be reached.

The conferees were then deadlocked on federal government payments to the states and localities for costs associated with providing services and benefits to newly legalized aliens. Simpson, after consulting with President Reagan and his cost-conscious budget advisors, insisted on a $1 billion per year ceiling on the federal reimbursements, while a slim majority of the House conferees (by a 15–13 vote) resisted that cap. Some observers believed the Simpson proposal would adequately cover the states' costs, but members from states that expected large numbers of aliens to be legalized in their states, especially California, argued the cap would force their states to accept financial burdens for what should be entirely a federal responsibility. The conference never officially adjourned, but ran out of time when the 98th Congress adjourned on October 12.

Even if the conference had reached final agreement on all issues, passage of the conference report through the House and Senate and signature by the President were not assured. Some of the compromise in the conference meetings had further alienated the special interests, and they would have fought hard to kill the conference agreement when it reached the floor of the House and Senate.

The outlook for immigration reform legislation in the 99th Congress beginning in January of 1985 is cloudy. The legislative process has to begin over again, because every Congress is unique. Simpson has indicated his willingness to move ahead for a third try, but Mazzoli and Rodino have not made their plans known. If President Reagan's second term Attorney General supports immigration reform in principle, that will give hope to the backers of Simpson-Mazzoli.

One wild card might have been presaged by the statement of Congressman Bill Richardson (D.-N.M.), the new chairman of the congressional Hispanic caucus, at a press conference near the end of the congressional session. Richardson said the Hispanic caucus would have to consider seriously some form of employer sanctions, realizing the strong support in the House and the Senate for them. Whether this means that accommodation between the supporters of sanctions and the Hispanic caucus is possible remains to be seen, but the statement does raise a glimmer of hope.

4

EDWIN HARWOOD

How Should We Enforce Immigration Law?

When he declared that America had "lost control over its borders," the Reagan administration's Attorney General, William French Smith, was merely stating a truism familiar to all. References to the "revolving door" at our southern border or, more generally, to the "immigration crisis" have become stock cliches. They refer to a breakdown in immigration enforcement that began during the late 1960s, accelerated during the 1970s, and continues to the present time. Although the number of illegal aliens living in the U.S. is not known, a conservative estimate of from three to six million is accepted by most scholars. Estimates of the net annual influx of illegal immigrants coming to the U.S. range from 200,000 to 500,000.[1] Whether the level of illegal immigration constitutes a "social problem" for our society is hotly disputed by scholars. Economists and policy analysts can be found on both sides of the fence. What is not in dispute is that the Immigration and Naturalization Service (INS) can no longer effectively deter illegal immigration.

Though it is almost certain that more illegal aliens are entering today than twenty to thirty years ago, it is much harder to know whether the level of illegal immigration is high by historical standards, especially when one adjusts for changes in the size of the U.S. population. America's extensive land and coastal borders have never been heavily patrolled. Even today, there are fewer than 3,000 border patrol agents to patrol approximately 6,000 miles of land border.

Arrests for entry without inspection (EWI) surged past one million in both 1983 and 1984. However, INS arrests are a poor indicator of the actual volume of entries. Paradoxically, they are probably high in large part because deterrence is so ineffective. Border Patrol agents are heavily concentrated in a few places having heavy illegal traffic, among them Chula Vista and El Paso. Despite a heavier patrol presence, crossings in these cities continue at high levels because they are *convenient* points for assembling and arranging transport into the U.S., compared with remote and more hazardous desert areas. Though illegal border crossers run the risk of apprehension, most are only briefly detained before being returned to Mexican customs. They can easily attempt entry a second or third time. Thus, though the Border Patrol can cheaply produce large numbers of EWI arrests, its linewatch and traffic check operations produce little in the way of effective *deterrence* against entry. To draw an analogy from local criminal justice enforcement: would shoplifters be deterred if, upon being caught, they were merely taken outside to a patrol car, made to wait half an hour, and then were released?

Besides the issue of whether INS has the capabilities needed to enforce the law, which at root is an issue of resource sufficiency, one must also consider the public's *attitude* towards immigration. Weak public support is an important political constraint facing the agency. INS officers refer to the public's "statute of liberty" syndrome. And the fact is that many Americans are highly ambivalent towards immigrants whether they come here legally or illegally. Though most Americans will tell pollsters they favor strict enforcement of the law, many are clearly much less supportive when the INS actually seeks to enforce the law against individual aliens, especially those who have managed to establish community ties in the interior. Citizens will often mobilize on the alien's behalf.[2]

The Problem

Although some argue that immigration control began to unravel when Congress moved to terminate the contract ("bracero") labor program with Mexico in the mid-60s, other factors are involved in the dramatic increase in illegal immigration. In the less developed countries of the Third World, political repression, increasing military conflict, economic destabilization, and high rates of population growth have emerged as potent "push" factors. To put it in economic terms, the "demand" for entry into the U.S. began to push hard against the "supply" of available preference (immigrant) visas.

Because of the visa bottleneck, many overseas aliens who cannot qualify for visas simply decide to come anyway. Today, in countries where the wait for an immigrant visa can stretch to seven, ten, or even more years, travel agencies and street vendors can be found close by U.S. consulates offering "shortcuts" to entry in the form of photo-substituted passports and forged visas. Some travel agents offer "package deals." They assist their clients in getting fraudulent supporting documents to enter as nonimmigrant visitors. Then, upon arrival, they arrange fraudulent marriages with U.S. citizens, which will qualify the alien for lawful residence—unless the INS is able to catch the fraud.

These foreign nationals, who enter *with inspection* but with fraudulent papers or visas obtained through fraud, constitute the "upscale" end of the market for illegal entry along with those aliens who enter legally as nonimmigrant visitors but then violate the terms of their visitor or student visas. At the other end of the market are the large numbers of Mexican and other Caribbean basin nationals who enter *without inspection* by surreptitious landings along the Florida coast or by walking across the land borders. In the case of many Mexicans, permanent residence is not the objective. Most are "guestworkers" who intend to return to Mexico.

Though Mexicans and other Latin Americans are believed to account for roughly two-thirds of illegal immigrants, the problem is both multinational and multifaceted. Besides the well-publicized mass crossings by Mexican nationals at the southern border, often occurring in plain view of outnumbered U.S. Border Patrol agents,

the issue of immigration control also involves *interior* enforcement
actions by INS' approximately 900 plainclothes investigators. Stationed mainly in the cities, INS' criminal investigators accounted
for almost 10 percent of the 1.2 million arrests made in FY1983.[3]
Interior arrests are costlier for INS than border arrests, not just in
terms of resources but also politically. Aliens who have lodged
themselves in the cities are more apt to resist deportation, and are
increasingly aided by ethnic and other activist groups whose
depleted treasury of civil rights causes is being replenished by the
crusade on behalf of illegal aliens, some of whom are refugees
from rightist Central American regimes.

Although Mexicans account for 95 percent of all arrests in the
U.S., INS officers encounter a diverse assortment of foreign nationals, including many middle-class aliens who work without
authorization or overstay their visitor (nonimmigrant) visas.
Still, INS believes that it apprehends only a very small percentage of the total number of illegal aliens living and working in
the cities.[4]

Prohibitory Approaches to Controlling Illegal Immigration

Both Congress and the public have tended to conceptualize the
solution to the *control* problem in terms of *prohibitory* as distinct
from tariff or other kinds of regulation. Athough the Simpson-
Mazzoli Immigration Reform and Control Act was not enacted by
the 1984 Congress, it may yet be resubmitted. It envisions curb-
ing illegal immigration through a combination of a strengthened
Border Patrol presence along with employer screening of new job
applicants. (This second control feature is referred to as the
"employer sanctions" provision.) If the bill passes, employers
would be required to verify the immigration status of their
workers.

Although the Simpson-Mazzoli bill is considered "innovative"
because of its novel and highly controversial employer sanctions
provision, it represents a continuation of the traditional *prohibitory* approach—of seeking to *bar* the entry and employment of illegals through civil and criminal penalties.

Unfortunately, prescriptions for immigration policy have

suffered from a serious vacuum of knowledge about the day-to-day operations of the INS and other federal agencies involved in immigration control. When the Hesburgh Select Commission on Immigration and Refugee Policy (SCIRP) reported its recommendations to the President and Congress in 1981, the voluminous research reports commissioned by SCIRP had almost nothing to say about the day-to-day administrative operations of the INS.[5] Given SCIRP's failure to commission research on the operations of INS and the immigration courts, the Simpson-Mazzoli bill is truly a shot in the dark. But equally surprising was SCIRP's failure to review the extensive research literature on the deterrent effectiveness of federal regulatory law in other contexts, a *sine qua non* for a policy remedy such as employer sanctions, which would move INS into the kind of employer-centered enforcement characteristic of EPA, OSHA, the FDA, and other agencies.

The assumption that the borders could be sealed by additional patrol agents was another unresearched premise in the SCIRP recommendations. Yet it cannot be known, for example, how many border patrol agents would be required to seal the southern border without knowing something about the deterrent impact of linewatch and other Border Patrol activities. Additions to the linewatch will increase the number of arrests but, barring a full "militarization" of the border, it is very unlikely to prevent determined aliens from entering. At best, the addition of 1,000 to 3,000 more agents might increase the inconvenience and cost of entry. But an increase in the cost of entry—what Herbert Packer has called the "crime tariff"—could, as will be discussed below, have perverse effects for interior enforcement. Moreover, with the exception of aliens who are abusive towards patrol agents or who are recognized as flagrant, repeat crossers, there is no penalty upon apprehension. (The small percentage of arrested aliens who are written up for formal deportation processing rather than returned directly to Mexican Customs may be inconvenienced by five to ten days in detention while awaiting their hearings. However, many of those processed for hearings will still be offered voluntary return in order to reduce the number of appeals to the Board of Immigration Appeals as well as pressures on INS' limited detention space.)[6] With the increase in the number of Central Americans being apprehended at the Mexican border, whom Mexican authorities refuse to take back, these pressures on detention space will continue.

Constraints on resources (available officers, alien detention and travel funds, immigration judges, federal prosecutors, etc.) leave INS with very few options. It must induce as many alien violators as possible to depart voluntarily. It achieves this in the case of most Mexican EWIs because of the ease with which they can reenter.

Besides a porous border, INS enforcement must contend with a legal system that began to impose heavier enforcement burdens on the agency during the 1970s. With *pro bono* assistance from civil rights and legal aid organizations, more aliens have begun to make full use of their appeal rights in deportation hearings. Though they will usually fail to obtain substantive benefits or relief after all appeals have been exhausted (e.g., Section 244 suspension of deportation, or political asylum), they can often delay their departure for months and even years. Many aliens who come to the U.S. for economic reasons can gain up to two years by putting in political asylum requests.[7] According to Yale Law professor Peter Schuck, the main thrust of the federal judiciary over the past two decades has been to expand alien rights in the manner of the liberalizing trends found in other public law contexts. As professor Schuck argues, and as I found in my field work, the main effect of a rights-centered liberalizing trend by the courts is that INS must invest more scarce resources to achieve a given enforcement outcome (e.g., deportation or criminal prosecution and conviction). Consequently, the bargaining position of aliens vis-à-vis the government improved considerably during the 1970s and early 1980s.

Sanctions deteriorate when the cost of enforcement is inflated by judicial intrusions that impose burdensome requirements on the agency.[8] Any view to improving immigration *control* requires looking beyond the borders to the impact of court-driven case law on INS enforcement efforts in the interior.[9] However, the major constraint on INS enforcement operations, especially in the interior, continues to be the woefully inadequate resources available to the agency. In many district offices the level of arrests made through raids on businesses ("employer surveys"), pickups on streets where day laborers congregate, etc., is a function not of the

number of illegal aliens INS officers could pick up but of judgments on the number of arrests that can be accommodated, which
in turn depends on the number of officers available to service
violators, the availability of interpreters (for groups that are non-
English speaking), whether local detention space can be found
(for aliens who cannot post bonds), etc. INS investigators,
moreover, have other duties involving alien benefit applications
("dual action" cases) that often have priority because aliens
awaiting benefit adjudications will complain over delays.

The enforcement dilemma posed by inadequate resources is well
expressed in the satirical lore of the field officers whenever they
pass a construction site where illegals are spotted: "They must be
citizens because we didn't have time to stop and talk to them." The
impact of an increase in arrests on the immigration courts must
also be taken into account. If too many aliens demand deportation
hearings, this will crowd calendars that are already heavily bur-
dened in some cities. In the case of Mexicans having no immigration equities, the officers may try to induce them to accept voluntary return (VR). A VR can be processed in fifteen to thirty
minutes but a deportation case may require one or two hours to
write up. And if the alien cannot post the bond, he will have to be
detained at a cost of $40 to $70 a night.

Resource constraints become the organizational imperative and
drive both official and unofficial policies at all levels. The gearing
of officer discretion is towards lenient rather than rigorous enforcement because of the imperative need to maintain equilibrium
between caseloads and resources. For example, patrol agents and
investigators may decide *not* to question certain groups of
suspected aliens for reasons of administrative expediency
("women with children take more time to clean up" or "if we
bring in deportable Poles, they'll just be given extended voluntary
departure with authorization to work").

The prototype policy adjustment occurred in the mid-60s when
uninspected entries began to escalate and important social control
tools had to be shelved. Whereas before, Mexican EWIs might be
detained a couple of weeks until the FBI kicked back their
fingerprint checks, the Border Patrol finally had to abandon the
policy of routinely fingerprinting all aliens. Expedited voluntary
return directly to the border also emerged as the most frequent

administrative action for most violators. Though the lenient policy of voluntary return was used for most first-time offenders even during the 1950s and 1960s, it became even more prevalent as the arrest caseload at the border began to escalate after 1965.

The threshold requirements for criminal action also rose. In the 1950s, simple EWI cases were sometimes charged and prosecuted for the misdemeanor of entry without inspection because federal magistrates apparently had the time to take such cases. Even in the busier sectors, repeat EWIs might be fined and given jail time in the 1950s and 1960s. (More typically, identifiable repeat offenders were repatriated back into the Mexican interior by bus or plane.) By the late 1970s, however, the EWI charge (8 U.S.C. 1325) was reserved almost exclusively for plea bargaining purposes in smuggling cases.[10] And smugglers, unless they are identified as principals or major operatives of professional rings, frequently get minimal sentences or probation because of the rising caseload pressures on the federal courts.

Rethinking Simpson-Mazzoli

Even prior to the end of the 1984 Congress, passage of the Simpson-Mazzoli Immigration Reform and Control Act appeared very much in doubt. Although the Senate approved its version of the bill (S. 529) in 1983 by a large plurality, the House's separate version (H.R. 1510) had passed with only a five vote margin (216 to 211) in June 1984. Given the thin margin in the House, it was questionable whether the Senate-House Conference Committee could have reconciled their differences in a way that would have been acceptable to the House. Not only was the Hispanic caucus in the House intractable in its opposition toward the employer sanctions provision of the bill, but the Democratic presidential and vice-presidential contenders Walter Mondale and Geraldine Ferraro had also announced their opposition to the legislation.

However, Simpson-Mazzoli will probably be resubmitted. In the event that it is eventually signed into law, it would represent the most far-reaching overhaul of U.S. immigration policy in over thirty years. It also would be likely to have major consequences for INS enforcement policy. For these reasons, a brief review of the bill's possible policy impacts is warranted.

First, Simpson-Mazzoli would confer amnesty on an estimated two to four million aliens who have been living illegally in the U.S. How many would receive amnesty will depend on which date Congress finally sets as the cut-off for establishing continuous residence in the U.S. (The 1984 Senate wanted 1980, the House 1982.) But it would also depend on how many aliens decided to come forward to apply. Though the amnesty measure is by no means popular with many legislators, some have taken the view that amnesty is a necessary even if distasteful "trade" for the bill's control features, in particular employer sanctions, a strengthening of the border patrol, and expedited exclusion hearings (which apply to aliens barred from entry at the time they present themselves for inspection or who have otherwise not effected a legal or illegal "entry").

Though most Hispanic lawmakers have no objection to amnesty, they will have none of employer sanctions. The Hispanic lobby believes the worker verification requirement might lead to discrimination against brown-skinned or other "foreign-appearing" workers. Civil libertarians are also upset over the possibility that a new identification document may eventually be authorized by Congress despite the fact that neither the 1984 Senate nor House version required a new identification card for Americans.

The *political* flaw in Simpson-Mazzoli is that it is a "public interest" as distinct from a "pork barrel" bill. This is the reason why it could pass the Senate without too much difficulty but had an uphill struggle in the House. To be successful, controversial "public interest" bills, even if approved by a majority of Americans (as determined by surveys) must mobilize interest group support. However, the groups that *dislike* various of the bill's provisions have been much more forceful in mobilizing opposition to "restrictionist" (control) features of the bill than the much weaker restrictionist lobbies have been in holding together a necessary consensus coalition. For example, the agricultural interests have been able to get a provision into the 1984 bill that would have prohibited warrantless open-field searches by the Border Patrol, which would have effectively hobbled the patrol's farm and ranch checks. (That provision weakened INS' interest in supporting the bill and it also triggered opposition from other law enforcement interests concerned over how a warrant requirement might have affected their activities, for example, in pursuing marijuana growers.) The congressional disarray mirrors the relative weight of public attitudes on illegal immigration. Americans say they support more effective immigration controls but their support is shallow. And they do not give the illegal immigration problem a very high priority in comparison with other policy issues.

If the bill would pass in a similar form in a future session of Congress, what would be the likely consequences for immigration control? First, additions to the Border Patrol would be apt to be quite modest—perhaps 1,000 or so additional agents. They would not be likely to do much more than increase the number of border apprehensions—perhaps by half a million according to INS estimates.[11] Though this would entail additional resource costs for INS since the arrestees would have to be processed and transported—with a certain percentage requiring detention and deportation hearings, etc.—it cannot be known how many other illegal entries would be *deterred*. If deterrence is minimal, then the government has boughten only additional enforcement costs for itself.

The employer sanctions provision, which the bill's sponsors touted as the most important control feature, would have penalized employers who knowingly hired illegal aliens after a grace period. However, in the last House version, employers would have a complete defense against possible civil or criminal penalties if they followed the procedures set forth in the bill for verifying the immigration and citizenship status of workers hired after the bill's passage. It is not altogether clear whether employers would have been *required* to check worker identification. (The 1984 Senate wanted worker verification mandatory for all employers, but the House resisted a mandatory verification requirement.)

The problem, however, is that without a mandatory verification procedure, INS would have a harder time proving that an employer *knowingly* hired illegal aliens. Conceivably, some prosecutions might be made on the basis of testimony from illegal workers—assuming they would agree to testify that their employers knew they were unauthorized to work. But given the proof burden apt to be required of the agency, it is more reasonable to assume that successful prosecutions would be limited to those firms where illegal aliens who had previously been identified by INS are found working again. This, at any rate, was the State of Virginia's experience when employers suspected of hiring illegal aliens were prosecuted.[12]

But whether or not worker verification would be mandatory, employer sanctions could continue to flounder for several important reasons. First, employers lack the expertise to make immigration status determinations. While they can go through the motions of checking a worker's identification, they cannot be expected to detect counterfeit or fraudulent identification. Thus, the hoped for leverage of having employers screen out illegal aliens could well prove a mirage. Employers would risk civil rights lawsuits if they turn away workers whose documents they merely *suspected* are bogus. They could, of course, refuse to hire aliens who admitted to being unauthorized aliens or any who refused to permit their ID to be checked. The likelihood, however, is that most illegal aliens would simply borrow or purchase the identification required. There is also the risk that employers might only ask Hispanic or other "foreign-appearing" workers for identification but neglect to require this of those they consider to be "obvious" citizens. This would constitute *screening* discrimination, as distinct from *hiring* discrimination. Though it has not been raised as an issue by Hispanic opponents of the bill, it would very likely emerge as a major civil rights issue once the bill became law.[13]

Employers would be put into a difficult bind. Many citizens would resent the inconvenience of having to establish their right to work every time they changed jobs. No doubt many citizens who lacked the required documents would complain at having to first obtain proper documents. Employers who sought INS assistance in checking the papers of suspected illegal aliens would be unlikely to get prompt assistance from INS—if they got help at all. Would they defer hiring a worker they suspected might be illegal, which could risk a lawsuit? This dilemma would be especially intractable for employers in industries with high labor turnover.

INS would have plenty of dilemmas of its own. First, the burden of employer sanctions enforcement would fall on INS' 800 to 900 criminal investigators. There is no mention in the 1984 Congressional Record of additions to the Investigation Branch for the purpose of monitoring sanctions.[14] Considering how understaffed the Investigation Branch already is in relation to its current caseloads, one wonders where the officers required for monitoring employer compliance would be found. If employer sanctions were to be given priority, then investigators may well be taken away from cases involving more serious INA violators, which could severely damage the quality of interior enforcement overall. How many fraud or alien smuggling cases would have to be shelved in order to assemble the evidence required to slap civil fines on one or two garment manufacturers?

Without a substantial increase in the number of officers assigned exclusively to employer sanctions investigations, along with government trial attorneys and other support personnel, employer sanctions enforcement might, after an initial burst of agency attention, develop into a token symbolic effort. True, some notorious violators would be hit with stiff fines. A few might go out of business or even go to jail. But unless employers perceived a sufficient risk of both discovery *and* punishment, employer sanctions would be unlikely to deter violators any more effectively than other provisons of the INA currently deter alien smugglers, fraudulent benefit applicants, false citizenship claimants, etc.

Moreover, if the cost in resources to INS for successfully levying fines from employers was perceived as being too high, INS officers would begin to lose interest and assign investigators to higher priority cases. It happens already with respect to the vast multitude of INA cases that are theoretically open to the Service to prosecute criminally.[15] In sum, it is a real possibility that INS enforcement resources would be diluted and dispersed to deter the less serious violator categories (employed illegal aliens) and their employers. This could jeopardize the agency's recent drive in interior enforcement to target aliens involved in crime, entitlement (welfare) fraud, smuggling, and immigration fraud.

Furthermore, there are hazards in the amnesty provision, which would legalize the status of illegal aliens who could establish their continuous residence in the U.S. before the cutoff date. Legalization could do serious damage to INS enforcement during the eighteen months period for submitting legalization applications.

Why is this so?

The House version instructed the Attorney General not to exclude or deport any alien who presents a "nonfrivolous application" for amnesty. More than that, INS officers would have been required to notify apprehended aliens that they have a right to apply for amnesty during the eighteen month period.

If Border Patrol agents encountered persons they suspected were illegal aliens — even if apprehended close to the border — and the individuals claimed to qualify for amnesty, how would the agents have been able to handle these claims? How would they decide in the field that an alien's oral claim to amnesty was not frivolous? One could hardly have expected aliens to carry on their persons the tax returns, rental, and other receipts that might establish a non-frivolous claim. Border Patrol agents conceivably might try to "break" amnesty claims they suspect are fraudulent in the field through adroit interrogation of aliens, something they already do when they encounter aliens whose citizenship and lawful residence claims they suspect.[16] But with suspect amnesty claims, the agents would have considerably more difficulty testing their veracity. Because the House version gave the alien the opportunity to contact a community or voluntary agency for an opinion as to whether his claim was frivolous, INS officers operating under the constraints of limited time and resources would probably have had little choice but to release amnesty claimants in the field, though they might have felt warranted in processing some for deportation hearings. (Court interpretations of the statute may well have barred INS officers from offering voluntary return to amnesty claimants whom the officers suspected might have been bluffing. Typically, patrol officers are lenient with false citizen and "green card" claimants, and allow them to return voluntarily once they "fess up.")

Neither lawmakers nor, for that matter, most immigration policy analysts understand the microscopic complexities of field operations — what makes the engine of enforcement work. They probably do not realize that INS border and interior enforcement depend crucially on the willingness of illegal aliens to concede both their alienage and deportability. This is especially true for Mexicans who account for roughly 95 percent of all apprehensions. If most Mexicans did not accept voluntary return to Mexican customs but instead insisted on deportation hearings, immigration enforcement would collapse. *Any* policy innovations that might tilt the balance of incentives in favor of an increasing demand for hearings by Mexican EWIs risks doing severe damage to INS' enforcement tissues as well as to the immigration courts.

This could happen if illegal aliens learn that an amnesty claim would require that they be released with authorization to work pending a decision on their application. As noted, INS might require the alien to post bond pending a deportation hearing (in lieu of being detained). However, the agency cannot detain very many Mexicans because of the severe shortage of detention space, not to mention the limited number of immigration judges.

The key to an understanding of how immigration enforcement works is to note how *equilibrium* is maintained between the various component elements of a very complex and delicately cantilevered system. Disturbing this equilibrium can have far-reaching and unanticipated effects. For example, if the border were to be successfully tightened through the addition of a significantly large number of agents, somewhat fewer Mexicans might try to enter. However, powerful incentives to demand deportation hearings would be created for those who did get through (or who are already in the U.S.) because of the increase in the "unofficial tariff" (inconvenience and/or the prices charged by smugglers.)

Much the same applies to the amnesty option. It could ratchet incentives *against* Mexicans agreeing to accept voluntary return, which in turn could gear the system into a downward spiral by demolishing the Service's most important line of defense—it's ability to maintain a sufficiently high bond to induce aliens to accept voluntary return.

As more Mexicans asked to have amnesty claims adjudicated (or asked for hearings on whatever grounds), more would find that an amnesty claim would secure their release on a minimum bond of $500 or even on their personal recognizance while also, as the House version of the bill would have allowed, granting them authorization to work. In this way, amnesty might stoke up increasing resistance to voluntary return. Upon being released on a minimum bond (or no bond at all), aliens would then have the choice of either developing the documentation required to support their claim or going back underground.

One hesitates to publicize INS' vulnerabilities. But the fact is:

INS will probably not be able to investigate more than a small fraction of amnesty applications for fraud. (Nor would it be a rational policy for the agency to invest heavily in thorough screening of legalization applicants.) The agency might hope that publicizing successful prosecutions of vendors of bogus legalization documents, along with *ex post* denials of amnesty to the aliens who purchased the documents, might deter fraudulent applications. But it cannot do very much more than that. Individual aliens caught using forged tax returns, utility bills, etc. to pass the "continuous residence" requirement would have the same risk of prosecution as aliens who currently make felony misrepresentations (18 U.S.C. 1001)—in short, next to no risk of criminal prosecution at all.[17]

Additional Considerations for Stopping Illegal Entry

The problem with Simpson-Mazzoli is not just that it was unlikely to "turn off the magnet" to continuing illegal entry but that it might actually aggravate the current enforcement crisis by adding a new and more intractable enforcement caseload to INS. Given Congress' unwillingness to adequately fund the agency for its mission, which no doubt reflects the lower priority America places on immigration violations by comparison with drug smuggling, espionage, or other felonies whose social harm is indisputable, the bill had much more chance of destabilizing the perilous equilibrium currently being juggled by the agency than it had of improving the enforcement environment.

The options open to the government for controlling illegal immigration are very limited. Barring political upheaval in Mexico, it is unlikely that Congress and the Executive Branch would authorize a "militarized" southern border with the American equivalent of a "Berlin-wall" type of solution. (On the other hand, it would be irresponsible of the government *not* to consider such contingency planning well in advance. Though a Mexican political collapse must surely be rated a low-probability event at the present time, it *might* happen. If it did, national security considerations would clearly be relevant and might well justify draconian policy measures.)

For the present, and hopefully the future as well, draconian

remedies that might staunch illegal immigration will inevitably
run afoul of the many other political and economic interests that
must be accommodated in our polity. Many Americans benefit
from having large numbers of foreign visitors. Many also benefit
from having illegal alien labor, or at any rate they do not consider
the presence of aliens sufficiently injurious to mobilize and petition Congress on behalf of a serious enforcement effort, one that
would insure that INS had ample resources to deal with the
problem.

What is intractable at present is primarily the *political* aspect of
the problem. If illegal aliens *were* perceived as a serious threat,
then surely the resources would be found to deter their entry—
even if it required 20,000 patroal agents and investigators.

Absent a widespread public perception that illegal immigration
poses a major threat to the society, *prohibitory* regulation alone
will not work because it is unlikely to receive the level of resources
required.

What, then, might be done?

Immigration enforcement should seek to achieve a more optimal allocation of resources by looking at the differential social
costs imposed by different categories of INA violators. In interior
enforcement, INS should continue to refine its current new case
management system so that aliens who are perceived as imposing
the highest costs on our society are served first from the tray of
available investigative and prosecutorial resources.[18] Aliens (and
citizens) who are involved in organized smuggling, immigration
fraud, document counterfeiting, along with aliens involved in
crime or entitlement (welfare) fraud should have priority. In the
case of unauthorized aliens who apply for federal or state welfare
benefits, INS can obtain maximum enforcement leverage as well
as substantial public support by assisting other agencies with
screening. Indeed, screening state and local welfare agencies to
prevent illegal aliens from obtaining unauthorized benefits is probably the highest leverage activity INS could achieve because the
agency's cost is very low in relation to the taxpayer dollars saved.

Congress should give serious consideration to *tariff* regulation
as a supplement to the civil and criminal sanctions that are
alone inadequate to the task of immigration control. If more Mexican EWIs were to be "legalized" on a temporary basis through a

generous guestworker program, INS could deal more effectively with alien smuggling. Mexican guestworkers could be charged for the privilege of entering the U.S. for a nine to twelve month period to work in certain specified low-wage industries. If the fee were competitive with what smugglers charge, then the unofficial tariffs currently paid out to smugglers could be converted into an official tariff collected by the Treasury. The funds generated could be used to strengthen INS border and interior enforcement at no added cost to American taxpayers.

In addition to a "user fee" for two to four million Mexican guestworkers, an "abuser fee" could be levied against visa aliens who enter as visitors and students but then overstay or work without authorization. Under such a policy, aliens would be required to post a bond of two to three hundred dollars before an overseas consulate issued their nonimmigrant visas. Either a flat bond amount might be required regardless of the country or visa classification or the amount might be set according to the assumed likelihood of visa abuse by nationals of a particular country. In any event, aliens caught working without authorization or found to have stayed beyond their expiration dates (without having notified INS) would forfeit the bond to the government. The funds generated by these "abuser fees" could also be used to augment INS enforcement activities at a savings to taxpayers.[19]

There would be several advantages to a tariff model of regulation using both "user" and "abuser fees." First, the money that aliens pay to smugglers would go instead to support INS enforcement efforts against smugglers and other INA violators. (Research would, of course, be needed to determine what proportion of the smuggling charge accounted for efforts to circumvent the INS and to minimize apprehension risk as distinct from other services smugglers provide aliens; for example, job referrals or transit through a land whose language is unfamiliar.) If the tariff is competitive, then smugglers should become less so. Secondly, a tariff bracero program would be easier to administer than the expanded H-2 farm labor program contemplated by Simpson-Mazzoli. Alien fee payers would be free to work for whomever they pleased as long as they stayed within the industry and job guidelines set by agency regulations. Aliens who played by the rules would be allowed to renew their permits.

Third, although the integrity of the tariff system would require continued border and interior enforcement, the administrative violator category (EWIs and visa abusers) would become a less intense focus of INS preoccupation. Employed aliens pose much less social harm—if indeed they pose any harm at all. The agency would continue to take administrative deportation action against visa abusers or guestworkers caught violating the terms of their permits. However, collection of prior fees and confiscation of bonds would mitigate the sense of enforcement concern over this category—by far the largest violator group. INS will have more freedom of manuever, as well as more ample resources, to take action against more serious INA violators who impose costs on the society.

Though an optimal enforcement policy will require INS to make more of an effort to calibrate the social utilities to be gained by targeting different violator categories in relation to resource expenditures, it would be wrong to assume that immigration law enforcement can simply juggle social utilities. For if that were so, then probably almost all enforcement officers would be assigned to screening welfare programs and apprehending aliens involved in crime. Indeed, most immigration enforcement probably constitutes a deadweight economic loss to the nation since most enforcement resources are directed against aliens who probably (in the view of some economists) do not impose costs on our society.

Calculations of the social cost or potential harm posed by different categories of violators cannot alone frame an optimal policy. Though immigration law and policy are shaped partly by considerations of America's economic and foreign policy interests, they are more fundamentally rooted in conceptions of national sovereignty. Though national sovereignty may be at a steep discount as a political value among some groups, it is still of vital importance to the polity as a whole. Setting the terms under which aliens can enter and reside among the citizenry is inherent to the sovereignty of the modern state. And though there may be sound reasons why a state might decide to forego a maximalist policy of rigorous enforcement, it cannot abandon its legitimate right to regulate immigration without jeopardizing that sovereignty.

Ironically, when one considers the political and resource tradeoffs that drive many INS policies—for example, past and present policy decisions to raid businesses but not hospitals and churches, to focus resources on the border where cheap arrests can be made rather than on costlier interior arrests, which are also legally and politically problematic—one realizes that the agency, whether consciously or unconsciously, seeks to contrive a politically optimal policy. Though immigration policy is in many respects *inherently* incoherent—as, indeed, the inconsistencies in our refugee and asylum policy suggest—much of the agency's behavior suggests an effort to achieve a "weighted" enforcement outcome, one that will maximize the agency's political capital as well as maintain its imperative requirement for equilibrium.

These pirouettes of policy mirror the tug and pull of a multitude of competing interests in conflict in our society. Where societal consensus is firm, the agency will "go to the wall" despite the substantial resource costs. The most conspicious example is the strenuous effort by INS and the Justice Department to denaturalize former Nazi collaborators or to deport aliens suspected of serious criminal activities. It would be quite in error to say that immigration enforcement has no teeth. The teeth can and will be found when the occasion warrants.

Finally, though immigration enforcement against most administrative and EWI violators is clearly ineffective, the fact remains that the law *is* enforced against many such violators. Because this is so, INS enforcement provides more than just symbolic affirmation of the important value of national sovereignty. At a minimum, it creates tariffs to entry while also imposing costs and inconvenience for those who have been apprehended in the interior.

But absent draconian measures, which—aside from the enormous cost—Congress is unlikely to authorize because of public ambivalence and a lack of consensus, INS can only continue to muddle through with its present policy of a token enforcement effort against most violators. A more coherent and rational policy would seek to capture for the public treasury more of the unofficial tariffs illegal aliens are already paying to enter and work in the United States and to use these funds to strengthen enforcement against the smugglers who exploit and abuse aliens as well as against those aliens who pose a clear threat to the society.

5

RODOLFO O. DE LA GARZA

Mexican Americans, Mexican Immigrants, and Immigration Reform

"Love the country where you live"

Statement engraved on a plaque at the entrance of a Mexican American Mutual Aid Society Club in San Marcos, Texas.

Mexican Americans are at the center of the nation's recent debate over immigration reform. Whatever effect Mexican immigrants have on the nation, their presence is *first* felt by Mexican Americans. Any policy aimed at controlling immigration will therefore also immediately affects Chicanos. (Chicanos, Mexican American, and Mexican-origin citizens will be used here synonymously to refer to American citizens of Mexican heritage.)

While Mexican Americans have seldom played a role in national policy deliberations, it is appropriate that they do on this issue

This paper was prepared with the assistance of Ana Juarez.

93

since proposals such as the Simpson-Mazzoli bill would probably affect them more than any other group of Americans. Mexicans, after all, are the largest single segment of the immigrant population, and Mexican American barrios serve as settlement houses through which most of these immigrants enter U.S. society.

Chicano leaders have been concerned about immigration reform because of the effects of proposals like Simpson-Mazzoli on longer-term resident Mexican Americans, rather than on new Mexican immigrants. To be sure, some spokespersons are also committed to defending the rights and well-being of these later arrivals. They, however, represent a secondary concern for most Chicanos. What is clearly of primary importance to them is the threat that these proposals may pose to the established Mexican Americans, in their status and rights as citizens. Rather than open-ended support for continued Mexican immigration, this is the principal reason Mexican American leaders have ardently opposed current immigration reform efforts. To appreciate this concern it is necessary to understand how it originated. My purpose here is to describe how this attitude developed, and then to explain how Mexican Americans evaluate some key reform proposals and how they assess the impact new Mexican immigrants have on the Mexican American people and the nation at large.

Chicanos and Mexico

Mexican American attitudes toward immigration policy, and specifically toward Mexican immigration, are the result of two conceptually distinct but experientially related processes. The first encompasses the relationship that Chicanos have developed with Mexico and Mexicans. The second concerns the Chicano relationship with American society.

The end of the U.S.-Mexican War in 1848 established the conditions that led to the creation of a Mexican American community. The first step came in 1849 when all Mexican citizens who remained in the territory acquired by the United States automatically became American citizens. They became citizens merely because they preferred to continue living where they usually had lived rather than uproot themselves and "return" to a "homeland" that many never had visited.

That political transformation began a gradual process of resocializing, of "Americanizing" the Mexican-origin people of the Southwest. The economic and political consequences of this transformation became clear almost immediately as Mexican-origin citizens throughout the region lost their lands and were denied their political rights. The social and cultural consequences of the conquest set in more gradually.

Throughout the Southwest, and especially in communities close to the border, Mexican-origin people continued to live as always, as Mexicans. Many of their settlements remained untouched by "Anglo-Americans." Where Anglos settled, the Mexican American barrios remained intact and apart. With some ease, therefore, instead of developing integrated communities, Anglos successfully segregated the Mexican-origin population to specific areas. The barrios became institutionally complete. They had their own shops, their own churches, and their own cemeteries. The public schools they attended were known as "Mexican schools," but these were controlled by Anglos and served few students.

Movement across the border also continued as if the border were nonexistent. Throughout the nineteenth century and the early years of the twentieth, Anglo officials deliberately avoided taking any actions that would impede Mexican immigration. This was, in part, because southwestern agriculture and mining were dependent on Mexican immigrant labor. A regular but gradual inflow of immigrants continued until 1910, the first year of the twentieth-century Mexican revolutionary upheaval, when several large waves of immigration began. This influx greatly expanded the size of the Mexican-origin population in the U.S. as a whole, and reinvigorated Mexican culture in the Southwest region.

In sum, during the 1800s the border did little to separate Mexicans from Mexican Americans. On the U.S. side, Mexican immigrants and Mexican Americans functioned as one community; in addition to their commonalities, U.S. society did not distinguish between them, and segregated them into unified barrios.

Chicanos and the U.S.

As the twentieth century progressed, however, relations between Mexicans and Mexican Americans underwent important changes.

In part, this was due to changes in southwestern society. By the 1920s, American institutions had fully established themselves in the area. These institutions penetrated Mexican American society despite the persistence of segregation, with gradual "Americanization" of an important minority of the Mexican-origin population.

Economically well-off compared to the great majority of Chicanos, this group began articulating "Americanness," and differentiating itself from Mexican immigrants. The principal exponent of these attitudes was the League of United Latin American Citizens (LULAC), the first major Mexican American organization. Its goals included developing "within members of our race the best, purest, and most perfect type of a true and loyal citizen of the United States of America." Among its most successful activities was an educational program designed to teach English to the Mexican-origin population.

World War II further accelerated the Americanization of the Chicano population. Whether in the military or as members of the urban industrial labor force, more and more Mexican Americans developed an identity as Americans and became aware of the differences between themselves and Mexican immigrants. This is one of the reasons that groups such as the American G.I. Forum, a Mexican American veteran's organization, LULAC, and other groups vociferously opposed the bracero program for licensed entry of agricultural labor, and even supported efforts to *repatriate* Mexican immigrants on the grounds that these immigrants were detrimental to Mexican American progress.

Mexican luminaries such as Octavio Paz were for years incapable of understanding that Mexican Americans were developing a new identity, one related to but distinct from the Mexican. Middle- and working-class Mexicans have been equally confused by the development of Mexican American culture and even more critical of it. They openly criticize Chicanos for betraying their traditions and for speaking a "bastardized Spanish." The perception that Mexican society has held of Mexican Americans is reflected in the following statement by an undocumented Mexican worker.

[I] started to learn a little bit about the United States, especially about the pochos, the Mexican Americans who lived around here. To me a pocho was kind of dumb, because they didn't try to advance themselves. . . . If a person is born in Mexico the Mexican American laughs at you and calls you a dumb person because you come from a dumb country. There is a lot of discord, you see. We don't look like brothers. We are not united. We don't feel the brotherhood.

Mexican Americans, thus, had become "pochos," a term one Chicano writer defines as "a Mexican slob who has pretensions of being a gringo sonofabitch."[1]

While it is not uncommon for tensions to exist between nationals and emigres, Mexicans appear to be unusually critical of Mexican Americans. This may be because Mexican Americans are a permanent reminder of the repeated failures of Mexican society. They came into existence because of Mexico's inability to defend its territory in the nineteenth century, and contemporary immigrants are testimony to the continued inability of Mexican society to meet the needs of its citizens. Unlike European immigrants who came to this country with the expectation that they rather quickly would be accepted, for over a century millions of Mexicans have exposed themselves to life-threatening journeys to work and participate in a society where they knew they would face harsh discrimination and exploitation. Yet many preferred living as second-class Americans rather than full-fledged Mexicans.

Within the continuous interaction between Mexican and Mexican Americans, the difference between Mexican and American society is emphasized daily. Some Mexican Americans may express an intense desire to maintain Mexican culture and traditions, particularly the Spanish language. However, few romanticize the old country and almost none show interest in repatriating. Most who go to Mexico "seeking their roots" quickly recognize that they are undeniably American.[2]

Mexican society must find ways to explain this continuously high emigration. At the official level this involves never acknowledging internal governmental responsibility for the conditions that force Mexican workers to leave. At the private level individual citizens, especially among the middle and upper classes, assert (falsely) that those who leave represent Mexico's worst: the illiterate, the lazy, and the irresponsible. Since there are presumably no good reasons to leave Mexico, it is reasonable to look down on those who do; it is a short step from there to looking with disdain on the entire Mexican-origin population of the United States.[3]

Since 1848, the self-identity of the Mexican-origin population of
the United States has undergone an extensive transformation.
Where once there were no differences between Mexicans on either
side of the border, by the end of World War II, and possibly earlier,
the differences were undeniable. This was manifest in the 1950s
and the 1960s when Mexican American leaders were among the
most vociferous of the opponents to continued Mexican immigration. To an extent unparalleled by the activities of any other
American immigrant group, the leaders of the Mexican American
community saw their interests as independent of and in conflict
with the interests of their "countrymen."

Although the 1848 treaty of Guadalupe Hidalgo guaranteed all
the rights and privileges of U.S. citizenship, the Mexican population that remained in the Southwest thereafter was, as we have
noted, relegated to second-class status. Chicanos denied political
and legal rights were thus unable to prevent speculators and settlers from taking over their lands.[4] Powerless and desperate, Mexican Americans turned to Mexican consular officials for protection. Although the consuls sometimes tried to help, there was
little they could or would do.

Reaching to the Mainstream

Frustrated and unaware of distinctions between themselves and
later Mexican immigrants, important elements of the Mexican
American community in the twentieth century sought further access to mainstream U.S. society. Taking a multiple approach, they
first differentiated themselves from Mexicans. In prior years,
Mexican American groups identified themselves *in Spanish* with
names such as La Alianza Hispana-Americana; beginning in the
1920s, they took on English names.[5] Organizations such as
LULAC and the American G.I. Forum made explicit their commitment to integrate into American society, to learn English, to foster
patriotism. These organizations restricted their membership to
U.S. citizens. They directed their attention to improving conditions for Mexican Americans within the United States. They no
longer looked to Mexican officials for assistance; instead, they involved themselves with U.S. legal and political processes. Furthermore, when they did become involved with the one key issue

affecting Mexicans, immigration, they did so in specific opposition to Mexican interests. They argued that Mexican immigrants were taking jobs that belonged to American citizens.

The Mexican American has, irreversibly, moved from Mexican to American society. Because the transition has been gradual, observers in the U.S. ironically conclude that, unlike other immigrants, Mexican Americans are unwilling to become part of U.S. society. It is, by contrast, more likely that Mexican Americans have retained a "Mexicanness" only because they were so long denied access to American institutions. Segregated in schools (those who could go to school), in the workplace, in church, and in neighborhoods, it is not surprising that Mexican American culture retained traditional aspects for so long. The continual addition of Mexican immigrants into Mexican American communities has reinforced and reinvigorated those traditions.[6] The great majority of these immigrants has been overtly or covertly recruited by American business interests. U.S. *policies* have therefore made it very difficult for Chicanos *not* to retain their Mexicanness, but American institutions punish them for doing so.

U.S. society since 1848, to emphasize, has lumped Mexican immigrants and Mexican Americans, many of whom are third- and fourth-generation citizens, into one group and treated both as undesirable but needed foreigners. U.S. citizens of Mexican origin were among "Mexicans" deported during the economic crisis of the 1930s. In 1984, immigration officials are once again asking Chicanos on the street and in the workplace to prove they are Americans. And, because they are perceived as foreigners, Mexican Americans see their political loyalties questioned intermittently, as they have been since the mid-nineteenth century.[7]

Perspectives on Immigration Reform

The experiences and processes described above have shaped the perspective from which Mexican Americans view immigration reform in general and Mexican immigration in particular. Certain patterns characterize Chicano attitudes toward these matters.

To begin, neither issue is of primary concern to the majority of Mexican Americans. What concerns Chicanos most is how immigration reforms will affect *them,* and they pay little attention to effects on Mexican immigrants. Mexican Americans remain divided with regard to assessing the effects the immigrants have on them and in their evaluation of the impact of Mexican immigrants on American society.

Immigration is, therefore, not a salient issue to Mexican Americans. Neither elites nor the general public include immigration among the most important issues affecting their local communities or the nation at large.[8]

This lack of relevance persists when attention is focused on Mexican immigration. During the 1984 Texas Democratic Primary, Representative Kent Hance organized his campaign for the U.S. Senate around his opposition to Mexican immigration. Criticisms of Simpson-Mazzoli and charges that Mexican undocumented immigrants were displacing American workers became central questions in the election. A decided underdog midway through the campaign, Hance won a plurality in the primary, forced a runoff, and eventually lost the nomination by less than one percent.

A survey focusing on attitudes toward immigration was coincidentally conducted between the primary and runoff in two Texas counties, one along the border and the other in the center of the state (this survey will be referred to as the Texas Survey). The survey interviews were completed just as the immigration issue was closely covered by the media and debated by political leaders across the state. Respondents were asked to rank the importance of the following issues: the environment, unemployment, education, immigration, welfare programs, social security, crime, and nuclear war. Among Mexican Americans, immigration received fewer "most important" or "very important" rankings than any other issue. Sixty-four percent ranked it in these categories. By comparison, the next lowest issue was welfare with 76 percent, and the issue of greatest concern was education with 96 percent ranking it as most or very important.

Elected Mexican American leaders as well as the heads of national organizations, in reaction to Simpson-Mazzoli and other immigration proposals, initiated no legislation or discussions until reform seemed imminent. This contrasts sharply with the conduct of these individuals with regard to bilingual education, voting rights, and general civil rights issues.

The response of Mexican American leaders and the community to immigration reform efforts, and to Simpson-Mazzoli in particular, reveals that greatest concern is for the potential impact of these reforms on Mexican Americans.[9] The consequences these reforms will have on Mexicans is clearly a secondary issue. The Mexican American Legal Defense and Education Fund (MALDEF) opposes Simpson-Mazzoli as a threat to Mexican American civil rights: "As we are often indistinguishable from the undocumented, our enjoyment of rights in large part depend (sic) on the way our legal, political, and social institutions perceive and react to immigrants and, in particular, to undocumented immigrants." MALDEF also fears that history will repeat itself: "the image of thousands of citizens and legal residents of Hispanic descent being deported along with the undocumented still burns fresh in our collective memory." MALDEF and others are convinced that national identity cards will exacerbate discrimination by making Mexican Americans a "suspect class" and providing employers an "incentive to stop hiring Hispanics altogether, in order to avoid paperwork, disruptions of operations, and penalties."

This likelihood may explain why 60 percent of Mexican American local and national leaders surveyed by the Southwest Voter Registration Project oppose employer sanctions, compared to the 70 percent of the Anglo community in California who support such provisions.[10] In the short run, the Mexican American community may suffer because of the nation's attempt to restrict immigration. Mexican Americans expect their leadership to prevent that from happening, and the leadership will be criticized and replaced if it fails to act. This has already begun to happen.

Richard Salvatierra, a columnist for *Hispanic Link,* has charged that the Hispanic Congressional Caucus was derelict in not developing legislative proposals in anticipation of Simpson-Mazzoli.[11] He argues that Mexicans have no more right to emigrate to this country than do Europeans whose relatives came over on the Mayflower. He acknowledges that some of those supporting Simpson-Mazzoli may be racists, but nonetheless insists that the nation must formulate policies to control its borders, to defend the interest of Mexican Americans and the nation. Salvatierra argues that Mexican American leaders must help shape immigration policy.

A Question of Constituency?

Supporters of Simpson-Mazzoli allege that Chicano leaders oppose immigration reform because they see continued immigration as a way to increase their constituency. But from a practical perspective, Chicano leaders, especially elected officials, have little to gain from increased immigration.[12] As a group, the undocumented were not politically active in Mexico, and their educational and economic characteristics suggest they are unlikely to become active here even if they are eligible to do so. As illegals they will surely avoid activities that could lead to their arrest and deportation. If amnesty provisions ever pass, it will be years before many (the majority?) of the undocumented currently in the U.S. complete the transition to legal resident alien. Furthermore, if existing patterns continue, few of those who become resident aliens will ever become citizens. Immigration and Naturalization Service (INS) data show that legal Mexican resident aliens have the lowest naturalization rates of any immigrant group in this country. Large numbers of the undocumented will not increase the size of the politically mobilizable Mexican-origin population in the (near) future. As Simpson-Mazzoli illustrated, the presence of large numbers of undocumented workers could lead to policies detrimental to Chicanos. It seems untenable that Mexican American leaders opposed Simpson-Mazzoli because they would benefit politically from continued Mexican immigration.

Arnold Torres, Executive Director of LULAC, has explicitly rejected such allegations. "[T]he Hispanic community is not opposed to the reforms that are proposed in this legislation." Such charges "totally discount our experiences regarding discriminatory treatment. . . . Our fear of discrimination is not fabricated but based on real experiences. . ."

The lack of concern for the effect of these measures on Mexican immigrants is also clear in the attitudes of Texan Chicanos. A majority (52 percent) of Mexican Americans interviewed in the Texas Survey approved of employer sanctions, and over 40 percent were either neutral to or supportive of national identity cards. While these provisions *may* well lead to discrimination, as Mexican American leaders fear, there is *no doubt* they would have hurt undocumented workers. Supporting these provisions, Mexican

Americans clearly define their interests as separate from those of Mexican immigrants and seem willing not to consider the consequences for future Mexican immigrants.

The support for these anti-undocumented-worker provisions seems unrelated to the effects the undocumented have on the way Mexican Americans live. Forty-three percent of the Chicano respondents in the Texas Survey stated they had no contact with undocumented workers, and 72 percent indicated that Mexican immigrants had no impact on their daily lives. Seventy percent agreed that undocumented workers took jobs that no one else wanted, and only 28 percent indicated that they had personal knowledge of undocumented workers taking jobs from Mexican Americans. This pattern resembles elected and appointed elites' assessment of the impact of the undocumented on Mexican American workers. Only 22 percent of these leaders held that undocumented workers were displacing Mexican Americans.

These respondents suggest Mexican Americans are more concerned about immigration reform than about immigration itself. There is little evidence that most Mexican Americans are adversely affected by the presence of undocumented workers, and there is increasing data that Mexican immigrants are an asset to Mexican American communities.[13] On the other hand, the reform proposals are seen as likely to exacerbate discrimination. It is only reasonable, then, that Mexican Americans will oppose these reforms. To avoid the negative consequences of immigration reform and protect their civil rights, Chicanos must find ways to limit Mexican immigration even though the available evidence indicates that most Chicanos do not feel adversely affected by it.

Mexican American leaders are not consistent in their responses to Mexican immigration. Some who assert that the undocumented take jobs no one else wants and do not displace American workers, also opposed the guestworker provisions of Simpson-Mazzoli on the grounds that guestworkers would displace American workers. Arnold Torres, in congressional testimony, stated that his organization was offended by "the fact that we are talking about bringing in new workers when we cannot even take care of American farm workers that we presently have in this country." Polly Baca, a member of the Democratic National Committee and one of the nation's most politically prominent Mexican American women, has expressed a similar outlook. Those who make this argument do not specify why they think that guestworkers would displace American workers while the undocumented do not.

Certain Mexican American leaders do oppose the guestworker program and the immigration reforms in general because of the hardships they would impose on the Mexican immigrant population. Congressmen Edward Roybal, Robert Garcia, and Henry B. Gonzalez have been especially outspoken on this issue, as has MALDEF. Congressman Gonzalez, for example, has dubbed the guestworker provisions of Simpson-Mazzoli the "rent-a-slave" program. MALDEF has been strongly critical of the amnesty procedures included in the legislation:

> In all good conscience, MALDEF cannot support a legislative proposal that is a disguise for a whole new series of raids into the undocumented community. We cannot urge people to come forward and identify themselves to the Immigration Service with the knowledge that, by doing so, they risk deportation. The fear and distrust that are so deeply ingrained in the hearts of the undocumented arose in part from their experience with broken promises.

A Divided Community

Mexican Americans are divided in their evaluation of the overall impact that undocumented immigrants have on U.S. society. The Texas Survey respondents seem particularly critical of the undocumented. Forty-eight percent strongly agree or agree that the undocumented abuse welfare privileges, while 40 percent disagree. Only 33 percent agree, compared to 59 percent who disagree, that undocumented workers have a right to such services. Over one-half (53 percent), however, believe that public schools should admit the children of undocumented workers, a small proportion given that this right has been upheld by U.S. courts. Overall, 40 percent of respondents believe that the undocumented are harmful to this country, while 32 percent think they are beneficial. In contrast, 42 percent of a national sample of Chicano elites describe the undocumented as an asset to the country.

Texas Survey respondents are much less supportive of amnesty for the undocumented than are local elites from across the Southwest. Forty-nine percent of Texas respondents, compared to almost 90 percent of community leaders in California, New Mexico, and elsewhere support amnesty. By comparison, 39 percent of Anglos in California support amnesty for the undocumented currently in this country.

Mexican Americans, then, are less supportive of Mexican immigration than Anglo observers have suggested. Their attitudes are best understood within the context of that population's historical effort to establish itself as a legitimate and permanent part of American society. Anglo institutions, not Mexican immigrants, are the source of the problems that continue to confront Mexican Americans. It is not surprising that immigration has been and remains a secondary issue for Mexican Americans. What is of primary concern to Mexican Americans is that they be permitted to enjoy the rights and privileges that have been their due since 1849.

It is with this objective in mind that most Mexican Americans evaluate immigration policy. Suggestions that reactions to policy in this area are motivated by political commitments to Mexico, by personal attachments to Mexican culture, or by self-serving interests on the part of elected officials reflect ignorance of and insensitivity to the experience of the Mexican American people.

III

Immigrants and the Economy

6

THOMAS MULLER

Economic Effects of Immigration

Since the first large groups of immigrants embarked on the nation's shores, the economic effects of their presence became a matter of dispute. Not surprisingly, groups favoring immigration have been found in the business and agricultural sectors, which typically benefit from a growing population. On the other hand, some workers and organized labor frequently have argued that the presence of immigrants reduced job opportunities and lowered wages for native-born workers. Labor understood that in the absence of immigration, a worker shortage could develop that would increase their bargaining power and thus their ability to maintain relatively high wages.

After the Chinese entered California in large numbers, white laborers, in part reflecting their resentment that the Chinese

This chapter is based in part on research undertaken with the support of the Weingart Foundation.

109

were able to obtain and hold jobs even during economic down-turns, accused them of working at slave wages and taking jobs away from Americans. Worker pressure was the primary force that led Congress to pass the Chinese Exclusion Act in 1882 and a subsequent agreement to eliminate Japanese immigration.

During the 1920s the argument that since the nation was already settled from the Atlantic to the Pacific, the need for immigrants to open new Western lands no longer existed was frequently made by those favoring strict numerical immigration limits. New immigrants, according to this view, would compete with and take jobs from native-born urban residents because opportunities to obtain free land were gone. These economic arguments should not be interpreted to suggest that economic sentiments alone formed the basis for restrictive legislation. Anti-Chinese sentiment, for example, was also racially motivated, as were restrictions on the number of Eastern and Southern Europeans allowed to enter the United States during the 1920s. Nevertheless, economic arguments were frequently cited by both sides of the immigration debate.

Economic concerns associated with immigration have not abated. During the occasionally acrimonious debate in Congress during June 1984 on the Simpson-Mazzoli bill, the issue of immigrants and jobs was again at the forefront of the arguments. This time, however, the discussion on the floor of the House of Representatives focused on so-called "undocumented" or illegal workers. For example, Congressman Shaw (D.-Fla.) stated that "the people left out of the [immigration] debate are the American workers who are being discriminated against, because they are losing jobs to illegal aliens who are coming to this country and working for less."[1] Congressman Burton (R.-Ind.) shared this view: "Part of the unemployment problem is that not everyone employed in this nation is an American . . . illegal workers take jobs from Americans. There are nine million Americans looking for work. There are five to twenty million illegal aliens. These numbers suggest a solution to the unemployment problem."[2] Some even voted against the bill because certain workers already in this country would be granted amnesty. Thus, Congressman Hance (D.-Tx.) stated that, "For every job now occupied by an undocumented worker, it costs the country. Amnesty costs jobs for American citizens. It legalizes the theft of American jobs."[3] He cast a vote against the bill.

On the other hand, a conservative Republican leader, Congressman Kemp (R.-N.Y.), argued rather eloquently that immigrants do not take jobs from Americans.[4] He, too, voted against the bill. The vice-presidential nominee of the Democratic Party also voted "no" because it granted amnesty, an unpopular issue among her blue-collar ethnic constituents.

Most members of Congress appeared to share the view that undocumented immigrants were taking jobs from native-born Americans. These sentiments appear to have been shared by the general public. A national survey undertaken by *Newsweek* showed that 60 percent of the population believed undocumented workers contributed to unemployment.[5] A survey undertaken for The Urban Institute in Southern California, which focused on economic and long-range issues, found that about half the respondents believed that immigrants working illegally take at least some jobs from Americans.[6] That percentage was lower than the national response, despite the high concentration of undocumented immigrants in Southern California. This suggests that those most exposed to alien workers feel less threatened than others.

Jobs, Wages, and Immigration—A Historical Perspective

Although economists have been examining linkages between immigration and jobs for a century or more, economic theory alone does not provide a solid basis for determining what impact immigration has on job opportunities for native-born residents. From a theoretical perspective, the impact of immigration depends on the assumptions made regarding the labor market and immigrant characteristics. Under some conditions immigrants are substitutes for domestic workers, while under other circumstances they are complements. Most economists also distinguish between short-run and long-run effects, and consider any adverse impacts of immigration to be typically short-term phenomena.

The economic effects of immigration depend on a set of assumptions regarding the labor force, the structure of the economy, and the characteristics of immigrants themselves. Most labor economists now agree that there are several labor markets, with the basic distinction made between a primary market where wages are partially administered and jobs tend to be secure, and a secondary market where wages are totally set by supply and demand, with little or no job security. Low-skilled immigrants, such as many of those from Mexico or the Caribbean, tend to become part of the secondary market. This reduces any potential adverse impacts they may have on the majority of American workers, who fall into the "primary" category. To the extent that many of the secondary market jobs are "dead end" with harsh working conditions (e.g., fruit and vegetable pickers), competition is limited. Few native-born workers are willing to work at such jobs, even at wages higher than those paid to undocumented laborers, especially if less demanding work is available.

Models developed by researchers such as Chiswick support the view that at the aggregate level, income of native households rises as a result of an immigrant inflow.[7] Others, including Grossman and Rivera-Batiz, find that limited displacement of native-born workers may take place as a result of an immigrant influx, at least in the short run.[8]

Most of the research on immigration is based on examining direct linkages between immigrants and the labor market. Those who have viewed immigration from a broader economic perspective, examining such issues as the long-term impact of immigration on capital investment, find immigration to have a positive effect.[9]

Most non-economists tend to be dissatisfied with the short- versus long-run distinctions. Elected officials, in particular, view events from a very short time horizon. Thus, their interest in theoretical studies that conclude that at some distant time the presence of immigrants may be positive or negative is limited at best. From a policy perspective, results based on empirical data, (historical and particularly current sources) appear to be a more satisfactory route to explore.

An examination of immigration and unemployment over the last century suggests that between the end of the Civil War and World War I, immigration slowed during periods of domestic economic downturns, while return migration (immigrants returning to their place of origin) increased. During the Great Depression, immigration slowed to a trickle. Between 1930 and 1939, 700 thousand immigrants arrived, but 490 thousand also departed. For every unskilled worker who came during the decade, almost two left the country.

Thus, immigration prior to World War II acted as an employment safety valve for this nation, expanding and contracting with changing domestic economic conditions. The vast majority of immigrants who came during the first four decades of this century (and those who came earlier) were either unskilled or took unskilled jobs. These jobs tend to be particularly sensitive to fluctuations in the economy, explaining why immigration rates frequently reflected economic trends in the United States.

Blacks formed a large domestic pool of unskilled workers during the early decades of this century. As such, they would be the ones most likely to compete with immigrants for jobs. However, even in 1930, four out of five blacks continued to live in the South, a region generally inhospitable, both economically and socially, to "second wave" Eastern and Southern European immigrants. The large northern industrial cities where most new immigrants resided had few blacks. Indeed, some scholars have noted that blacks did not move North because immigrants held low-skill jobs.[10] Since native-born whites in Northern urban areas tended to be skilled workers, job competition between immigrants and native-born persons was limited.

What about wages? The impact of immigration on earnings has been a matter of concern to economists for decades. Based on their work, there is considerable evidence that wages of unskilled labor did not rise as rapidly as skilled worker wages during periods of large-scale immigration to this nation. The wage differential between the two categories of workers narrowed during periods of labor shortages, such as during World War I and World War II, when immigration slowed while the demand for labor increased dramatically.

The fact that unskilled worker wages were depressed during periods of large immigrant inflows is consistent with economic theory, which predicts that wages would fall (in relative terms) if the supply of workers increases. Following the same reasoning, however, lower wages can also produce more jobs as reduced prices increase demand. As long as immigrant workers are as productive as other workers and accept lower wages than others for similar work, a surplus is produced that benefits non-immigrants, employers, and ultimately consumers, in the form of lower prices. Thus, one could anticipate a redistribution of income, with higher living standards for nonimmigrants as one result of an increase in the supply of unskilled immigrants. Real income in this nation rose more rapidly between the 1870s and the 1920s, at the peak of immigration, than in most other industrial nations. While it is difficult to quantify the role of immigrants in this growth, they were unquestionably an important factor in the rise of the United States to the position of the leading industrial nation by the end of the nineteenth century.

Immigration ceased to be an economic issue after the restrictive quota legislation passed during the 1920s. The new laws and the Depression, followed immediately by World War II and severe constraints on the number of postwar refugees admitted, sharply curtailed the flow of immigration to the United States for several decades. Fewer immigrants entered between 1930 and 1960 than arrived during the 1920s. By 1965, however, a strong economy and civil rights activities created a favorable climate toward immigration, leading a liberal Congress to reform immigration laws by eliminating some of the quota provisions. Concurrently, Congress terminated the bracero program, which for two decades had legally provided mostly Mexican agricultural labor to the growers on a temporary basis. These two unrelated congressional actions substantially changed both the places of origin and the characteristics of immigrants since the late 1960s. The new immigration law increased the flow of immigrants from Asia, while the bracero program termination caused a flow of illegal immigrants to this nation to replace most of the previously contracted workers in the fields of California and Texas.

The New Immigrants

The "new" immigrants as described in this chapter are those persons who have entered the United States legally or illegally since 1969 when the 1965 Immigration Act became effective. In contrast to the pre—World War II period, the number of new immigrants entering legally has shown no signs of slowing down during recent economic downturns. The three recessions that marked the

1970–1983 period did not appear to have any measurable effect on the inflow of immigrants. (Whether return immigration was affected is not known, as information on those leaving the nation is no longer collected.)

The apparent lack of sensitivity on the part of recent immigrants to economic conditions in the United States can be attributed to several causes. First, given a quota system with limits on the number of persons admitted annually, few wish to lose their place in line, even if job opportunities are scarce. Second, post–World War II economic downturns, mostly as a result of public sector intervention, are less severe than those which plagued the nation during the 1930s and earlier. Thus, the chances of finding some work, even in the early 1980s, were considerably better than during pre–World War I downturns. Third, an increasingly large number of immigrants are dependents of U.S. residents, and thus may not be seeking work, at least not immediately following arrival. Finally, a higher share of new entrants (other than Mexicans) than in earlier periods are professional and other white-collar workers, less affected by economic downturns than those with limited skills.

Low-skilled undocumented workers continue to enter regardless of economic conditions because wage differentials between the United States and nations south of the border are so large that even if immigrant workers can find jobs for only part of the year, their income will surpass earnings from year-round work in their native country, even assuming such stable work could be found.

The new immigrants are highly concentrated in a few large urban areas. While earlier entrants and internal migrants from the rural South also tended to settle in metropolitan centers, the degree of urban concentration has increased compared to previous immigration waves. Between 1970 and 1980, two out of every five new immigrants became residents of the Los Angeles and New York consolidated metropolitan areas, while one out of five settled in four other urban centers: Chicago, San Francisco, Houston, and Miami. In most of the Midwest, however, few new immigrants could be found. Thus, only eleven thousand were enumerated in Indianapolis and fifteen thousand in the Milwaukee area during 1980, comprising only one percent of their population.

In contrast to earlier massive flows to northern industrial cen-

Table 1

Characteristics of Native-Born Residents and Immigrants in the U.S., 1980

Characteristic	Native-Born Residents	Pre-1970 Immigrants	1970–1980 Immigrants[a]			
			All	Asians	Europeans	Mexicans
Persons between 20 and 44 years old (%)	36	51	56	58	55	57
Labor force participation rate (%)	62	59	64	61	67	69
Unemployment rate (%)	6.5	5.8	8.1	6.2	6.7	10.3
Mean household income	$20,412	$19,545	$17,485	$19,430	$21,849	$13,618
Persons with 4 or more years of college (%)	16.3	13.2	22.2	37.4	20.4	2.7
Professional employees (%)	12.3	12.8	10.7	18.0	12.8	1.4
Total U.S. population (%)	93.7	3.8	2.5	0.8	0.3	0.6

[a]Immigrants are defined as all foreign-born persons.

Source: 1980 Census of Population, *Detailed Population Characteristics*, U.S. Summary, 1984.

ters, the majority of recent arrivals are found in the South and West, regions whose economic growth has outpaced northern states for several decades. Earlier centers of immigration, such as Pittsburgh, Cleveland, and Buffalo, now facing serious economic readjustment problems, are no longer attractive to newcomers— whether internal migrants or immigrants—seeking work.

In some respects, new immigrants do not differ from their predecessors. As shown in Table 1, about 56 percent are in the prime (20–44) working age categories, a demographic profile similar to earlier arrivals, while only 36 percent of native-born residents fall in this age bracket. Among immigrants sixteen years old and older, 64 percent are working. This is a somewhat higher percentage than those working among the nonimmigrant population. It means that the immigrant worker/dependent ratio is high, a key factor in estimating the short-term impact of immigration on the economy in general and on such trust funds as social security in particular. The new immigrant household has slightly more persons working than the general population, which is another indication that immigrants as a group are at least as likely to hold a job as nonimmigrants.

The most notable characteristic that distinguishes new arrivals from earlier immigrants is their educational achievement. Recent immigrants have a collectively higher education level than the native-born population. This differs sharply from earlier entrants whose education levels were typically lower than native-born residents. Perhaps the most impressive numbers are those that show the vast differences in educational attainment among groups by their place of origin. While 37 percent of all Asians have four or more years of college, only 3 percent of Mexicans have a similar education. The high educational status of Asians is reflected in their occupational structure, with one out of ten recent arrivals holding a professional job. Among those in the United States a decade or longer, the proportion holding professional jobs rises.

Household income is another measure of economic success. While the income of recent immigrants is below the average of the native-born population, most of the difference is attributable to the presence of Hispanics and persons from the Caribbean basin. The income of Asians approaches and the income of Europeans surpasses the level of the base population. And if the work of Chiswick and others is any indication, Asians and most other non-Mexican groups will surpass native-born Americans in earnings within a generation.

The Economic Effects of Immigration in Southern California

No state absorbed more immigrants during the last twenty years than California. In 1983, close to five million persons, or one out of five state residents, were foreign born. This is roughly one-third of the national total, although only one of ten Americans is a resident of the state. Among the population forty-five years of age or younger, the proportion of foreign born is even higher. It is in Southern California, principally in Los Angeles, that the foreign-born presence is the most visible. The number of immigrants in Los Angeles County during the early 1980s was close to a third of the population, about equal numerically to the foreign-born population of New York City during the 1920s. Since the recent immigration wave has left a greater imprint on Southern California than any other part of this nation, economic effects associated with this inflow, be they positive or negative, should be more discernible in this region than elsewhere.

Employment statistics bear out the impressive immigrant presence in the region's labor force, particularly in Los Angeles County. During the 1970s, employment in Los Angeles increased by 645 thousand (excluding undocumented workers who were not enumerated by the 1980 Census). Mexicans who arrived during the decade held 210 thousand of these jobs, and non-Mexican immigrants an additional 234 thousand jobs. In all of Southern California, which gained 8 percent of all jobs added nationally during the 1970s, one out of every three jobs added in the decade was held by a recent immigrant.

On first glance, these statistics would suggest possibly massive displacement of native-born (and earlier immigrant) workers as well as high unemployment among the base population and recent arrivals. An examination of employment statistics, however, does not support the massive displacement thesis, even in Los Angeles. Among the measurable effects of such displacement would have been higher average unemployment and lower labor force participation rates than in other regions. The data do not confirm such a pattern. In fact, unemployment in the Los Angeles area, which exceeded the national norm in 1970, fell below the national mean in the early 1980s. Teenage unemployment also increased less rapidly in the county than in the balance of the nation. Labor force participation rates in the Los Angeles area rose almost as rapidly as in the balance of the country, suggesting that the number of persons discouraged from seeking work did not rise as a result of the immigrant inflow. Other economic indicators, such as changes in the proportion of the non-Hispanic population below the poverty level, followed the national pattern. Among Hispanics, however, almost one-third fell below the poverty line, a reflection of their generally low earnings.

How were immigrants able to hold so many jobs in one region without displacing others? The type of jobs taken by immigrants provides at least part of the answer. Two out of three jobs added in the region were in the white-collar category. However, recent immigrants, Mexicans and others, held only one-quarter of these jobs, and comprised an even smaller share of high-wage professional, managerial, and technical jobs. By contrast, more unskilled jobs were taken by immigrants than were added during the decade.

Did immigrants displace these low-wage jobs holders or did they replace those leaving? Job gains by native-born workers were almost exclusively in white-collar occupations, with mean earnings twice as high as in occupations native-born workers were leaving, which would suggest replacement rather than displacement. This interpretation is supported by unemployment rates in Los Angeles, which as noted earlier exceeded the national average prior to the surge in immigration, but had fallen below the national average in the mid-1980s.

The massive immigration of the 1970s no doubt produced some economic dislocation in California and elsewhere during the sharp national and regional economic decline between 1980 and 1982. During this period, unemployment in California and Los Angeles exceeded the national level. However, both the state and county recovered more quickly from the recession compared to the balance of the nation. The number of unemployed in Los Angeles fell by one-third during calendar 1983, and by the first quarter of 1984 was below the national average. Since large-scale immigration continued during the early 1980s, this suggests that the economy quickly absorbed new immigrants as the pace of economic growth quickened.

Of course, another phenomenon could have been taking place: unskilled workers discouraged by low wages may have been leaving the region, rather than remaining and accepting lower wages, an issue explored later in this chapter.

What about minority workers, particularly blacks? The concern has always been that they would be hurt the most by the entry of low-skilled, low-wage immigrants. This, indeed, was the formal position of the National Association for the Advancement of Colored People (NAACP). In testimony to the Subcommittee on Immigration, the Association backed employer sanctions on the premise that "undocumented workers have a disparate effect on unskilled, unemployed, and marginally employed blacks."[11] This view should not be surprising, since black household income nationally is less than two-thirds of white non-Hispanic income. In 1980, 26 percent of all black families, but fewer than 7 percent of white families, had income below the poverty level, and the same pattern is evident in California, although average incomes of both whites and blacks are above the national mean.

An examination of metropolitan areas in the western states and Texas failed to show that black unemployment rose with the rise in Mexican immigration during the 1970s. Indeed, areas where the Mexican immigrant population was large had marginally lower unemployment than would be expected, holding other factors constant. However, the Southwest, particularly California, had a net inflow of blacks from other regions, although most of these entrants were skilled workers.

Unquestionably some competition between blacks and immigrants existed and continues to exist at the bottom of the occupational ladder. Fortunately, however, most jobs added by blacks in Southern California were not in these low-wage categories. Indeed, almost all of the net gains in black jobs between 1970 and 1980 in California were in white-collar occupations for several reasons, including the following:

(1) A sharp rise in black education. About 78 percent of all black employed males and 83 percent of all black employed

females in California during 1980 had a high school education, a sharp increase over the 1970 level. The percentage was virtually the same as the average for *all* male state residents, and slightly higher than the state female average. The proportion of blacks with college degrees in California also increased sharply during the decade.

(2) Black women accounted for most of the black employment gains within the state during the 1970s. Among these women, the vast majority of new job entrants accepted white-collar jobs, which few Hispanic immigrants hold. More black women left blue-collar and low-wage service jobs than entered these occupations.

(3) A rapid rise in the number of blacks, particularly women, holding public-sector jobs. One-third of all job gains for black women and over one-fourth for black men were in the public sector, although aggregate employment in this sector did not rise substantially during the decade.

(4) An influx of professional and other white-collar blacks to the region from other states.

The statistical data do not indicate a measurable adverse impact of the immigrant presence in the Southwest on aggregate black employment. While some nonimmigrants, both blacks and others, were probably displaced from low-wage jobs, others gained from the presence of a larger population. These persons included public-sector employees. This is of particular importance to black workers in California, and especially in Los Angeles County, where one out of four black males and one out of three black females worked for the government, compared to one out of ten white males and one out of seven white females.

For example, the demand for teachers in Los Angeles rose as immigrant children swelled enrollment, with the Los Angeles Unified District the only large urban system in the nation gaining students. Other city, county, and state agencies also added workers as the population expanded. However, since taxes to pay for schools and social services were derived primarily from nonlocal sources, the drain on the local economy of expanding the public sector was insubstantial.

One of the most important factors explaining the absence of adverse effects associated with immigration was the expansion of low-wage manufacturing jobs. During the 1970s the Los Angeles area expanded production in several manufacturing sectors where employment declined nationally, including apparel, textiles, furniture, and leather goods. While employment in these industries fell in most parts of the country, Southern California and metropolitan areas of Texas showed a growth in jobs. Although some proportion of this increase could be attributed to expanding demand (in part caused by immigrants), the availability of low-wage labor was no doubt a more important factor in explaining this rise. Wages in the manufacturing sector in Los Angeles, which exceeded the national average in 1972, had fallen below this average by 1980. Since most of the added jobs in highly internationally competitive sectors can be related to the presence of alien workers, the absence of these workers would not have resulted in more jobs for native-born Americans. Thus, these jobs are net additions to the economy, as the goods produced are in most instances substitutes for foreign imports. In the absence of finding workers willing to work at wages offered, at least some of these jobs would now be in the Far East, or perhaps on the Mexican side of the Rio Grande.

Do we want to maintain low-wage manufacturing jobs? It may well be that as a nation we should not retain the type of low-wage industries where many immigrants find work, but concentrate our resources on high technology sectors. Perhaps maintaining these jobs, one could argue, only demonstrates that immigrants may be an economic liability. It is true, of course, that a production job paying fifteen dollars per hour contributes more to the economy than one paying four dollars. If as a nation we could concentrate our resources on producing only high technology products, this would be preferable to weaving textiles or manufacturing shirts. Viewing the world's economy realistically, however, this is not a feasible alternative to a broadly based, diversified economy. Further, many immigrants, particularly Asians, come with advanced technical training. Their presence may enhance our ability to compete in the international market in electronics and related products.

This discussion leads to a more fundamental question: why should one expect immigrant workers to take jobs from Americans? The argument is seldom if ever made that the millions of native-born Americans who moved from northern industrial states to the South and West during the 1970s took jobs from native-born residents of these regions. While the employment characteristics of immigrants differ somewhat from internal migrants, the effects on local economies are similar for both groups. In both cases, a young, productive population is added. When the population of Houston expands due to either migration or immigration, so does the demand for goods and services, which induces the need for additional workers. From a policy perspective there is, of course, a difference. Even if Michigan residents took jobs from native Texans, the process can be described as economically efficient and in the best tradition of a free-enterprise system. On the other hand, if immigrants were taking jobs from Texans, this would be a legitimate concern, since immigration is subject to federal law. While one cannot and should not constrain internal migration, we can, to some extent, control the level of international migration. From an economic perspective, however, one can expect the local private sector to be stimulated by population-induced growth that results in a productive labor force regardless of its origin. The demand for locally produced apparel and furniture in Southern California increased during the 1970s in part because immigrants purchased some of these goods. Except for the fact that immigrant purchasing power was lower than the purchasing power of internal migrants, the presence of the additional population induced a higher demand for goods and services.

While immigration does not appear to have an adverse impact on native-born employment in California, it appears that Hispanic immigrants reduced *average* wages in low-skill occupations. The likely effects of large-scale immigration during the decade on 1969–1979 wage increases for selected occupations are shown in Table 2. The average male Hispanic wage during the 1970s rose only 50.7 percent, or substantially more slowly than the California average. Wages for Hispanic women also increased at a lower rate, but disparities between Hispanics and others were not as large as among men. The gap between Hispanic and black women, however, widened. Several factors account for the slow wage growth among Hispanic workers, including immigration, age, and education. The large influx of Hispanic immigrants whose wages were below the average of other workers pulled average wages of all

Table 2

Changes in Median Wages in California, 1969–1979, By Occupation and Ethnicity

Sex and Occupation	1969			1979			Percentage change 1970–1980		
	Blacks	Hispanics	Others	Blacks	Hispanics	Others	Blacks	Hispanics	Others
Males									
Total	$6,627	$6,993	$8,925	$12,386	$10,535	$16,595	86.9	50.7	85.9
Professional-managerial	8,632	10,505	12,311	16,965	16,441	22,272	96.5	56.5	80.9
Skilled blue collar	7,432	8,242	9,353	15,121	13,190	16,736	103.5	60.0	78.9
Operatives	6,710	6,790	7,646	12,914	10,748	14,654	92.5	58.3	91.7
Laborers	6,218	5,849	5,494	9,511	8,633	8,439	53.0	47.6	53.6
Females									
Total	3,928	3,525	4,378	8,847	6,427	8,363	125.2	82.3	91.0
Clerical	4,613	4,363	4,911	9,435	8,250	9,092	104.5	89.1	85.1
Operatives	3,708	3,412	3,855	8,100	6,228	7,081	118.4	82.5	83.7

Source: Bureau of the Census, 1970 and 1980 Censuses, *Characteristics of the Population.*

Hispanics down. Since the typical Hispanic worker, particularly the immigrant worker, is also younger and less educated than his or her non-Hispanic counterpart, this implies less experience and possibly less skill, and thus lower pay. Another element, more difficult to quantify, is discrimination. Researchers have found that when other worker characteristics are controlled, undocumented aliens receive somewhat lower pay than others.

A comparison of wage growth between California and the United States indicates that in low-skill jobs, increases in California were less than elsewhere in the nation. As shown in Table 3, Hispanic wages in particular increased more slowly in California than in other states. In most occupations shown, including three out of four low-skill categories, black wage growth in California exceeded the national average. This growth is particularly significant since black earnings in the state during the 1960s were above the national average. Personal income of black families increased most rapidly in parts of Southern California, Houston, and San Diego, while the slowest growth was observed in the older northern industrial cities.

Table 3
Median Wage Increases in California Between 1969 and 1979 as a Percentage of National Wage Growth

Occupation and Sex	All Workers	Hispanics	Blacks
Males			
Engineers	97.5	99.5	98.3
Craftsmen	97.0	83.7	93.1
Laborers (manufacturing)	77.0	85.3	103.1
Operators	77.6	71.4	97.7
Females			
Registered Nurses	93.4	84.0	103.1
Administrative Support	96.2	95.1	99.3
Service Workers	81.3	78.5	82.1
Operators	82.3	80.8	101.5

Source: Bureau of the Census, 1970 and 1980 Censuses of Population, *Characteristics of the Population.*

The Public Sector

The discussion so far has focused on the private sector, ignoring local, state, and federal governments which comprise one-third of the national economy. For over a century this country excluded from entry immigrants who could become public charges (paupers). However, the public sector, particularly the federal sector, was not a significant element in the economic structure of this nation during earlier periods of mass immigration.

In most instances, welfare agencies formed by immigrant groups and other volunteer agencies assumed responsibility for the care of indigent immigrants. Although government officials frequently complained that immigrants were a burden on their resources, data supporting this contention are limited, with the possible exception of statistics from California. There, the large and mostly poor Mexican population comprised one out of seven persons in state hospitals in the 1920s, with the number of sick Mexican persons requiring public health services close to one-third of the total. About one out of ten recipients of state aid in the 1920s was Mexican, and the percentage in Los Angeles County, with its large Mexican concentration, was even higher.[12]

Since statistics on Mexicans are incomplete, the total Mexican population in California is difficult to estimate. It appears, however that the number receiving services was greater on a per capita basis than in the non-Mexican population. This, of course, should not be surprising, considering the meager wages paid to Mexicans in the state.

Since the New Deal and Great Society eras, programs aimed at low-income persons have mushroomed, and the public sector at all levels expanded more rapidly than the private sector until the late 1970s. Given the current economic importance of this sector, there is reasonable concern that immigrants, particularly undocumented workers are or could become a financial burden on government. The Simpson-Mazzoli bill specifically excluded from eligibility for amnesty persons who may become public charges.

Los Angeles County has been particularly insistent in its public comments on immigration reform measures that such legislation include provisions requiring that the federal government reimburse localities for the costs of providing health or other care to undocumented aliens. The county argues, based on its own study undertaken in 1982, that the cost of providing services to undocumented aliens in that year totaled $214 million, but that the aliens contributed only $95 million in taxes, leading to a substantial deficit, which its nonimmigrant residents had to offset through their tax payments.[13]

The Simpson-Mazzoli bill, and particularly the version of the bill passed by the House of Representatives in June 1984, included provisions for the federal government to assume most of the social, health, and related costs for services provided to immigrants. The potential cost of these provisions led the Director of the Office of Management of the Budget (OMB) to issue a memorandum in early 1984 citing the multibillion dollar cost of these programs to federal agencies, an action many political observers considered to be an indirect statement of opposition to the bill by the Reagan administration. Indeed, the President stated in July 1984 that he was opposed to the version of the bill passed by the House because it would be "too costly." The opposition to fully compensating states for services provided to immigrants contributed to the failure of the conference committee to agree on a compromise, thus sealing the fate of the bill. This and other statements by public officials lead to the more general question: what is the effect of immigration on the public treasury at all levels of government?

Based on an extensive analysis of 15,000 immigrant families, one researcher has shown that the typical immigrant uses substantially fewer public services than a native-born resident from the time of entry until twelve years later.[14] These results were based on data from a national sample of immigrants residing in the United States during 1976. As shown in Table 1, however, immigrant groups differ sharply in their economic characteristics. In particular, Mexicans have lower earnings than their European or Asian counterparts. In view of these differences, one would not expect Simon's conclusions on service demands to necessarily include Hispanic immigrants. For example, the income of a typical household headed by a Mexican immigrant in Los Angeles is a third less than other households, while the income of recent Mexican immigrant households is closer to one-half the state average. It should not be surprising to find that Mexican immigrants produce a substantial fiscal deficit, particularly at the state level.

Since the California state tax structure is progressive, the average Mexican household in 1980 contributed only $1,515 in revenue, or just over one-half the state average.[15] Expenditures are also above the state average, but only modestly. At the local level, revenue payments by Mexican households were estimated at 77 percent of the average, and expenditures slightly above average.

What explains above-average outlays? Welfare services are not the culprit. Since well over half of all Mexican immigrants in the country are undocumented, they are ineligible for most social services. Los Angeles County has developed an extensive system to minimize abuse by those not eligible to receive these services because of their status. Public school costs account for the largest share of above-average public outlays, which is understandable since the typical Mexican household has more than twice as many children enrolled in these schools as non-Mexican households. In California, the state government pays for most public education from kindergarten to graduate school, which helps to explain the large state deficit. A recent study of undocumented Mexicans in Texas found that illegal aliens pay more in taxes than they receive in services at the state level, but produce a deficit at the local level.[16]

The concern many public officials have expressed is that if amnesty is granted and undocumented persons become eligible for services, demand will rise sharply. Since the federal government funding to states and localities may be terminated after a few years, the burden on nonimmigrant taxpayers would rise.

Is this concern reasonable? The majority of non-Hispanic immigrants is likely to demand less in services than it contributes in taxes. While the cost of providing services for Hispanics may exceed the average for all residents, at least part of this deficit may be offset, at the national level, by other immigrant groups. A distributional problem can exist if low-wage immigrants with large families are the dominant group in an area, since this would lead to an additional burden on local taxpayers. In the longer run, as the income of Hispanics rises, the burden they may impose would be reduced or eliminated.

It should be noted that the largest public outlay is for education. In the public school system, four dollars out of every five is spent for personnel. Most teachers are middle-class non-Hispanics, and the economic benefits from this outlay accrue to them (as well as to the children, since improved language and other skills will increase their chances of higher earnings). If most public funds for immigrants were spent on cash transfer payments, this could present a serious drain on middle-income residents. Currently, this is not a major concern because most jurisdictions carefully check eligibility for transfer payments.

Distributional Effects of Immigration

There is little doubt that from an aggregate economic perspective, immigrants, including those who are part of the current "fourth wave," have benefitted the nation—and themselves. Nevertheless, massive immigration has subtle internal distributional effects which need to be considered.

The income distribution in California has been altered by the presence of Mexican and other Hispanic immigrants, since the average income of these entrants is sharply below the native-born resident level. In California the mean income of households who came during the 1970s from Mexico, Jamaica, Haiti, and Central America was about $14,000 compared to $23,000 for native-born households. About 22 percent of all recent immigrants to the state are below the poverty level, while fewer than 8 percent of all native-born households fall into this low-income category. The high poverty level exists despite the fact that the typical immigrant household has 1.7 workers, a somewhat higher number than other households. This, of course, is attributable to low earnings and large family sizes among some immigrant groups.

In Los Angeles, immigrants comprise a substantial share of the total population considered to be below the poverty level. Whether wide income disparities among groups have an adverse effect on the total economy is by no means certain. Unquestionably there can be an added impact on the public sector, particularly if immigrants are eligible for social services. The adverse effects are more likely to be social rather than economic, at least in the short run. Large concentrations of low-income households, when combined with unrealized expectations of higher living standards, can create serious social tensions, as the urban riots of the 1960s attest. This concern is tempered by the fact that large numbers of low-income households come from Hispanic nations where income disparities are much wider than in the United States. And since most Hispanic immigrants, despite their low earnings, enjoy a higher living standard than all but a minority of their brethren in Mexico or Central America, their tolerance for income disparities tends to dampen social dissatisfaction among the first generation. However, income disparities, if they continue to widen, will unquestionably produce social tension among future generations.

Immigration affects the population not only vertically (across income categories) but also spatially. During periods of large-scale immigration to this nation, states which absorbed large numbers of immigrants, such as New York, were states with substantial outmigration of native-born residents. Concurrently, states with few immigrants tended to be those where substantial inmigration from other parts of the United States was taking place. This phenomenon was observed in all regions of the nation with the exception of the West between 1870 and 1920.[17] Both immigrants and internal migrants streamed to this nearly empty region in the late nineteenth and early twentieth centuries.

Is there any evidence that the new immigration wave is shifting the internal distribution of our population? California data for the 1970s and early 1980s indeed suggest that the internal movement of workers has been affected by immigration. Since the 1840s California has attracted internal migrants as well as immigrants in large numbers. Even during the Great Depression, net migration to the state exceeded one million. World War II resulted in probably the largest and most concentrated internal migration ever during a three-year period in American history, as millions moved to fill jobs in the state's mushrooming defense industries. The westward movement continued into the 1950s and 1960s. However, concurrent with the sharp immigration rise, internal migration slowed to a trickle from the mid-1970s to the early 1980s. During this eight-year period, more non-Hispanic whites and Hispanics left California than entered.

From an economic perspective, the most significant factors in migration are the economic characteristics of migrants. During the 1970s, about 250 thousand persons with a college education came to California from other states, while close to 100 thousand with little education left, a pattern also observed in the early 1980s.

Most recent entrants from other regions of the nation were professional workers and, to a lesser extent, persons with non-professional white-collar skills. At the same time, large numbers of semi-skilled as well as unskilled blue-collar and farm workers were leaving. Thus, persons leaving the state have the same characteristics as Mexican immigrants. Is this relationship coincidental? Probably not, since more unskilled workers continued to move into other Western states than were leaving these states. A more likely explanation is that as wages in low-skilled occupations declined relative to other wages, fewer persons in these occupations found California economically attractive. On the other hand, demand for professional workers was rising, stimulating the continuing inflow of these persons to the state.

From an economic perspective, this population exchange was probably efficient. However, the process may have reduced employment opportunities in California for unskilled workers from the Northeast and Midwest where unemployment rates during the late 1970s were high.

Conclusion

It is almost inevitable that the century-old debate on the economic impact of immigrants will continue regardless of revisions to the existing immigration legislation that may ultimately be passed by Congress and signed into law. This discussion will continue for two principal reasons. First, there will always be native-born workers at the bottom of the economic heap. These workers and groups who represent their interests will continue to fear those who may compete with them for unskilled jobs. Immigrants, particularly undocumented workers, are the most likely group in that category. Second, there has always been and will continue to be an element of the population opposed to immigration for reasons other than economic. These opponents will express economic arguments for restrictive measures because such positions are more socially acceptable than arguments based on race, ethnicity, religion, or place of origin. These noneconomic positions, widely expressed both publicly and privately half a century ago, are less acceptable in today's society. Thus, economic issues will continue for some to be a mask hiding their real concerns.

An examination of historical data, while deficient from a contemporary analytic perspective, nevertheless indicates that there were short-term adverse effects associated with mass immigration, primarily in the form of lower wages for unskilled workers. On the other hand, there is no evidence that any sizable unemployment resulted from the large immigrant inflow, perhaps because immigration slowed during periods of economic decline. It is important to recall that the deepest and longest depression in the nation's history followed the most restrictive immigration laws this nation ever promulgated. This is not to suggest any direct linkage between the two events. Nevertheless, states where internal migration continued, notably California, fared better economically than other states during the 1930s. Whether internal migrants (or immigrants) come to an area in response to jobs or create jobs is one of the oldest "chicken or egg" disputes in the economic literature. But despite our limited understanding of linkage between population growth and economic growth, it is evident that immigrants, just as internal immigrants, typically expand an economy. Thus, one finds the rate of per capita economic growth somewhat more rapid in places with net inmigration compared to those with net outmigration.

Minorities, specifically blacks, do not appear to have been adversely affected by the presence of Mexican immigrants. This is probably a reflection of the new opportunities which became available through a combination of affirmative action programs, higher education levels, and, at least in California, an expanding economy. Whether this favorable outcome will continue during the 1980s and beyond will depend to a considerable extent on the level of economic growth. If opportunities in more skilled and higher paying jobs continue to be available to minorities, the scale of job competition between immigrants and minorities should remain modest. Should opportunities for blacks to advance become constrained, conflicts will inevitably arise.

Viewing the issue broadly, there are numerous winners in the immigration game: businesses that hire undocumented workers and thus increase their profits, consumers who may pay lower prices and are able to obtain domestic help at affordable rates, and most importantly, immigrants themselves. Whatever arguments are made by organized labor and others that this nation exploits these workers, most derive more economic benefit from working in this nation than business enterprises who hire them or consumers.

Having identified some of the beneficiaries of immigration, we now turn to the other side of the coin: who are the losers? Groups in this category include marginal business firms unable or unwilling to hire immigrants but competing with firms that have such workers on their payroll; unions representing unskilled workers in areas where undocumented workers are a major component of the local labor force; and some low-skilled native-born workers unable to improve their occupational status and unwilling (or unable) to move from areas with large numbers of low-skill, low-wage immigrants to other regions.

Tax burdens for residents in areas with large numbers of low-income immigrant families can be expected to be somewhat above average. However, in most instances economic benefits to the aggregate local economy are likely to outweigh fiscal deficits which may accrue.

On balance, the economic benefits of immigration, based on our knowledge so far, tend to exceed private and in some areas public costs. However, serious research on the impact of recent immigration has merely begun. Further analysis may show that as a result of structural changes in the nation's economy, the effects of immigration are less positive than current information suggests. More likely are future findings showing that from an economic perspective immigrants are a plus to the nation. This should lead to a more thorough assessment of such noneconomic issues as social integration, language, and the environment.

7

VERNON M. BRIGGS, JR.

Employment Trends and Contemporary Immigration Policy

There have been few influences more important to the development of the population and the labor force of the United States than immigration. The descriptive phrase "a nation of immigrants" correctly portrays both the quantitative magnitude of the numbers of people who have come and the qualitative characteristics of their skill and educational contributions to the process of nation building. The fact that the United States continues to receive substantial inflows of immigrants remains a practice that distinguishes the nation from virtually all other countries. Through the 1970s and early 1980s, the United States has legally admitted twice as many immigrants and refugees for permanent settlement as the remaining nations of the world combined. If an allowance is made for the number of illegal immigrants who entered and settled during this same period, the gap is even more pronounced.

There are only two ways for a nation to acquire its labor force: people are born within its boundaries or they immigrate from other nations. Throughout most of the nineteenth and the early twentieth centuries, immigration was perhaps the most important aspect of U.S. human resource policy. The imposition of the nation's first ceilings on immigration in the 1920s was followed by several decades of depression, war, and their aftermath. As a consequence, immigration receded significantly, in terms of human resource importance, from the mid-1920s to the mid-1960s. Because of this diminished role over that forty year period, many scholars and policymakers have been slow to recognize that since the mid-1960s, immigration—in all of its diverse forms—has again become a major feature of the U.S. economy. During 1980, for example, it is probable that more foreign-born people came to the United States for permanent settlement than in any previous year in the nation's history. Moreover, the 1980 Census revealed that since 1970 "the number of foreign-born Americans has increased sharply after declining [each decade] since 1920 and [that] one of every ten people reported speaking a language other than English at home."[1] Noting the emerging trends, the demographer Leon Bouvier observed in 1981 that "immigration now appears to be almost as important as fertility insofar as U.S. population growth is concerned."[2] As the labor force is the principal means by which population changes are transmitted to the nation's economy, Bouvier warned that "there is a compelling argument for close coordination between the formulation of employment and immigration policy."[3]

The Data Dilemma

A persistent barrier to the study of the effects of immigration on the labor force is the gross deficiency of available data. Part of this inadequacy can be attributed to the decline in the relative importance of immigration to the nation from the mid-1920s to the mid-1960s. Since 1965, a myriad of other domestic human resource issues—such as youth unemployment, shortage of scientific and technical manpower, minority employment patterns, the job dislocation effects of changing technology, women in the labor market, anti-poverty concerns, and regional employment shifts— have diverted attention from the gradual re-emergence of immigration as a major concern.[4] As a result, there has been little pressure from scholars and policymakers for better collection and dissemination of immigration data despite major improvements in most other labor force data sources over this same time interval. The influence of immigration on the labor market is thus the weakest link in the nation's contemporary labor market statistics system.[5]

As a consequence, a recent congressional report on immigration concluded that despite "long established data collection programs, immigration-related data are still deficient in scope, quality, and availability," and that "immigration statistics are particularly inadequate as tools for policy analysis and demographic research."[6] Reliable information on the economic characteristics of legal immigrants and refugees is scant, and, for illegal immigrants, essentially nonexistent. Likewise, data on emigration flows have not been collected since 1958. Hence, net immigration cannot even be approximated.

The lack of reliable data has been consistently used by persons and groups who oppose reform of the nation's inadequate immigration system. This problem, however, must be put into proper perspective. Gross data deficiencies are not unique to the study of immigration. The lack of reliable and useful data plagues virtually every important area of public policy. Yet the lack of good data has in no way retarded the initiation of significant policy interventions in these other areas of public concern. It is only with respect to immigration reform that the argument has been effectively used to forestall reform efforts.

The Ability of Policy to Affect Labor Force Trends

The preponderance of labor force trends that occur within the economy are beyond the ability of policymakers to influence even if they want to do so. Labor market research has repeatedly shown, for instance, that race and gender can influence employment and income experiences. As the number and proportion of minorities and women have increased in the labor force, human resources policymakers can only respond with adjustment policies to reduce the influence of the factors that cause outcome differentials. The same is true for demographic changes in the age distribution of the labor force; for the shift in social values that contributed to the dramatic increase in female labor force participation; or for the effects of the pace and scope of technological change on the preparation of workers for jobs. The control of immigration flows, however, is considered an exercise in the use of the discretionary powers of the state. As such it is one dimension of a nation's human resource policy that *should* be capable of directive action rather than forced reaction.

Immigration has economic implications for the participants and for the receiving society. It can determine labor force trends as well as respond to them. For this reason, the efficacy of policies that regulate immigration must be judged in terms of how they relate to broader labor force trends at any prevailing time. As will be apparent, this is decidely not the case in the United States today.

The Influence of Administrative Structure

Because the magnitude and composition of immigration flows are supposedly subject to direct regulation by human institutions, it is important to understand the policy process. Although there is only scant mention of immigration in the Constitution, by the late nineteenth century the Supreme Court had concluded that the federal government was the exclusive governmental body to exercise this authority.[7] After a brief assignment of administrative power to several different agencies, the responsibility for immigration policy was ultimately shifted to the newly established U.S. Department of Labor (DOL) in 1914. This action represented a clear recognition by policymakers that labor market considerations should be a primary concern in the administration of immigration policy. In 1933, by executive order, immigration and naturalization functions were joined into one DOL body—the Immigration and Naturalization Service (INS).

With the recognition in 1940 of the likely involvement of the United States in World War II, a critical decision was made that has had lasting influence on the course of immigration policy. In

June 1940, the INS was shifted from DOL to the Department of Justice. Ostensibly, the shift was necessary for national security reasons; rapidly-changing international events dictated a more effective means of control over immigrants and nonimmigrants. Concern over subversive elements in the population was elevated to the highest priority of the agency. Labor market considerations —the historic concern—were shunted aside. When the war ended, the agency remained in the Department of Justice. The long run effects of this change have been disastrous to efforts to build a coherent immigration policy—especially if one of the concerns is that immigration policy should be congruent with domestic labor force trends. The Department of Justice has multiple responsibilities, and, when compared to its numerous other important duties, immigration matters have tended to be neglected or relegated to a low order of priority. Moreover, the Department of Justice is one of the most politically sensitive agencies in the federal government. It has often opted for short-run expedient solutions for immigration issues. It has seldom manifested any interest in the economic aspects and consequences of immigration.

Another lasting effect of the shift of immigration policy to the Justice Department has been that the two Judiciary Committees of Congress gained the responsibility for immigration and the INS. Traditionally, membership on these committees has been reserved (often exclusively) for lawyers. The result, as noted by David North and Allen LeBel, is that "as immigration problems arise, be they major or minor, perceived or real, the response of lawyer-legislators is that the law should be changed."[8] As a consequence, immigration law in the United States has become extremely complex. Over the years, the labor market implications of immigration policy have either been ignored or, in the best of circumstances, given superficial attention.

Immigration Trends since 1965

The revival of legal immigration as an influential force dates to passage of the Immigration Act of 1965. This represented the culmination of decades of efforts to purge the nation's immigration system of the overt national chauvinism that had been the central focus of the "national origins system" adopted in 1924.

After years of active struggle, the civil rights movement achieved its capstone goal—the passage of the Civil Rights Act of 1964. Just as racism could no longer be tolerated in the way citizens were treated by fellow citizens, neither could something like racism be practiced in the way non-citizens were considered for immigrant admission.

The restrictive "national origins system" had done more than shape the racial and ethnic composition of immigrant flows. It had sharply distorted the total flow of immigrants. Some nations with large quotas (e.g., Great Britain, which was entitled to about 40 percent of all of the available visas) did not use all of the available slots, while other nations (e.g., Italy and Greece) with small quotas prevented backlogs of would-be immigrants from entering. During the period 1952 to 1965, for example, only 61 percent of the available quotas were actually used despite the fact that tens of thousands of persons were precluded from admission because they came from the "wrong" country. Succeeding administrations in the post–World War II era were forced, to seek *ad hoc* legislation and use parole powers given to the Attorney General to admit hundreds of thousands of refugees for both humanitarian and national interest considerations. One of every three persons admitted to the United States from 1952 to 1965 entered outside the terms of the prevailing immigration system. Because the system was outdated by both worldwide and domestic events, the Immigration Act of 1965 was adopted.

It is important to note that while the changes enacted in 1965 significantly changed the system, the reform movement could not entirely escape the heavy hand of the past. Thus, while overt national chauvinism was eliminated in 1965, under the new act family reunification became the dominant factor in preferences for immigrant admission. This might *seem* to be a humane feature, but motivation for the change was far less noble. The change was made in the Judiciary Committee of the House of Representatives where some congressional supporters were more concerned with finding a way to covertly retain the older national origins system. Obviously, if certain groups had been excluded or had a low quota in the past they would have had fewer relatives who could use their presence to enter as new immigrants. Even though the Johnson administration sought to retain the emphasis on labor market considerations as the highest criterion (which had been the case since the use of a preference system to determine immigrant priorities was formally established in 1952), Congress made family reunification the main factor. Labor market considerations were downgraded to lower preferences and a reduced number of visa allotments. The ostensible reason for the reversal of priorities was that, during the era when labor market factors dominated the admission criteria, the system did not use all of the available slots. But as already noted, the reason for the inability to use all of the available slots between 1952 and 1965 was the distortion imposed by the "national origins system" — *not* the concept of labor priority.

In the years since 1965, there have been minor changes in the immigration system but it has retained a focus on family reunification. The system in early 1984 set a single worldwide admission ceiling of 270,000 visas per year. No more than 20,000 visas are allotted to the immigrants of any one country. The "immediate relatives" of each visa holder, however, are not counted in either ceiling. Immediate relatives are spouses, children, and parents of U.S. citizens over age 21. To decide which specific individuals are granted a visa under these numerical ceilings, a six category preference system exists. Four preference categories (accounting for 80 percent of the visas) are reserved for persons who are family related. Two of the categories are based on labor market principles. For these two categories, a person must secure a labor market certification from the DOL stating that the presence of the immigrant will not adversely affect the job opportunities and prevailing labor force standards of citizen workers. In addition to these considerations, Congress has established thirty-three separate classes of people who are specifically excluded from being admitted (e.g., paupers, prostitutes, Nazis, Communists, fascists, homosexuals) even if they are otherwise eligible.

Between 1965 and 1980, a separate preference group existed for refugees, with 17,400 slots. During that interval, however, the actual number of refugee admissions greatly exceeded this ceiling (averaging about 50,000 persons a year). The excesses were admitted through the use of the parole authority given to the Attorney General to admit persons for emergency reasons. Because the use of the parole powers was finally admitted to be a means of

circumventing the existing immigration statutes, refugees were
removed from the immigration system in 1980. With the Refugee
Act of 1980, refugees are now admitted under an entirely new procedure. Since 1982, the President has submitted to Congress the
number of refugees to be admitted in advance of the next fiscal
year. The number of refugees approved for 1984, for instance, is
72,000 persons.

The Refugee Act of 1980 also created for the first time an asylee
policy for the United States. As opposed to a refugee (who is
usually a person living outside of his or her home nation and who
fears persecution if forced to return, but who is *not* presently in
the United States), an asylee is a person who also fears similar
persecution if he or she returns to his or her homeland but is
already physically present in the United States. The Refugee Act
of 1980 authorized up to 5,000 asylee admissions a year. In early
1984, there were over 173,000 asylee requests pending approval
and it is likely that this number will continue to grow.

In addition to the "front door" approach to the nation's labor
market, there is a massive "back door" as well: the problem of illegal immigration. Although the legal system is extremely complex in its objectives, the entire system can be easily circumvented
by those who simply enter on their volition. All evidence indicates
that most illegal immigrants come to the United States to find
jobs—not to secure welfare or for criminal purposes. The exact illegal immigrant population or annual flows are unknown. In its
final report in 1981, the Select Commission on Immigration and
Refugee Policy cited from 3.5 to 6 million illegal immigrants
believed to be in the United States. Their estimate, however, was
based on a review by the Census Bureau of studies conducted in
the early and mid-1970s. Making this estimate, the bureau concluded "we have, unfortunately, been unable to arrive at definite
estimates of the number of illegal residents in the United States or
the magnitude of the illegal immigrant flow".[9] Whatever the
validity of the estimates included in the Select Commission report,
those estimates are based on the averaging of data for the
mid-1970s—not the mid-1980s. Given the certainty that illegal
immigration has increased since the mid-1970s, the stock and
flows are now greater than those cited by the commission's report.

Unfortunately, the only data series on illegal immigrants that is

Table 1

Illegal Immigrants Apprehended

Year	Number of Apprehended Illegal Immigrants
1965	110,371
1966	138,520
1967	161,608
1968	212,057
1969	283,557
1970	345,353
1971	420,126
1972	505,949
1973	655,968
1974	788,145
1975	756,819
1976	866,433
1977	1,033,427
1978	1,047,687
1979	1,069,400
1980	910,361
1981	975,780
1982	962,687
1983	1,248,000

Source: U.S. Department of Justice, *Annual Reports* of the Immigration and Naturalization Service.

consistently available is on apprehensions by the INS. This series, shown in Table 1 for the years 1965 to 1983, indicates a consistent upward trend. The problem with these data, of course, is that they cannot be corrected for multiple captures of the same individual in any one year. Yet there is no reason to believe that the multiple entry problem is proportionately any more substantial in the 1980s than it was in the 1960s. This series is probably reliable as a general indicator of the trend toward larger numbers of illegal immigrants in the U.S. labor force. Somewhat reluctantly, the General Accounting Office, in its exhaustive review in 1982 of the literature on the size of the illegal immigrant population came to the conclusion that, despite its limitations, the apprehension statistics are "the most comprehensive data on illegal aliens" available.[10] Of course, this series counts only those caught; apprehensions are only the tip of the iceberg.

With respect to immigration policy and the labor force, there remains the subject of nonimmigrant workers. For legitimate reasons, permission may be given to non-citizen workers (about 360,000 persons) to be employed in the United States. These are foreign ambassadors, the foreign news media, visiting professors, athletes, rock bands, and a wide assortment of other classifications. In most instances, there is little concern over labor force displacement effects. There is, however, one category of foreign workers in this grouping that has been a consistent source of debate as to the legitimacy of their need and their possible displacement effects. These are H-2 workers, admitted on a temporary basis. Some 23,000 H-2s were admitted annually in recent years; about one-half are agricultural workers. The number of H-2 workers, however, is not specified by law so the number can fluctuate depending upon employer demand and the willingness of the Department of Labor (and sometimes the Attorney General, who can override denial of a request by the DOL) to admit them.

Labor Market Impacts of the Era of Renewed Immigration

There is a paucity of credible research on the precise employment experiences of all groups of post-1965 immigrants. There is no data base to measure the labor force status of immigrants comparable to the information compiled in the monthly *Current Population Survey* of the U.S. Census Bureau for all workers in the United States. There is no published data series that indicates employment, unemployment, or labor force participation for immigrants. All that are available are administrative statistics, and *ad hoc* studies conducted over the past decade. From these disparate sources, it is possible to discern tendencies as well as conclusions. An awareness of these is a prerequisite to understanding the macroeconomic effects of immigration on the nation.

   The immigrant infusion to the supply of labor has increased. Legal immigrants since 1965 have more than doubled the annual flow for the period 1924 to 1965. For the earlier period, the annual flow was 191,000 immigrants and immediate relatives a year; for the period 1965 to 1981, the number increased to an annual average of 435,000; for the years 1978 to 1981, it was 547,000. These figures do not include refugees who have yet to adjust their status to become resident aliens, asylees whose status is still pending, or any illegal immigrants. If all flows are considered, it is likely that immigration in the 1980s accounts for as much as half of the annual growth in the population and probably an even greater percentage of the real growth of the labor force.[11]

The size of the annual flow of immigrants has no regard for domestic labor market conditions. The aggregate number of immigrants and immediate relatives admitted each year is completely independent of the prevailing labor market conditions. If allowance is also made for refugees admitted since 1965 and for the tide of illegal immigrants during this same period, there is no doubt that immigration has steadily added substantial numbers of workers regardless of the cyclical ability of the economy to provide sufficient jobs for either citizen or immigrant workers. This practice is unique among the handful of countries that have been admitting immigrants during this period.

Immigrants have a higher labor force participation rate. Legal immigrants are asked at the time they apply for a visa to specify an "occupation." The answers to this question have traditionally provided the scant occupational information that exists for immigrants. David North and William Weissert, in the early 1970s, found in a small sample survey that those adult immigrants who, at the time of entry, specified an "occupation" soon entered the labor force. In other words the answer to the question tended to be a rough proxy for a labor force participation rate. Using this procedure they found that the labor force participation rate of adult immigrants who entered the United States in the 1960s was only fractionally higher than 59 percent rate for the general population.

More importantly, North and Weissert compared the original data supplied at the time of entry with registration cards completed by immigrants two years later. They found a 20 percent increase in the number of persons who indicated that they had an occupation.[12] The additional workers came largely from the immediate relatives of legal adult, female immigrants who had previously listed themselves as "housewives" and from some of their children who were initially classified as "students." North and

Weissert contended that the estimates provided by other studies
that relied only on labor force information at the time of entry
seriously "understated" the real impact of legal immigrants on the
labor market because of their failure to allow for these subsequent
labor force entry decisions.

There are no such data, of course, for illegal immigrants, but it
is obvious that their labor force participation rates are as high, if
not higher, than those of legal immigrants. Illegal immigrants are
primarily job seekers, and as such they are ineligible for many of
the transfer programs that might provide alternative income
sources. The situation of refugees, however, is not quite so clear.
Refugees prior to the 1970s seem to have adjusted to labor force
entry more easily than did the refugees from Southeast Asia who
have entered since the mid-1970s. Refugees have been eligible not
only for federal income transfer programs but also for local and
state programs.

On balance, however, it seems certain that the labor force participation rate of all immigrants since 1965 is considerably higher
than that of the labor force as a whole.

**Immigration supplies workers without regard to the
macro human resource needs of the economy.** The overwhelming proportion of all those persons who have emigrated to
the United States have been admitted regardless of their skill,
education, or geographic settlement preferences. Eighty percent
of the persons who received visas to immigrate are admitted
because the immigration system gives preference to family
reunification. Immediate relatives of all immigrants are admitted
regardless of their labor force credentials as are all refugees and
would-be asylees. This is not meant to imply that those who are
admitted under these procedures lack talents but, as David North
and Allen LeBel have observed, they "do so accidentally."[13] Accordingly, it is estimated that only about 5 percent of all persons admitted to the United States are required to have labor certifica-
tions indicating that they are meeting established labor force
needs. If illegal immigrants are included this small percentage
of labor certified workers would be reduced to an even smaller
number.

The immigrant flow is mainly composed of members of minority groups. The most important qualitative change in the personal characteristics of immigrants that has occurred since the end of the national origins system has been the complete shift in the immigrants' regions of origin. Almost 80 percent of the immigrants and refugees admitted during the 1970s were from Latin America and Asia. In the 1980s, the percentage is closer to 84 percent. Beginning with the decade of the 1960s, Europe was replaced for the first time in the nation's history by Latin America as the leading source of immigrants. By the 1970s, Asia, free from the discriminatory features of the previous immigration system, was challenging Latin America for that distinction.

The shift in the source of immigrants is revealed vividly by an examination of the nations that have become the primary source of immigrants since 1970 (Table 2). The last time a European nation was included in this ranking was 1973 (when Italy placed fifth). Mexico has clearly become the country producing the most immigrants and the Philippine Islands have tended to be the runner-up. The other leading source countries vary from year to year, but since 1974 all have been located in either Asia or the Caribbean Basin area.

The predominance of immigrants from Latin America and the Caribbean area can be easily explained in terms of the priority given to family reunification in the admissions system. For Asians, the explanation is more complex. It would seem that the family reunification system should have worked against many Asian groups, given the exclusionary features that were in effect for much of the pre-1965 era. The answer to this paradox lies in the fact that Asians have made astute use of the occupational preferences, and in the fact that they have overwhelmingly dominated the massive refugee flows since the mid-1970s.

Likewise, the illegal immigrant flows have been dominated by flows from Mexico and the Caribbean area. The best approximations are that about 60 percent of the illegal immigrants to the United States come from Mexico and about 20 percent come from other countries of the Caribbean area. The remaining 20 percent come from other nations of the world.

Without a doubt, the combined immigrant flows are overwhelmingly composed of persons from minority groups (Hispanics,

Table 2
Legal Immigration Figures

Year	Total Legal Immigration		Rank Order of Immigrant Source Countries					Percentage of Total Accounted For By Five Highest Countries
			First	Second	Third	Fourth	Fifth	
1969	358,579	Country Total Percent	Mexico 44,623 12.4	Italy 23,617 6.6	Philippines 20,744 5.8	Canada 18,582 5.2	Greece 17,724 4.9	34.9
1970	373,326	Country Total Percent	Mexico 44,469 11.9	Philippines 31,203 8.4	Italy 24,973 6.7	Greece 16,464 4.4	Cuba 16,334 4.4	35.7
1971	370,478	Country Total Percent	Mexico 50,103 13.5	Philippines 28,471 7.7	Italy 22,137 6.0	Cuba 21,611 5.8	Greece 15,939 4.3	37.3
1972	384,685	Country Total Percent	Mexico 64,040 16.7	Philippines 29,376 7.6	Italy 21,427 5.6	Cuba 20,045 5.2	Korea 18,876 4.9	35.8
1973	400,063	Country Total Percent	Mexico 70,141 17.5	Philippines 30,799 7.7	Cuba 24,147 6.0	Korea 22,930 5.7	Italy 22,151 5.5	44.2
1974	394,861	Country Total Percent	Mexico 71,586 18.1	Philippines 32,857 8.3	Korea 28,028 7.1	Cuba 18,929 4.8	China-Taiwan 18,056 4.6	42.9

Year							
1975	386,194	Country	Mexico	Philippines	Korea	Cuba	China-Taiwan
		Total	62,205	32,857	28,362	25,955	18,536
		Percent	16.1	8.5	7.3	6.7	4.8	43.4
1976	398,615	Country	Mexico	Philippines	Korea	Cuba	China-Taiwan
		Total	57,863	37,281	30,803	29,233	18,823
		Percent	14.5	9.4	7.7	7.3	4.7	43.6
1976 TQ[a]	103,676	Country	Mexico	Philippines	Korea	Cuba	China-Taiwan
		Total	16,001	9,738	6,887	6,763	5,034
		Percent	15.4	9.4	6.6	6.5	4.9	42.8
1977	462,315	Country	Cuba	Mexico	Philippines	Korea	China-Taiwan
		Total	69,708	44,079	39,111	30,917	19,764
		Percent	15.1	9.5	8.5	6.7	4.3	44.0
1978	601,442	Country	Mexico	Vietnam	Philippines	Cuba	Korea
		Total	92,367	88,543	37,216	29,754	29,288
		Percent	15.4	14.7	6.2	4.9	4.9	46.0
1979	460,368	Country	Mexico	Philippines	China-Taiwan	Korea	Vietnam
		Total	52,096	41,300	29,264	24,248	22,546
		Percent	11.3	9.0	6.4	5.3	4.9	36.8
1980	530,639	Country	Mexico	Vietnam	Philippines	Korea	China-Taiwan
		Total	56,680	43,483	42,483	32,320	27,651
		Percent	10.7	8.2	8.0	6.1	5.2	38.2
1981	596,600		na	na	na	na	na	na

[a]Transitional quarter

[b]Projected estimate

Source: Select Commission on Immigration and Refugee Policy, *U.S. Immigration Policy and the National Interest*, Staff Report, Supplement to the Final Report, (Washington, D.C.: Government Printing Office, 1981), pp. 230–231.

blacks, and Asians). As will be discussed later, there is a strong clustering pattern of immigrants in local labor markets of the central cities of a few large states that are already partly composed of persons from similar racial and ethnic backgrounds. As a result, it is very likely that many immigrants compete directly with other citizen minority workers for available jobs. The competition is likely to be most severe in the lower-skilled occupations. For the higher-skilled legal immigrants, as indicated earlier, the competition for employment opportunities is more broadly based. It is likely, therefore, that since 1965 immigration in general— but illegal immigration and refugee flows in particular—has tended to adversely affect the employment opportunities of minority citizens. To the degree this has happened, uncontrolled immigration has worked at cross purposes with other human resources policies initiated over these same years and designed principally to increase the economic opportunities available to these minority citizen groups.

The occupational pattern of immigrants is radically different from that of the labor force as a whole. With specific reference to the occupational pattern of immigrants, the occupational distribution of those admitted as legal immigrants is skewed toward professional, technical, and skilled workers. This is due largely to the bias of the complex admission system toward those who have family connections as well as the time and the money to work their way through the labyrinth of the legal immigration system. The minority admitted under the two occupational preferences are primarily those with high skills and/or extensive educational backgrounds. Persons who are likely to become "public charges" are specifically excluded from becoming legal immigrants regardless of their national origin. Furthermore, because of the extensive backlog of visa applications (over 1.2 million visa applications were pending at the end of 1982) there have been no visas available since 1978 for the non-preference residual category that theoretically exists. It is not surprising that the occupational characteristics are skewed differently from the distribution of the labor force as a whole. Yet, it should also be apparent that given this occupational distribution, it is likely that legal immigrants do compete extensively with the citizen labor force for jobs in white-collar and skilled blue-collar occupations. Even though 80 percent of the legal immigrants are admitted under family reunification principles, it is a mistake to believe that there are no labor market consequences that flow from their presence.

David North's studies of a cohort of 1970 immigrants and a study by Barry Chiswick of the foreign born who entered the U.S. prior to 1970 indicate that the earnings of immigrants initially tend to be below those of citizen workers in comparable occupations, but the differences gradually vanish in eleven to fifteen years.[14] Moreover, Chiswick found that male immigrants actually end up doing better than citizen workers in comparable occupations after about twenty years in the country. He was unable to make conclusive findings about female immigrants. Interestingly, Chiswick found that immigrants from Mexico and the Philippines (the two countries that have been the largest sources of legal immigrants since 1965) were the least likely to sustain these favorable results.

In reviewing Chiswick's ambitious research on this subject, it is vital to note that his analysis is of all foreign-born persons who had entered the United States prior to 1970. Since 1970, the full effects of the Immigration Act of 1965 and the Refugee Act of 1980 have become manifest. North emphasizes that the 1970 Census data on the foreign born concerns a group composed of persons of above-average age, most of whom came to the U.S. many years earlier and under provisions of earlier legislation."[15] Consequently he warns against the use of this data as a reference group since "one must not assume that the profile of the foreign born which emerged from the 1970 Census will be similar to that emerging from the 1980 or 1990 Censuses."[16] For example, the sizeable increases in the number of illegal immigrants since the 1960s—especially those from Mexico and the Caribbean Basin— have been dominated by low and unskilled workers. In Chiswick's work, there is no way to separate the experience of legal immigrants from illegal immigrants since the foreign born as reported by the census are a collective statistical grouping. It is certain that the illegal immigrant population is severely undercounted in the census and, accordingly, it is likely that its experiences are not adequately captured by this data base.

One study that has made use of the 1980 Census and its data on the foreign born was done by Gregory DeFreitas and Adriana Marshall. It found that over one-third of all immigrants were employed in manufacturing (compared to 23 percent of native-born workers).[17] In many metropolitan areas, the concentration was even more pronounced—75 percent of all manufacturing workers in Miami were immigrants, as were over 50 percent of those in Los Angeles and New York City, 25 percent in San Francisco, and 20 percent in Chicago and Boston. In thirty-five metropolitan areas with a population of more than one million, immigrants comprised 19 percent of all production jobs in manufacturing. Not surprisingly, given the occupational, industrial, and geographic concentration of the immigrant work force, the study found that the rate of wage growth in manufacturing was inversely related to the size of the immigrant population in those metropolitan areas. The high concentration of foreign-born workers had a statistically significant negative impact on wage growth compared to the experience of large metropolitan areas with lower percentages of foreign-born workers. The study does have some of the same data problems that confronted Chiswick (i.e., all forms of immigrants are lumped together, the data is cumulative in that it fails to make distinctions among individuals based on the length of their residency in the U.S., and illegal immigrants are likely to be undercounted), but it does have the real advantage of using 1980 data.

Given that the illegal immigrant flows into the labor force since 1965 are likely to have matched and probably exceeded the legal flows, it is essential that the labor market experiences of illegal immigrants be specifically included in any effort to assess the overall impact of immigrants on the labor market. There are only two major studies that have attempted to analyze these patterns. One is a 1976 nationwide study by David North and Marion Houstoun of apprehended illegal immigrants.[18] The second is a 1979 study by a research team from the University of California at Los Angeles (UCLA) of unapprehended illegal immigrants in Los Angeles.[19] Both studies were funded by the U.S. Department of Labor. In the North and Houstoun study, the respondents had been in the United States for an average of two and one-half years while in the UCLA study the mean was four years.

Table 3

**Employment Patterns of Illegal Immigrants from
Two Research Studies Prepared for the U.S. Department of Labor**

	Detention Site Study, 1974–1975	Los Angeles Community Study 1972–1975		
	All Apprehended Aliens	Total	Apprehended Aliens	Apprehended Aliens
White Collar:	5.4	10.5	6.6	12.1
Professional and technical	1.6	4.3	2.7	5.0
Managers and administrators	1.3	0.7	.8	.7
Salesworkers	1.1	1.9	.8	2.3
Clerical	1.4	3.6	2.3	4.1
Blue Collar:	55.2	73.0	79.0	70.4
Craft workers	15.3	28.8	32.8	27.1
Operatives	25.1	31.8	31.1	32.1
Non-farm laborers	14.8	12.4	15.1	11.2
Service Workers	20.6	16.1	14.2	16.9
Farm Workers	18.8	.4	.2	.5
Total percent	100.0	100.0	100.0	100.0

Sources: For detention site study: David S. North and Marion F. Houstoun, *The Characteristics and Role of Illegal Aliens in the U.S. Labor Market: An Exploratory Study.* (Washington, D.C., Linton & Company, 1976) p. 104. For L.A. community study: Maurice D. Van Arsdol Jr., Joan Moore, David Heer, Susan P. Haynie, *Non-Apprehended and Apprehended Undocumented Residents in the Los Angeles Labor Market.* Final Draft submitted to the U.S. Department of Labor under Research Contract No. 20-06-77-16, (May, 1979), p. 65.

The occupational patterns of the respondents in the two studies are shown in Table 3. Clearly, the illegal immigrants are concentrated in unskilled occupations such as farm workers, service workers, non-farm laborers, and the semi-skilled blue-collar occupations of operatives. A significant number are also in the skilled blue-collar occupation of craft workers. Few were found in any white-collar occupation.

A comparison of the data in Table 3 with the employment patterns of the nations black and Mexican-origin workers will show that workers from these groups are employed disproportionately in exactly the same occupations as are most illegal immigrants in the cited studies. The employment pattern of Mexican-origin workers better resembles the patterns of illegal immigrants than it does the general distribution pattern of the nation's labor force.

It seems certain that the illegal immigrant workers are concentrated in the secondary labor market of the U.S. economy where they often compete with the millions of citizen workers who also work or seek work in this sector. Indeed, Under-Secretary of Labor Malcolm Lovell in his testimony to Congress in support of immigration reform, stated that "in 1981, close to 30 percent of all workers employed in this country, some 29 million people, were holding down the same kind of low-skilled industrial, service, and farm jobs in which illegals typically find employment."[20]

Illegal immigrants are by no means the only cause of unemployment and persistent low income patterns among certain subgroups of the American labor force, but they certainly are a factor. The formulation of any serious full employment strategy for the United States in the 1980s, therefore, will have to include measures to curtail illegal immigration.

It would appear that the occupational impact of legal immigrants is at the upper end of the nation's occupational structure while the impact of illegal immigrants is at the lower end. Studies that combine these two groups to obtain an average measure of the impact of immigrants on the labor force (e.g., those that use the data for the foreign-born population) miss the significance of this dichotomy. The important point is that in both segments of the labor force there is competition with citizen workers and in both cases there is no guidance provided by the immigration system.

**The locational impact of immigrants is extremely un-
equal.** One of the most pronounced effects of the unguided immigration system is that legal immigrants are highly concentrated into a few major labor markets. Since 1966 California and
New York have consistently accounted for about 46 percent of the
intended residences of all legal immigrants. Texas, Florida, New
Jersey, and Illinois account for about 25 percent of the remainder.
Thus, six states have received almost three-fourths of all legal immigrants. Data from the 1980 Census also confirm this high concentration rate of the total foreign-born population in the same
states (the percentage of foreign born in California was 14.8 percent, New York 13.4 percent, New Jersey 10.3, Florida 10.9, Illinois 7.3, and Texas 6.0).[21]

Legal immigrants in the 1970s have consistently settled in the
large central cities of those states.[22] Although the exact percentages vary from year to year, a central city was the destination of
about 55 percent of the immigrants who were admitted between
1960 and 1979. Urban areas—with a population of between 2,500
to 99,000 people—were the clear second choices while rural areas
were a distant last. These initial residential patterns differ from
those of the general population, for whom urban areas have
become the overwhelming first choice since 1960 (accounting for
almost half of the population) followed by an almost equal
preference (of about 25 percent each) for central cities and rural
areas.

The census information on the foreign-born population in 1980
vividly demonstrates the effect that immigration is having on the
population of a few large metropolitan areas. In 1980, for instance,
the metropolitan area with the highest percentage of foreign born
within its population was Miami, with a phenomenal 35.2 percent.
The second highest was Los Angeles (21.6 percent), and the third
was New York City (20.8 percent). Thus, the burden of accommodating the growing immigrant flow has not fallen evenly. Only
a few states and a handful of cities have borne the brunt of the
revival of immigration that has occurred since 1965. Moreover,
the settlement pattern of illegal immigrants has closely resembled
the locational preferences of legal immigrants. In their quest to
avoid detection, illegal immigrants often seek to blend into communities that already have large numbers of persons from similar

ethnic backgrounds. This tendency, of course, only intensifies the pressures on these few states and cities to accommodate immigrants.

The uneven distribution of immigrants means that studies focusing on the national level and using aggregate labor force data miss the actual impact of immigration. The labor forces in many states and localities are largely unaffected by this phenomenon. But the states (and their central cities) forced to accomodate massive immigration account for a significant portion of the total employment in the nation. Thus, the differential impacts of immigration affect the economy as a whole.

In the short run, it is likely that immigrants contribute to higher unemployment rates. Although the available research is very limited, Chiswick found that foreign-born males take about five years to reach the same number of weeks worked and to accumulate the same number of weeks unemployed as native-born men.[23] His finding suggests that, in the short run, immigrant males tend to experience a higher incidence of unemployment than is generally the case. Chiswick also found that the foreign-born males from Mexico, Cuba, and China tended to take longer to reach parity with native-born men than did the foreign-born men from other nations. As indicated in Table 2, since 1970 all three of these countries have consistently ranked among the largest sources of legal immigrants and refugees. Again, it is important to keep in mind all of the limitations of the Chiswick analysis—especially the fact that his work is based largely on the experiences of the foreign born *prior to the 1970s.* It is logical to conclude that the experiences of the past decade should be less positive than those of the 1970s.

Concluding Observations

The prevailing immigration policy of the United States was largely conceived in the early 1950s and the mid-1960s when immigration was not a particularly significant influence on the national economy. As a consequence, the current immigration policy manifests a complete disinterest in its labor force implications. Perhaps the nation could continue to allow immigration policy to remain indifferent to America's economic welfare if the economy had not undergone significant changes and if the immigration flows of workers had remained relatively small. But this has not been the case. Hence, the "practice" of allowing immigration policy to continue to follow its own nepotistic, inflexible, mechanistic, and massively abused course is a "luxury" that this nation can ill-afford.

The contemporary economy of the United States is a far cry from the one into which earlier waves of immigrants entered. The resurgence of immigration since 1965 has coincided with a period of unprecedented changes in both the size and composition of the American labor force.

With regard to size, the civilian labor force increased by an average of 1.8 million workers each year from 1964 to 1973; and annually by 2.2 million from 1973 to 1980. Since then, the rate of annual increase—as officially measured (which means that it is doubtful that the full effects of growing numbers of illegal immigrants are included)—has declined slightly. Nonetheless, in 1984 the Bureau of Labor Statistics (BLS) announced that it is revising its long-term projections of labor force growth from the period 1982 to 1990 to 1.6 million new workers each year. Even this figure is likely to be conservative—as all similar projections by BLS in the past have been.

As for the composition of the labor force, the period since 1965 has been one in which racial and ethnic groups as well as women have dramatically increased their representation in the total labor force. The BLS projects that these patterns will continue— with women accounting for two-thirds of the annual growth in the labor force and blacks about 25 percent over the next decade. It is certain—especially if immigration continues the pattern of the past—that the Hispanic labor force will also increase its share disproportionately even though the BLS did not highlight this group in its projections.

In terms of the entire labor force, the next decade presents the nation with a unique situation. Because the baby boom generation has now come of age, it is projected that by 1990 the largest single age cohort of the population will be between the ages of 25 to 44— the prime working years. It is a period when labor force participation is at its highest for both males and females. During the late

1980s and early 1990s, it is predicted that there will be more persons in the labor force than not—including babies. By 1995, it is expected that 70 percent of the labor force will be between 25 to 54 years of age. Thus, it will be a period of mounting pressure to generate additional employment opportunities—especially for women and minorities.

It is clear that the last two decades of the twentieth century are going to be years in which the labor force of the nation will be confronted with immense pressures to accommodate both the growth in the number of jobs seekers and their changing characteristics. The quest to meet these challenges will be difficult enough without an immigration policy that is seemingly oblivious to its labor market impacts but that, in actuality, has important labor market consequences.

The broad outlines of the policy reform needed to make immigration policy conform to the economic welfare of the nation are easy to list. With respect to the annual levels of immigration, there need to be enforceable ceilings. But they should be ceilings and not inflexible numbers. The actual number of immigrants admitted should be responsive to unemployment trends in the nation. Annual immigration levels should fluctuate inversely with unemployment trends. The system should be capable of responding to changing economic circumstances. The boundary ceiling should be set by legislation but the precise levels in any given year should be set administratively. The administrative responsibilities for immigration policy should be shifted back to the U.S. Department of Labor (or some new agency that might be created to administer and coordinate all of the nation's human resource development policies) and away from the judiciary committees of Congress. Likewise, this agency should have complete control over the admission of nonimmigrant temporary workers.

The criteria for determining who will be admitted as a legal immigrant should give priority to the occupational preferences, which characterized the preference system from 1952 to 1965. (It should be recalled that such a change would *not* affect the status of immediate family members as they are not counted.) Family reunification should remain an admission criterion, but not the primary one. No other nation in the world allows such a nepotistic and discriminatory doctrine to dominate its admission system.

The occupational preferences should be increased to at least the pre-1965 level of 50 percent of the available visas. In addition, the occupational categories should be changed to allow the entire range of skill levels (i.e., unskilled, semi-skilled, and skilled) to be admitted with full discretion given to the administrative agency to decide which occupations are in greatest need at any particular time. Included within this discretionary power should be the right to give preference to immigrants willing to settle in regions where labor is scarce. The shift away from the dominance of family reunification would also allow opportunities for "new seed immigrants" (especially for immigrants from Africa who have the most trouble competing under the existing system) to enter.

The refugee and asylee policies of the nation are the most difficult to integrate into a policy design that focuses on economic priorities. Obviously, the United States should continue to participate in the worldwide effort to absorb, and to assist in the accommodation of, refugees. But experience clearly indicates that there must be some limitations on the number of refugees that are to be admitted and where they are to be settled. A legislative ceiling should be set on the number of refugees to be admitted with the understanding that, if special circumstances do arise, more refugees may be admitted, but that offsetting reductions will be made in the number of legal immigrants in the same or the following year. If a situation should develop that is truly extraordinary, Congress could legislate a temporary increase in the numerical boundaries to accommodate such a unique circumstance.

The asylee issue is presently too complex to discuss in this paper except to note that the current policy is hopelessly bogged down by judicial paralysis. It is essential that a more efficient system for reaching closure in these cases be designed. But the ultimate principle for admission should be the same as for refugees: namely, if asylee permissions are granted, legal immigration should be reduced accordingly. It is essential that the principle of choice be firmly established in the operation of the nation's immigration system. Otherwise, one is confronted with the chaos of the present system, in which the policy is essentially one that ratifies what has already happened. Moreover, the idea that total immigrant flows should fluctuate with domestic labor market conditions makes no sense if the entire process can be circumvented by flows from another source. There are already signs that the refugee and asylee system is being used for purposes other than those for which it was designed—to avoid persecution because of one's political views. The full cost of assisting refugees and asylees should be borne by the federal government.

All of the preceding suggestions, of course, are predicated on the assumption that a full-scale effort will be mounted to end the flow of illegal immigrants into the country. It would make no sense at all to attempt to construct a postive immigration policy that works in tandem with general economic policy if the entire process can be easily circumvented. The appropriate policies should be designed to address both the "push" and the "pull" factors that contribute to the illegal immigration process. They should include enhanced deterrent policies (e.g., employer sanctions, increased INS funding, and less reliance on the use of the voluntary departure system) as well as preventive measures (e.g., extensive economic and technical development assistance, trade and tariff concessions, and the absolute insistence on the adherence to human rights principles as a prerequisite for receipt of the economic aid and trade concessions).

The absence of any serious effort to forge an immigration policy based upon labor market considerations means that immigration policy today functions as a "wild card" among the nation's array of key labor market policies. Unlike all other elements of economic policy (e.g., fiscal policy, monetary policy, employment and training policy, education policy, and anti-discrimination policy) where attempts are made by policymakers to orchestrate the diverse policy elements into a harmony of action to accomplish particular objectives, immigration policy has been allowed to meander aimlessly. This is a situation that no sensible nation can allow to continue.

8

IVAN LIGHT

Immigrant Entrepreneurs in America: Koreans in Los Angeles

In the mid-1970s, Los Angeles became aware that a large and rapidly growing Korean colony had formed along Olympic Boulevard about three miles west of the Civic Center. Anyone traveling down this boulevard would notice the many English/Hangul-lettered signs proclaiming the presence of Korean small businesses. The growing Korean colony was the more striking because in 1970 hardly any Koreans had resided in Los Angeles. In recognition of the new Korean enclave, and in response to repeated requests from the Koreatown Development Association, the City of Los Angeles proclaimed the Olympic Boulevard neighborhood "Koreatown" in 1980, and posted signs so stating on major streets and freeways. Representing, by 1980, about four-fifths of one percent of the total population of Los Angeles County, 60,618 Koreans were still a numerically small minority even after a decade of immigration. Nonetheless, the Korean minority was conspicuous among those "persevering Asians" whom the *Los Angeles Times* editorially identified as the city's "new middle class" chiefly on the basis of their visibility in small business.[1]

The extent of Korean entrepreneurship was, in fact, remarkable. In 1982, the yellow pages of the Korean telephone directory enumerated 4,266 Korean-owned business firms in Los Angeles County, approximately 2.6 percent of all county firms. In retail trade, Koreans operated nearly 5 percent of all firms in the county. Since Koreans numbered less than one percent of county population, their "overrepresentation" was appreciable in business, especially retail business. However, other measures discovered even higher "overrepresentation" in business. A Korean-American scholar found that 40 percent of Korean heads of household were self-employed in 1978 compared to only 7.6 percent of the Los Angeles County population. Moreover, these Korean entrepreneurs employed an additional 40 percent of coethnics in their firms so that fully 80 percent of employed Koreans in Los Angeles County actually worked in Korean-owned firms, mostly service and retail proprietorships.

As these figures suggest, Koreans did not achieve so large a small-business sector by reliance upon coethnic customers. Of course, some Korean-owned stores specialized exclusively in coethnic trade. However, taking all the Korean firms together, only about one-fourth of their customers were Korean, while three-quarters were non-Korean. Blacks, whites, and Hispanics each represented about one-quarter of the Koreans' customers, but, in view of their representation in county population, blacks were overrepresented twofold and whites appreciably underrepresented by their quarters. Hispanics were represented at approximately their expected number.

Korean entrepreneurship did not develop in what mainstream business corporations regarded as an attractive business climate. Despite its glittering reputation, Los Angeles suffered the blighted conditions common among big American cities. Crime, unemployment, residential crowding, time consumed in the journey to work, and housing prices all increased faster than national averages in the 1970s. *De facto* segregation of public schools was not reduced, and educational quality declined. These changes accompanied demographic trends generally indicating lower socioeconomic population characteristics in the urban core relative to the ring—and increased residential segregation of whites from blacks, Asians, and Hispanics. The percentage white in the city's population declined from 59.0 in 1970 to 44.4 in 1980. In the surrounding county of Los Angeles, the percentage white declined from 65.9 percent to 49.4 percent.

More to the point, the growth of retail business firms was negligible in both the city and the surrounding county, but the suburban ring registered a 23 percent increase. As measured by employees, the average size of retail firms increased in the ring, but decreased in the core. Service firms increased 59 percent in city and county, but in the outer ring service firms increased 118 percent. Average size of service firms increased in the core as well as in the ring, but it increased much faster in the ring. Although typically small "mom and pop" stores, Korean firms were not the smallest firms in the non-agricultural economy. True, Korean firms in Los Angeles were smaller than the average of all firms in terms of employees, legal form of organization, and invested capital. However, since this average of all firms includes large corporations, it diminishes by contrast the relative stature of Korean firms. Compared to proprietorships, Korean firms were larger than average in employees and invested capital.

Benefits of Korean Entrepreneurship

Korean-owned firms conferred obvious economic benefits upon Los Angeles in that they serviced low income, heavily non-white neighborhoods generally ignored and underserved by big retail corporations. As a result, wheels of commerce ground where they would otherwise have been still, and the City of Los Angeles took a percentage in sales tax. Additionally, the Koreans injected foreign capital into the Los Angeles economy, thus stimulating employment and earnings. Some Americans had jobs in Korean-owned firms established with Korean capital. When these Americans spent their paychecks, other Americans became indirect beneficiaries of Korean immigration and entrepreneurship.

Despite these economic benefits, Koreans experienced conflicts with some Americans as a result of their rapid influx and concentration in mercantile roles. The most serious tensions arose between Korean merchants and black customers in central Los Angeles. Some blacks complained about high prices in Korean stores, discourteous service, non-employment of blacks in Korean firms, and the tendency for Korean merchants to reside outside the black neighborhoods in which they located their markets. Indeed, Los Angeles' black newspaper, *The Sentinel,* complained that when Korean merchants replaced Jewish predecessors, blacks who had been working in the stores lost their jobs and prices increased. Nonetheless, black efforts to boycott Korean merchants fizzled because black leaders opposed a boycott that they regarded as extreme, unwarranted, and impolitic. In addition, black consumers had no realistic alternative to shopping in Korean markets. Finally, Los Angeles Koreans made intelligent efforts to reduce intergroup tensions having learned about earlier black-Korean conflict in Washington, D.C.; Philadelphia; and New York City. Therefore, Los Angeles' Korean organizations arranged a "treaty" of cooperation with black civic organizations. Korean and black leaders toasted this treaty at a festive banquet. Although this treaty did not prevent tensions, it greatly reduced black interest in a boycott.

Korean entrepreneurship conferred social as well as economic benefits upon Los Angeles. The Korean influx tended to restore and revive the neighborhoods in which Koreans settled. In addition to Koreatown, residential home of one-third of county Koreans, Koreans clustered in a handful of widely scattered locations, often associating with other Asians. Koreatown itself developed in a deteriorating, underutilized area on the northern boundary of the city's black ghetto. As Koreans moved in, this neighborhood's appearance and prosperity revived. Property values increased. As the *Los Angeles Times* editorially observed:

Koreans have taken run-down structures, weedy lots, and neglected streets in the previously declining area, and turned them into thriving businesses interspersed with clean, landscaped areas.[2]

Further, residential and commercial interests compelled Koreans to take a stand against street crime. Unlike whites who fled to the suburbs, Koreans were tethered to inner-city businesses and to Koreatown. Crime rendered Koreatown stores and streets unprofitable as well as unsafe. Hard as it was for Koreatown residents to tolerate street crime, it was impossible for Koreatown merchants who required safe streets and parking lots in order to guarantee access to their business premises. Moreover, retail store and service proprietors lived in fear of armed robbers whose street culture had discovered the wisdom of routinely murdering victims and witnesses. Several Korean merchants died at the hands of gunmen. The Korean Chamber of Commerce accordingly undertook vigorous anti-crime campaigns in Koreatown. Koreans demanded additional police protection and, when politicians were insufficiently accommodating, Koreans conducted public subscriptions to pay for a bilingual police outpost in Koreatown, citizen patrols of Koreatown streets, anti-crime seminars, and even anti-crime billboard advertising in the Korean language.

Ambitious Koreans also raised the level of achievement in the public schools. Korean parents encouraged their children to excel in school. As a result, Korean students were outstanding academic achievers in the public schools, easily winning more than their share of honors, prizes, and college scholarships. In 1982 Koreans represented 2.9 percent of the undergraduate student body at the University of California, Los Angeles even though Koreans numbered less than one percent of Los Angeles County population. In a national context of deteriorating academic performance, the Koreans' academic achievements were the more noteworthy in Los Angeles, whose public schools suffered worse-than-average deterioration as a result of the flight of middle class and white households to secure suburbs.

Adverse Consequences of Entrepreneurship

Although immensely valuable to Los Angeles, Korean entrepreneurship did promote two adverse and usually ignored consequences. First, most Korean-owned garment firms employed undocumented workers. The garment industry in Los Angeles grew rapidly in the 1970s largely as a result of an influx of cheap but undocumented labor from Mexico. By the end of the decade, the garment industry generated more gross sales than the movie industry. Three hundred fifty Korean firms represented about 15 percent of garment factories in Los Angeles in 1979. According to a spokesman for the Korean garment contractors, the Korean firms employed 20,000 women workers in 1980. Like other employers in this industry, Koreans hired undocumented Mexican seamstresses. About 80 percent of workers in the Los Angeles garment industry were undocumented in 1979. Although growth of the garment industry brought welcome income into central Los Angeles, a depressed inner city, the price of this income was augmentation of the illegal worker population. Assuming that Korean garment factories hired the expected share of illegal workers, neither more nor less than the mean for their industry, Korean garment factories provided employment for 16,000 undocumented women, thus encouraging more migration of undocumented workers to Los Angeles. Since Korean-owned garment factories represented about one-tenth of Korean firms in 1980, the proportion of Korean firms that utilized undocumented labor was appreciable, and Korean firms made a small but consequential contribution to the county's population of undocumented workers.

Although garment employers were aware that the workers they hired were undocumented, they violated no laws in hiring illegals. However, under the Simpson-Mazzoli Immigration Reform and Control Act, debated in Congress in 1983 and 1984, employers would have incurred civil and criminal penalities if they knowingly hired undocumented workers. Whether passed intact in a future session of Congress or not, the Simpson-Mazzoli Act's employer sanctions provisions are proof that many people in Congress and in the general public believed that hiring undocumented workers was a harmful economic practice—and Korean garment factories were among those who hired undocumented workers.

Second, Korean entrepreneurship sometimes entailed violation of laws protecting public morals, health, or labor standards. In 1979 Los Angeles police undertook an investigation of 60 Korean-owned massage parlors mostly located in seedy Hollywood areas. Suspected of fronting for prostitution, the Korean massage parlors represented about 15 percent of massage parlors then licensed in the city of Los Angeles. No convictions resulted, but in April 1984 a Superior Court judge held two Koreans in contempt of court and fined them $1,000 for employing ex-prostitutes in their massage parlor. Police investigations of organized crime in Koreatown also turned up four extortion gangs of which the largest, the Korean Killers, was estimated to have as many as 250 members. According to police, a "favorite" business of Korean gangs was to extort protection payments from operators of massage parlors. A vice squad detective alleged that by 1984 Koreans owned "just about all the massage parlors in Los Angeles." This network of massage parlors required protection. In 1981 the Los Angeles Police Chief charged that a Korean "godfather" operated an organized crime syndicate with 400 hoodlums on the payroll. However, police only arrested three Koreans in a drive to break up this syndicate (whose alleged boss was never named although rumors circulating in Koreatown identified him as the president of a big Koreatown commercial association).

Other violations of law were undramatic but telling. Korean packing houses and restaurants came under investigation for violations of the labor and sanitary code. Inspectors found rat feces and vermin on the premises of Korean packing houses. Korean restaurant workers prepared food on the floor. In the garment industry, state task forces collected evidence of rampant sanitary and labor code violations. More than 95 percent of all garment firms were in violation of state or federal standards. Although Koreans were no more culpable than non-Korean garment factory owners, they were perceived to have participated in a general assault on labor standards characteristic of this industry. Police also charged Koreans with practicing acupuncture without licenses, and investigated allegations that Korean employers in a variety of industries were paying workers less than the statutory minimum wage. Admittedly, many Korean violations of business law arose because of language barriers and unfamiliarity with American law. Indeed, Korean industrial associations usually took as their first task the translation of the business code into Korean for the benefit non-English-speaking members. On the other hand, in order to squeeze into already crowded industries, Korean entrepreneurs sometimes had to shave legal corners. In this sense, Korean sanitary and labor code violations were symptoms of the hard struggle Korean entrepreneurs faced in the competitive sector.

Koreans and Other Immigrants

In the number, rate, and size of businesses, Koreans in Los Angeles represented an outstanding example of immigrant entrepreneurship in the United States. However, Korean entrepreneurship is a social force wherever Koreans settle. Since 47 percent of the nation's 355,000 Korean immigrants resided in seven metropolitan areas (of which two are in Southern California), the Korean impact outside Southern California was concentrated in New York, Chicago, Washington, D.C., and San Francisco. Illsoo Kim has provided a descriptive account of Korean entrepreneurship in New York City,[3] and other accounts have documented the same phenomenon in Chicago, Atlanta, and Philadelphia. Hence, the presumption is strong that Korean immigration had the same entrepreneurial impact in other cities that it had more powerfully in Los·Angeles.

Of course, Koreans are not the only entrepreneurially inclined new immigrants. Immigrants have been more frequently self-employed than native whites in every decennial census since 1880.[4] As Conk has also observed: "The proportional representation of the foreign born as traders and dealers is remarkably stable . . . over time."[5] In 1970, for example, the percentage of self-employed in twenty-two large metropolitan regions was 9.8 among foreign-born men, 9.6 among native-born men of foreign parents, and 6.0 among native-born men of native parents.[6] Some evidence suggests that a heavy concentration of foreign-born workers caused a city's business population to increase beyond national averages. For thirty-six metropolitan areas for which data was available, the 1980 Census indicated a positive and statistically significant correlation between percentage of the labor force self-employed and the percentage foreign born: the higher the percentage foreign born, the higher the percentage self-employed in a city.

Although the foreign born in general have always been more frequently self-employed than the native born in general, some foreign groups have always demonstrated higher rates of self-employment than others. Thus, Higgs found that the rate of retail merchants per 1,000 of population in 1900 was 124 among Russians, 58 among Italians, 29 among Irish, and 20 among Swedes.[7]

In their probability sample of Providence, Rhode Island, conducted between 1967 and 1969, Goldscheider and Kobrin found that Jews and Italians were still more frequently self-employed than French Canadians, Portuguese, or Irish.[8] Although rates of self-employment declined in every nativity origin group with successive American-born generations, the intergroup differences persisted. That is, in every generation, Italians and especially Jews demonstrated higher rates of self-employment than the other groups. According to Katzman, "Negroes, Mexicans, and Filipinos contain few entrepreneurs.... On the other hand, the Chinese and Japanese ... produce an extraordinary number of entrepreneurs as do the Russians (mostly Jewish)."[9] Between 1972 and 1977, Asians formed 20.7 firms per 1,000 population, Hispanics 17.2, and blacks 14.9. The U.S. Bureau of the Census also reported that in 1980 self-employed and unpaid family workers were 6.5 percent of urban Asians, 3.9 percent of urban Spanish-origin, 2.3 percent of urban blacks, and 5.7 percent of all urban persons.[10]

Although uncorrected for urban or rural residence, Table 1 provides comparative data illustrating the unequal entrepreneurship of nine nationality groups in 1980. The table distinguishes three components of the self-employed population: employees of their own corporation, self-employed workers, and unpaid family workers. Employees of own corporation are chiefly professionals, especially medical doctors. Self-employed workers are predominantly nonprofessional. Unpaid family workers and self-employed workers therefore constitute the small business population, which included 7.3 percent of all employed persons in 1980. Table 1 also shows that 13.5 percent of Koreans were in the small business population, the largest proportion of any detailed nationality group shown in the census. Among Asians, Japanese, Chinese, and Koreans were more frequently self-employed than the general population, but Vietnamese were noteworthy exceptions. Within the Spanish-origin population, Cubans were more frequently self-employed than Mexicans. European immigrants clustered around the national mean.

However numerous, immigrants do not fan out over the industrial spectrum, participating equally in every trade.[11] Instead, they concentrate in particular industries where they are usually overrepresented. For example, among Koreans in Los Angeles,

Table 1

**Self-Employed Workers as a Percentage of Employed Persons
by Detailed Nationality Origin: United States, 1980**

	Employees of Own Corporation	Self-Employed Workers	Unpaid Family Workers
All Persons	2.1	6.8	0.5
Japanese	na	7.9	0.6
Chinese	na	7.2	1.0
Korean	na	11.9	1.6
Vietnamese	na	2.2	0.5
Mexican	na	3.5	0.3
Cuban	na	5.8	0.4
Irish	2.0	6.6	0.5
Italian	3.5	6.9	0.4
Polish	2.5	5.9	0.4

Source: U.S. Bureau of the Census. *Census of Population*. Vol. 1. *Characteristics of the Population*. Ch. C. *General Social and Economic Characteristics*. Pt. 1. *United States Summary*. PC80-1-C1. (Washington, D.C.: United States Government Printing Office, 1983), pp. 159, 165, 173.

three-quarters of firms were retail or service proprietorships. Of these, gasoline service stations, wig stores, grocery stores, and liquor stores were the most common. Although case studies of specific immigrant minorities are sparse, documentation currently available identifies several new immigrant groups who have heavily utilized entrepreneurship in identifiable industries and localities. For example, Greeks dominate the pizza business in Connecticut towns;[12] Dominicans are a power in New York City's garment industry;[13] Soviet Jews operate about half the taxi cabs in Los Angeles;[14] and Arabs have taken over much of the grocery industry on Chicago's South Side.[15] Hong Kong Chinese have doubled the number of Chinese-owned businesses in Toronto.[16] Vietnamese merchants created a little-Saigon in Orange County, California where local merchants sought unsuccessfully to ban the posting of business signs in foreign languages. In Sea Drift, Texas, Vietnamese shrimp-fisherman provided unwelcome competition for the whites some of whom turned to the Ku Klux Klan for protection of their industrial interest. In Detroit and Toledo, 54 percent of Arabic-speaking Christians operate grocery stores.[17] Once mostly professionals, especially medical doctors and engineers,

South Indians in Southern California have begun to turn to import-export businesses.[18] Especially in big depressed cities, the entrepreneurship of immigrants has become a consequential economic force. Sassen-Koob observes that New York's potpourri of immigrant entrepreneurs generated employment, saved abandoned buildings, revived deteriorating neighborhoods, and generated tax and cash flows. Although the immigrants' investments were "small scale," Sassen-Koob finds them "not insignificant in the context of a city where economic decline affects large sectors of the economy and the population."[19]

North America is not distinctive in recent reports of extensive entrepreneurship among selected immigrant minorities. In Britain, recent sociological research has called attention to the extensive self-employment of Greeks, Italians, Gujaratis, Sikhs, Pakistanis, and Jews.[20] As in the United States, the entrepreneurship of new immigrants in Britain mostly occurs in central areas of depressed cities such as Manchester, Liverpool, and London. Aldrich *et al.* declare that minority business expansion is occurring "amid the physical and economic decay of the inner city, cheek-by-jowl with declining activity, employment, and population."[21] But the British experience has turned up one important anomaly. In the United States, West Indians have always enjoyed a reputation for entrepreneurship, and still do in Brooklyn, New York where they are most heavily concentrated. For reasons that are not clear, West Indians in Britain have not established a significant record of entrepreneurship in the last decade.

In the 1970s only the Cubans in Miami had developed a complex, interdependent ethnic economy that rivaled the Korean achievement in Los Angeles. Cuban-owned enterprises in Miami increased from 919 in 1967 to 8,000 in 1976.[22] Like Koreans, Cubans concentrated in identifiable industries rather than fanning out over the industrial spectrum in equal proportion. Textiles, leather, construction, finance, and furniture became Cuban specialties; cigar-making had always been Cuban-dominated. Cubans controlled 40 percent of the construction industry in Miami and 20 percent of the banks, in 1980. Another study found that in 1979, 20 percent of Cubans in Miami were self-employed and 49 percent found employment in Spanish-speaking firms owned by coethnics.[23] Moreover, workers in the coethnic economy received returns on their human capital (education, experience, knowledge) nearly equivalent to those paid in the most advantaged primary labor market and far superior to those paid in the secondary labor market, a junkpile of deadend jobs. Enclave employment did not disadvantage immigrant workers, and probably made better opportunities available than they would have found on the general labor market. These Miami results confirm those uncovered by Jeffrey Reitz who studied the economic performance of Slavs, Italians, and Chinese in Toronto.[24] Among Toronto's immigrants, those who worked in the ethnic economy (e.g., a workplace in which they spoke a language other than English) earned better returns on their human capital than immigrants in the English-speaking economy. "For members of minority groups with low levels of education," Reitz concludes, "work in settings controlled by their own group is quite attractive from the standpoint of income opportunity."[25]

Causes of Immigrant Entrepreneurship

The rediscovery of immigrant entrepreneurship in Britain, Canada, and the United States undermined the position of social scientists who, following C. Wright Mills, widely believed that small business had provided an important avenue of social ascent in the past but, in an era of giant corporations, was no longer of economic or social consequence.[26] The resurgence and profitability of immigrant enterprises partially contradicted Mills' claim that small business was an economic anachronism tottering into oblivion. For example, Gelfand reported that in 1880, 43 percent of Jews in Los Angeles were retail or wholesale proprietors.[27] A century later, 40 percent of Koreans in Los Angeles were proprietors, a level hard to reconcile with the claim that small business had become obsolete in the intervening century.

Indeed, the "enclave sector" emerged as an independent mode of structural incorporation to complement wage earning in the primary and secondary sectors of the labor force. Immigrants who developed a business sector enjoyed two major advantages over immigrants who did not. First, immigrant or ethnic business provided coethnics with an alternative to the general labor market, thus reducing the pressure of their numbers on the job supply.

Second, ethnic business provided more secure work and higher incomes, accelerating social mobility of the ethnic or immigrant minority. Since this conclusion rehabilitates the old-fashioned view of small business as a viable route of social ascent, the present has swung into closer compatibility with the past than sociologists had earlier believed possible.

The key element of historical continuity is the use of ethnic resources to support the competitive position of individual firms. This bootstrapping method builds entrepreneurship from elements of ethnic culture. Ethnic resources are the social features of a group, which coethnic business owners utilize in business, or from which their business benefits.[28] Ethnic resources include values, knowledge, skills, information, money and work attitudes, solidarity, an orientation to sojourning, and ethnic institutions. If one says, for example, that immigrants work long hours; assume the risk of criminal victimization; are thrifty; express satisfaction with skimpy money rewards; help one another with business skills, information, and purchase of ethnic commodities; cluster in particular industries; combine easily in restraint of trade; or utilize rotating credit associations, one is calling attention to the economic impact of the immigrants' ethnic resources. After all, if others had these resources, their possession would confer no economic advantage upon immigrants. Because ethnic resources cost no money, they are the natural basis upon which impoverished immigrants develop business firms.

One must distinguish ethnic resources from class resources that may, however, be simultaneously present in the same immigrant group. Class resources are cultural and material. On the material side, class resources are private property in the means of production or distribution, wealth, and investments in human capital. On the cultural side, class resources of entrepreneurship are bourgeois values, attitudes, knowledge, and skills transmitted intergenerationally in the course of primary socialization to a class culture.[29] Although hard to differentiate at the margin, class resources and ethnic resources are as different as class culture and ethnic culture. Either is capable of promoting entrepreneurship. According to currently fashionable speculation, class resources encourage individualistic styles of entrepreneurship whereas ethnic resources encourage collective styles.

In the specific case of Cubans and Mexicans (see Table 1), the superior class resources of the Cubans probably accounts for the higher rate of entrepreneurship among them. In the case of Cubans and Koreans, both ethnic resources and class resources were simultaneously supporting the entrepreneurship of group members. That is, pre-Mariel Cubans and Koreans alike were highly educated in their countries of origin, well endowed with money upon arrival in the United States, and middle or upper-middle class in social origin. Among the Koreans, surveys found that 70 percent of adult men were college graduates compared with only 15 percent of men in Los Angeles County.[30] Similarly, one-half of Korean men reported that their last occupation in Korea was professional, technical, or managerial. On the other hand, Koreans also worked sixty-hour weeks; saved one-half of their income by dint of painful thrift; accepted the risk of criminal victimization; passed business information among themselves; maintained expected patterns of nepotism and employer paternalism; praised a Calvinist deity; utilized family, alumni, congregational, and network solidarities; thought of themselves as sojourners; expressed satisfaction with poorly remunerated work; and utilized rotating credit associations in financing their small businesses. All of these culturally derived characteristics of the Korean immigrant community contributed to Korean entrepreneurship, but none required money.

Since the use of rotating credit associations was a particularly noteworthy feature of prewar Asian entrepreneurs, its persistence among the Koreans is a firm element of continuity with the past.[31] Kunae Kim undertook an ethnographic investigation of Korean rotating credit associations in Los Angeles. Eighty percent of Koreans she studied were kye (the Korean rotating credit association) participants, and she declared the institution "a significant part" of their strategy for "making it in America."[32] Kim and Hurh interviewed 96 Korean business owners in Chicago. Thirty-four percent of respondents indicated that they had "accumulated some of their own capital through the rotating credit system."[33] In sum, Korean entrepreneurship obviously benefitted from class resources, but Koreans also utilized old-fashioned ethnic resources for supplementation, and a similar conclusion fits the Cuban experience in Miami.

Although the persistence of ethnic resources represents a link with the historic past, old-fashioned verities that the world has not outgrown, the generous endowment of Cubans and Koreans with class resources represents a sharp cleavage with American immigration history. Americans must forego the habit of assuming immigrants were once the "wretched refuse" of benighted countries. With the exception of Mexican and some Latin American immigrants, the general level of socioeconomic status among new immigrants surpasses that of the American common man. As a result, new immigrants possess class resources in excess of the underdog Americans, blacks and Mexicans. This novel situation is called "leapfrog migration" to indicate the lodgement of immigrants in the middle rather than, as previous known, at the bottom of the social ladder.[34] Leapfrog migration arises in substantial measure because U.S. immigration laws have awarded priority to professional and technical workers in "short supply" occupations and to persons prepared to invest in a business enterprise they own and manage. When unable to find suitable employment in the general labor market, educated immigrants have the motive and resources to start their own small business enterprises. Moreover, under the terms of the "investor's exemption," an administrative category introduced by the Immigration and Naturalization Service, persons with $250,000 to invest in a business they own and manage may circumvent labor certification requirements, taking a place at the head of the immigration queue. Some proportion of the foreigners investing in business enterprises here do so because entrepreneurship offered them their only access to the United States.

Immigrants of middle or upper-middle class origin react with chagrin to the manual jobs they obtain in the general labor market. Immigrant doctors, pharmacists, engineers, or attorneys may pump gasoline in service stations, but they are looking for escape from this level of employment. Hence, their labor force disadvantages (poor English, unrecognized professional degrees, under- and unemployment) confer on educated immigrants a motive to open their own businesses. Of course, the entrepreneurship-stimulating effects of disadvantage in the labor force have always been present, and the rate of self-employment among the foreign born has, in consequence, been higher than among the native born

since at least 1880. However, as the underutilized human capital
of immigrants has risen, a function of their middle and upper-middle class social origins, their motives and capability for entrepreneurship have also risen. Even if the path of small business owners is harder now, contemporary immigrants are better prepared
for entrepreneurship than were the unskilled, uneducated immigrants of the prewar epoch. Therefore, new immigrants surmount
business hurdles that still obstruct the social mobility of low status
blacks, whites, and Hispanics. When the *Wall Street Journal* won-
dered why Cubans in Miami could open numerous businesses
whereas blacks in Miami could not, the newspaper concluded that
the question unfairly ignored the money, Latin American import-
export connections, and bourgeois social origin of at least a substantial minority of Miami's Cubans. This conclusion underscores
the hazard of assuming that intergroup differences in rates of
entrepreneurship reflect only ethnic resources. Ethnic resources
do affect entrepreneurship, but before their effect can be identified in empirical cases one must discount intergroup differences in
class resources.

A neglected and unwelcome point of continuity with the past is
the copresence of organized crime and immigrant entrepreneurship in Koreatown. This copresence is reminiscent of Chicago in
the 1920s. After all, Al Capone is part of American immigration
history and, precisely insofar as one looks for continuity with
immigration history, one expects his like among new immigrants.
Daniel Bell's "queer ladder of social mobility" still beckons disad-
vantaged foreigners.[35] Racketeering offers a fast profit for those
willing to risk murder or incarceration, unrecognized as forms of
entrepreneurial risk. Organized crime has some structural basis
in America's free enterprise economy. That is, as entrepreneurial
minorities saturate legitimate business opportunities, some ambitious immigrants or, more commonly, the children of immigrants begin to bend, then to stretch, and finally to break the law
either to make a living or to make a better living. Unable to comprehend this historical continuity with the past of his adopted
country, a Korean-born sociologist expressed his rage and humiliation at the public indictment of racketeers among his countrymen. However, capitalism has allowed the crossing of the boundaries of legality in pursuit of profit, a portion of the bountiful

rewards earned being thereupon earmarked for protection. Like Prospero and Caliban, ethnic entrepreneurship and ethnic racketeering often appear together, so that those who applaud the former have ruefully to accept some measure of the latter.

Because the economic benefits of immigrant entrepreneurship are so massive, timely, and well targeted, creating veritable enterprise zones in America's depressed inner cities, people overlook the social costs of excessive entrepreneurship. High rates of immigrant self-employment became necessary because immigrants could not find wage and salary jobs at a level befitting their training and expectations. Obviously, American society benefits more from self-employed immigrants than from unemployed immigrants. However, an economic strategy based on self-employment compels immigrants to find ways to circumvent the normal restraints upon expansion of the business population. Innovation and niche-finding are positive results of this search. Violations of law, decency, and public welfare are negative results. Laws protecting labor standards, sanitation, professional competence, and decency do restrain the expansion of the business population. So do common standards of decency that are not written into law. Someone who cannot squeeze into the business population otherwise can often do so by violating these laws or public standards, thus obtaining a commercial advantage over non-violators. For example, employers who pay less than the minimum wage, a violation of law, obtain a commercial advantage over employers who obey the law. Violating rules is a kind of entrepreneurial risk that, if unpunished could permit otherwise unemployed or underemployed people to operate lucrative businesses. In the long run, however, individual violations of laws turn into endemic violations that, having rendered the laws unenforceable, reintroduce the evils laws were intended to avoid.

As violations become endemic, the social benefits of immigrant entrepreneurship are increasingly counterbalanced by social costs until, in an extreme case, what started as a beneficial influx of entrepreneurial talent in depressed central cities ends up as a destructive and terrifying assault upon labor standards, sanitation, health, child welfare, and human values. Although that tipping point has by no means been reached, reliance upon immigrant entrepreneurship to make jobs for immigrants does move society in that direction. As matters stand, these evils are not hypothetical. They exist now, albeit in moderate amount and heavily overbalanced by the great social and economic contributions of foreign entrepreneurs. However, these evils could grow, and given a policy of central city *laissez faire,* probably will. Like fire, guns, chemicals, and pregnancy, entrepreneurship is both useful and dangerous, but unlike the others, the dangers of entrepreneurship are usually overlooked.

IV

Becoming American

9

PETER I. ROSE

Asian Americans:
From Pariahs to Paragons

Chinese exchange students. Japanese salesmen. Korean greengrocers. Recent immigrants from Hong Kong and the Philippines. Thousands upon thousands of refugees from Vietnam, Laos, and Cambodia. Asians are everywhere. Some say they are taking over but, more often than not, the comment is made only in mock horror.

Although "takeover" is a far from accurate image, in recent years the United States *has* become a magnet for any number of people from Asia. While many have come to study or to ply their wares, many more have come to stay. Between 1970 and 1980 the number of persons who specified Asian or Pacific Island ancestry to United States census takers increased 146 percent, making it the fastest growing segment of the population (see chapter 1, figure 1). Since 1980 the pace has accelerated considerably, augmented by several large waves of Indochinese refugees. In the years ahead, the "Asian cohort" will continue to grow because of high birth rates and because of the effects of chain migration (i.e., once citizenship is attained by an individual, his relatives move up on the priority list for entrance into the U.S., and many do come).

A hundred years ago the prospect of such a "yellow tide" would have—indeed had—evoked hysterical outcries against imminent inundation, urgent calls for measures to stay the flow, and ruthless attacks on those who were already here. Not today. While some still feel that too many immigrants—including Asian immigrants—are being allowed to enter the United States, concerns about threats to our way of life, when expressed, are far more apt to be directed against those crossing the Rio Grande than those crossing the Pacific.[1]

The images of those who used to be called "Orientals" (they prefer the term "Asian") have changed dramatically. No longer viewed as kowtowing inferiors—the sort of folks Ralph Waldo Emerson once suggested were only good for serving tea[2]—or as inscrutable heathens, Mongolian scabs, or untrustworthy neighbors loyal only to their motherlands, they are now seen by many as members of "model minorities." In a remarkable inversion, old negative stereotypes have been replaced with positive new ones. "Conniving" has turned into "competitive," "clannish" into "community-minded." Those who were once seen as inferior have been vested with most ennobling qualities. The pariahs have become paragons, lauded for their ingenuity and industry and for embodying the truest fulfillment of the "American Dream." Ronald Reagan has called them "Our exemplars of hope and inspiration."

Such encomiums are reinforced today not only by an increasing appreciation for the carefully made products of the East—electronic gadgetry, photographic equipment, and compact cars—but by the economic success and widely reported accomplishments of Americans with names like Wang, Yamaguchi, Kim, and Tran. Moreover, in recent years there have been a number of glowing feature stories in the national press about the winning ways of recent arrivals, people like Chi Luu, the twenty-five-year-old boat person from Vietnam who graduated valedictorian from City College of New York and won a full scholarship for graduate study at M.I.T., and Linn Yann, the twelve-year-old Cambodian refugee who placed second in a regional spelling bee in Chattanooga, Tennessee (Linn Yann missed on "enchilada").

Such accounts signal an important phenomenon. Already note-worthy in the fields of science, medicine, and the arts, Asians are increasingly found at the top of honor rolls, high on lists of academic prize-winners and scholarship recipients, and prominent in student rosters of elite universities. They are also beginning to swell the ranks of law schools and to seek careers in politics—areas where, in the past, they were rarely to be found.

Jews of the East?

Often compared to Jews, many Asian Americans do seem to share certain values, modes of acculturation, and patterns of mobility with those once called "Orientals" themselves. The characteristics are familiar: a deep sense of ethnic identification and group loyalty; a high level of filial respect; a heavy emphasis on proper demeanor and on the seriousness of life; a firm belief in the importance of education; a tendency toward extrinsic assimilation (taking on the superficial trappings of dominant groups—speech, dress, musical tastes—while remaining socially separate); and an overriding attitude that one must advance as far as possible not just for oneself, but so that parents can enjoy the Chinese, Japanese, Korean, or Vietnamese equivalent of what in Yiddish is known as *nachas fun die Kinder,* "pleasure from the [accomplishments of] children."

Of course, there are un-Jewish Asian Americans (and un-Jewish Jews) who do not toe the mark, who reject traditional mores, who disobey their parents, who do not want to delay their gratifications. There are those who start work in restaurants, factories, and sweatshops and do not advance up the socioeconomic scale or simply drop out or join gangs. But most do stay the course. Demographic studies show that, along with Jews, Asians are the most upwardly mobile group in the country.[3] As an aggregate, they have caught up to and are even surpassing the Joneses and the Smiths, as well as the Cohens and the Levines.

William Petersen, the demographer most closely associated with the use of the "model minority" term,[4] indicates that their comparative rate of progress is remarkable. He points out that what the Chinese and Japanese had to endure might well have resulted in a pattern of poor education, low income, high crime rates, and unstable families. Instead, notes Petersen, "[they] broke through the barriers of prejudice and, by such key indices as education and income, surpassed the average levels of native-born whites."[5]

In a May 1982 issue of the *New York Times Magazine,* Robert Lindsey profiled a number of Asian American artists, architects, artisans, doctors of medicine, captains of industry, political leaders, and small businessmen. Citing census figures, Lindsey showed that those placed under the rubric "Asian Americans" (members of twenty different "nationality groups") had the highest median family income when compared to all others.[6] Lindsey's account failed to reflect two things: (1) that Asians are disproportionately located in urban areas where wages are higher, and (2) that more members of their families are apt to contribute to the household coffers and are more likely to stay at home for a longer time to do so than those in most other groups. However, such mitigating factors notwithstanding, Asian advancement has a very solid basis. At the time of Lindsey's report, 75 percent of the Asians were high school graduates compared to 69 percent of the whites, 51 percent of the blacks, and 43 percent of the Hispanics. Even controlling for the age distribution of the different populations, those differences are not statistical flukes—they have to do with cultural norms, modes of adaptation, and the manner of seizing available opportunities.

Many others have tried to explain why so many Asians are moving up the socioeconomic ladder with such alacrity. Those who know Asian ethnic groups most intimately—that is, from the inside—often use the same terms to describe them. But they are cautious. While agreeing that many have attained much and that many more will be successful in the future, in certain quarters there is a gnawing disquietude about the image of widespread Asian-American *embourgeoisement.* Close observers have begun to note that both pressures on the young from within the communities and expectations from others outside it are beginning to take their toll. Asian youths, finding themselves on rather narrow career trajectories (requiring a major in math or science, for example) that demand high grades and unstinting effort, and that emphasize the necessity to stay the course or lose face, are feeling the effects of psychological and emotional strain. Reports from college health services indicate that more and more Asian American students are seeking counseling and that their concerns are usually related to the fear of failure.

Public awareness of this phenomenon increased in the spring of 1984 when a series of stories appeared in national news magazines, including the campus edition of *Newsweek*. The lead *Newsweek* article, "Asian-Americans: The Drive to Excel,"[7] provoked several sharp responses from those who felt that the cumulative effect of such reporting was to create a new stereotype, that of neurotic overachiever.

Almost as if anticipating such reactions, the authors of one such piece quoted several social scientists who tried to provide some perspective—or perhaps in a spirit of egalitarianism, to imply that after all Asian Americans are just like everybody else. Russell Endo of the University of Colorado is reported to have said, "In all groups you'll find that some people are sort of in-between. That's true of Asians as well."[8] It is. But such a statement does not address what individuals do with their endowments, especially in those situations where there is a high priority placed upon success and youngsters are socialized to excel by parents and teachers—and expected to do so by everybody else.[9]

A year before the flap over the *Newsweek* piece, Diane Mei Lin Mark and Ginger Chih had already expressed the concerns and ambivalence of many Asian Americans. In their social history, they claimed that one of the primary obstacles to the improvement of conditions for Chinese Americans is the persistence of the "myth of the model minority."[10] They objected not to the praise extended to those who succeed in overcoming great hardships, but to new "exaggerated" characterizations which are seen as being nearly as unrealistic as the old ones. They and others worry about a seeming insensitivity to the inclination of many Asians to mask their real feelings and put on their best face(s) for the outside world. In addition, they point to the persistence of stratification within various communities and continuing problems of health care, housing, employment, and social welfare, especially for new immigrants and refugees, the elderly, and the growing teenage population.

Of late there *has* been a tendency to gloss over the inglorious history of American anti-Asian attitudes and practices, to look at demographic attributes rather than underlying psychodynamic phenomena, and to ignore the continuing division between those now moving into and through the system and those still left behind. The latter is reflected in what some call the "occupational dichotomy" between managers and workers.[11] It is evident in other places, too. Nonetheless, what is most striking is that Mark and Chih and many other Asian Americans writing about the dilemmas of being both a part of and apart from this society return again and again to the model minority motif themselves. They often end their assessments by conceding that, after all, the "myth" is still more real than not.

The sociologist Harry Kitano has said, "the judgement of Japanese Americans as the 'model American minority' is made from a strictly majority point of view. Japanese Americans are good because they conform—they don't make waves—they work hard and are quiet and docile."[12] Kitano suggests that, "Ideally, members of the ethnic community should share in any evaluation of the efficacy of their adjustment." In view of this obligation, he concludes:

In spite of different definitions of what constitutes success and of philosophical discussions that may show Japanese as short of being an "ideal" group, they have achieved a niche in American society. They have been effective in social organization, in socialization, in controlling deviant behavior, and in coming to grips with "success" in American terms. When we look back on the past prejudice and discrimination faced by Japanese we find that even their most optimistic dreams have been surpassed.[13]

Insider Kitano's words echo what outsider Petersen has written: "As extraordinary as have been the positive achievements, the lack of a countervailing negative record is even more astounding."[14] Anyone with a modicum of exposure to American history can understand why this seems so remarkable. No people who came to these shores of their own volition ever suffered as much discrimination or ostracism as did those from China and Japan. None were made to feel less welcome.

Sojourners and Settlers

Things might have been different had this vast land become an oriental outpost rather than an occidental one. The historian

George Stewart once whimsically speculated on such a prospect. Suppose, he suggested, instead of the English, Dutch, and other Northern Europeans crossing the Atlantic and settling the eastern seaboard of North America, the approach had been from the West. Asians, rather than Europeans, would have disembarked and established political control and, for all intents and purposes, cultural hegemony over the new land. In Stewart's imaginary account, a Chinese navigator named Ko Lum Bo stumbles upon the pristine continent and it is *his* descendants who populate it:

> The Chinese colonists introduced their own well-established ways of life. They continued to speak Chinese and to practice their own religion. Being accustomed to eat rice, they still ate it, as far as possible. Vast areas of the country were terraced and irrigated as rice paddies. The colonists continued to use their comfortable flowing garments, and pagodas dotted the landscape.[15]

Stewart's scenario is a wonderful piece of social science fiction. Had it been real, this country would have been very different indeed.

The Chinese. Of course some of "Ko Lum Bo's" descendants, like many of Columbo's, did come here. The Chinese came as early as the 1850s. They labored in gold fields, helped to build the railroads, and sacrificed much to enjoy what others were to take for granted. They were ostracized, demeaned, and rejected; they were also the first group to have their further entry restricted by specific laws. The Chinese Exclusion Act of 1882 was a landmark decision, a crucial watershed in American immigration history and in race relations. It set a precedent for the restrictive legislation of the 1920s that was to prevent many other "undesirables" (mainly from Eastern and Southern Europe) from entering the country.

It is reasonable to assume that, whatever the political motivations for keeping them out, to many unworldly, xenophobic, and competitive Americans, the Chinese "coolies" they saw in the mining areas and seaport towns were a strange lot. They wore pigtails (required at home to indicate their submission to Manchu rule, and since they saw themselves as sojourners, kept to allow their re-entry into China). They wore garments that were comical to western eyes. They ate foods that others abhorred. They spoke an incomprehensible gibberish. But they were also perceived as a threat to other laborers because they were willing to work long hours for low wages. When times were good this was a boon to the railroad magnates and mine owners, many of whom had contracted for them, but it was rarely seen as an advantage for "native" workers, many of whom were, of course, immigrants themselves. (No less a labor leader than the AFofL's Samuel Gompers was a major spokesman against admitting Chinese—or any "Orientals"—to trade unions.)[16] And whenever there was a labor surplus, they were not wanted by anyone.

Convenient scapegoats upon whom to vent all sorts of frustrations, the Chinese became frequent targets for abuse by the rednecks of their day. Anti-Chinese rallies were staged in many western towns—often ending in violent outbursts, the forced "deportation" of the unwanted aliens, and in some instances, such as the Rock Creek Massacre in Wyoming in 1885, brutal killing.

Few raised their voices to protest and the Chinese, numbering approximately 100,000 at the time, deserted the sparsely populated areas. They concentrated—and insulated—themselves more and more in the cities and their own enclaves within them, in what came to be known as "Chinatowns."

Like the Jewish ghettoes of the Middle Ages, the boundaries of San Francisco's Chinatown, and some others, were demarcated by authorities. Those who cooperated by residing within the area, sometimes called a "safe zone," were left to their own devices. In their still predominantly male immigrant societies, life could not center about the nuclear family, but organizations based on kinship and clan membership abounded; so did district associations, *hiukuan*, made up of people from the same home area.[17]

The Chinatowns began to develop an infrastructure of their own and a class structure as well: workers at the bottom; small businessmen (restaurateurs, grocers, launderers) in the middle; merchants and professionals at the top. The rank order remains, although the players have shifted. The original workers, many of them the "old bachelors," are now replaced by new immigrants from Hong Kong and mainland China and some Chinese refugees from Southeast Asia. Members of the new bottom rung are sometimes referred to by the "ABCs" (American-born Chinese) as "FOBs" (those "fresh off the boat").

Chinatowns still exist. To outsiders they are exotic enclaves in the city, places to wander early in the evening to peer into odd curio shops and to buy condiments from tiny groceries before "eating Chinese." For the residents, they are enclaves of solace and security, cultural expression, and bustling activity. They can also be places of considerable exploitation. Above and behind the neon dragons and the main rooms of the enamel-red restaurants are tight-packed living quarters and kitchens, factories, and sweatshops where many of those newcomers from Taiwan, Hong Kong, the People's Republic of China, and Indochina often find their first jobs in America.

For some there still exists the problem of what Norbert Wiley once called "the ethnic mobility trap" but it is less pronounced today than in the past. Wiley's idea is that many community members move up through the local stratification systems, sometimes with considerable swiftness, by providing specialized and ethnically-specific services.[18] They have far more difficulty moving into mainstream occupations. In recent years more and more young Chinese Americans have begun to spring the trap of confinement mainly by following occupational paths that are viewed with favor both within their community and in the wider society. Even they, however, maintain links to their urban bases. New relationships with non-Chinese college friends, business associates, or professional colleagues often tend to be and to remain, in the lingo of the sociologists, "secondary." Close, comfortable, and intimate relationships are far more likely to be with fellow "ethnics." (This pattern, as shall be seen, is also characteristic of some other Asian Americans, like Koreans, but is far less pronounced among the Japanese).

In their thoughtful ethnography, *Longtime, Californ'*, Victor and Brett Nee give vivid evidence of the vitality of San Francisco's Chinatown and the people within it. Often quoting at length from those they interviewed, they indicate the character of a community at once riven with political factions and generational rivalries and interdependent, linked by common bonds and organizational structures.[19]

Melford Weiss, author of another ethnography, *Valley City: A Chosen Community in America*, suggested that people in such ethnic neighborhoods may be understood best by putting them into three categories: "traditionist, modernist, and activist."[20]

The traditionalists are those who adhere to the values and traditions of Chinese society, who try to maintain the "sojourners" lifestyle. It is they, more than any of the others, who embody the old stereotypes of the "mandarin" and the "coolie." The modernists, by contrast, are in many ways mainstreamers who try to adhere to the ways of life of those in the dominant culture. Some might call them "CASPs" (Chinese Anglo-Saxon Protestants) but in many cases their dissident and politically-active children, caught up in the ethnic revival, want to be considered Asian and are wont to refer to their parents as "Bananas," yellow on the outside, white in the middle.

Today there are nearly 900,000 Chinese citizens and aliens residing in the United States: 40 percent of them in California, 18 percent in New York, 7 percent in Hawaii, and between 3.5 and 1.4 percent of the rest located in Illinois, Texas, Massachusetts, New Jersey, Washington, Maryland, Florida, Pennsylvania, and Michigan.[21] (See Table 1.)

Japanese Americans and Korean Americans are also concentrated in many of these same states and, as fellow Asians, are often compared to the Chinese. Examination of their experiences suggests that the tripartite model obtains for them as well, although certain modifications have to be made. For example, neither group is apt to have as high a proportion of "tradi-

Table 1

America's Asian Population

(Distribution based on ancestral identification in 1980)[1]

	Number (in thousands)	Percent distribution			
		West	North-Central	South	Northeast
Chinese	894	55%	9%	12%	25%
Filipino	795	68	11	11	10
Japanese	701	77	9	9	7
Korean	377	43	18	20	18
Asian Indian	312	19	23	23	35
Vietnamese	215	44	14	33	9

[1]American-born and immigrant people of Asian descent.

Source: Census Bureau.

tionalists" or "activists" in its overall ranks as the Chinese. Most are modernists and many are mainstreamers as well.

The Japanese. Leaving home, even as temporary sojourners, was not a common activity for many Asians, at least not until fairly recently. For many it was long forbidden. Nowhere were restrictions tighter than in Japan where, from the sixteenth to the nineteenth centuries, no Japanese were allowed to venture beyond their island home or to have contact with the West.

It wasn't until the period of the Meiji Restoration, which began in 1868, that things began to change. Under the directives of Emperor Meiji's administrators, trade relations began to develop between the Japanese and the *gaijin,* the foreigners the Japanese had long been taught to fear. With the desire to become part of the wider world, to learn as much as possible about the ways of others, especially about their technologies, many contacts were established through official channels and business enterprises. Laborers and students were encouraged to go abroad to work and to study.

In the early years of the opening to the West, a number of Japanese urban dwellers were recruited for plantation work in Hawaii. This did not prove very satisfying either to the workers or their employers. Later, rural Japanese were enticed by the opportunity to improve their financial lots by becoming "guestworkers" of sorts. Like the several million Southern Italians who came to this country during the period (for both groups, the peak decade was 1900–1910), many Japanese saw themselves as "birds of passage"—individuals whose single-minded goal was to make their fortunes and return home. Some did, but many ended up staying in Hawaii, where they eventually became the dominant "minority," or on the American mainland.

The Chinese, who began coming to the United States in the early days of national expansion, found pick and shovel work in the hinterlands and frontier towns of the West. When the economy began to falter, they were driven back into the seaboard cities. The Japanese, most of whom arrived on the West Coast after the Chinese Exclusion Act of 1882, settled in those same cities. Many worked in small businesses and in service occupations. Others began moving out of town to obtain employment as agricultural laborers, tenant farmers, and contract gardeners.

From the early days the Japanese favored self-employment and family assistance. In a relatively short time, the Japanese proved to be "too good" at what they did and were resented not only for their foreignness but also for their skill and industry. Moreover, because they appeared to be more eager and able than the Chinese to become a part of the American system and to assimilate, at least in terms of outward signs of acculturation and economic achievement, they were viewed as threats not only to those in the working class but also to people who themselves were upwardly mobile. The prejudice against the Japanese was pervasive: discrimination was widespread, and restrictions slowed but never quite stifled their own advancement.[22]

The fate of the Japanese Americans is well known. First, the *Issei* (first generation) had to face the enmity of their American hosts when they settled in the United States; second, their community was hardly permitted to grow in the early decades of this century owing to a "gentleman's agreement" between President Theodore Roosevelt and the Japanese government; third and perhaps most baneful of all, they and their children (the *Nisei*) were humiliated and imprisoned in the wake of the attack on Pearl Harbor in 1941 when pervasive anti-Japanese sentiment was turned into legalized harrassment. Under FDR's Executive Order 9066, 110,00 Japanese, both American citizens and aliens, were removed from the West Coast and interned in "relocation" centers scattered across the country, some as far away as Arkansas. The majority remained in the internment camps until the Supreme Court, ruling in a case brought against the government by American-born Mitsuye Endo that the federal government had clearly violated the rights of loyal Americans by incarcerating them without proper cause, ordered their release.[23] In the years that followed, numerous other suits were to be brought to correct the injustices and offer reparations for psychic and financial damage.

Those who have studied the episode most closely point to the loyalty to the U.S. that persisted despite the persecution. While still in the camps, *Nisei* men were offered the option of volunteering for military service. A large number did so. Many of them saw combat in the European theater. Their units suffered some of the highest casualty rates of the entire war and they received an unusually high number of commendations for their valor under fire.

One of those wounded in battle was Senator Daniel Inouye of Hawaii. He, along with Senator Spark Matsunaga, also of Hawaii, and Congressmen Mineta and Matsui and former Senator Hayakawa, all of California, are often cited as examples of the extent to which Japanese Americans were able to survive their ordeal, reenter society, continue their quest for full participation, and gain entry into the highest circles of power.

While there are cases of those who never fully recovered from the camp experiences and of others who are still fighting for recognition as members of a separate and unique ethnic group, there are very few Japanese Americans languishing in poverty in the ghettoes that are home to many other American minorities (including some of the other Asians).

In 1971 William Petersen reported that, "of all types of crime, delinquency, dependency, or social disorganization about which we have usable statistics, the incidence is lower for Japanese than for any other ethnic group in the American population, including native whites of native parents.[24] That remarkable record remains to this day. Moreover, the evidence of considerable socioeconomic achievement, especially of the *Nisei* and *Sansei* (third generation), are to be found in various studies of the differential mobility of American ethnic groups.[25] Numerous examples of their increasing integration in the wider society are also available.

If, as Milton Gordon has suggested, intermarriage is the last stage in the process of assimilation, then the Japanese Americans are much farther down the road than any other non-whites, including most other Asians.[26] As long as a decade ago, Akemi Kikumura and Harry Kitano found that interracial dating and marriage between Japanese Americans and Anglo-Americans had risen to 50 percent in Fresno, Los Angeles, and San Francisco.[27] How the offspring will define themselves remains to be seen. However, one clue is offered in that some, now entering universities, rather than trying to "pass," seem to be taking pride in their dual heritage and showing particular interest in things Japanese.

Today, in addition to some 800,000 Japanese Americans, there are many Japanese businessmen in the U.S., later-day birds of passage who come to feather their nests or those of the companies they represent. The increasing ubiquity of Japanese enterprises has led to a resurgence of animosity in certain sectors, such as among the hardpressed automobile workers in the early 1980s. Frustrations were manifest in calls for protectionist policies and attacks on those thought to be Japanese. An extreme case in point was the vicious murder in Detroit of Vincent Chin, a young man who turned out to be Chinese.

Such rash vengefulness, while quite rare today, is an old story. To a small number of Americans, "A Jap is [still] a Jap"—even if he is really Chinese or Korean. Many remain insensitive to the dual character of individuals who are Asian but also genuinely American. Few *Sansei* and fewer *Yonsei* (fourth generation) know Japanese; most Koreans here are not Buddhists but Christians.

The Koreans. To be sure, there are some historical parallels to be drawn when one looks at the experiences of the major Asian groups that immigrated to the United States. The Koreans, like the Chinese and the Japanese, also began their North American experience in Hawaii and on the mainland as contract laborers.

What is ironic is that in 1882, the very year the Chinese Exclusion Act was passed, the United States became the first western nation to sign a treaty of friendship and trade with Korea. In the years that followed, some 7,500 Korean workers were contracted by Hawaiian planters to replace the Chinese "coolies" barred from the country by the Exclusion Act. Some of the Koreans returned home; many remained on the islands. And, according to several reports, 2,000 males and twelve females settled in California, forming the first Korean community here.[28] Successive waves were to even out and then reverse the gender balance, establishing a pattern of surplus females that was to dominate well into the 1960s.

Between 1907 and 1924 most female Korean immigrants were, like their Japanese counterparts, "picture brides," sent for through marriage brokers by older males. Ultimately this led to the anomalous situation described by Vincent Parrillo as follows: "As a result of the age disparity between the picture brides and the older males, many second-generation Korean Americans spent a good portion of their formative years with non-English-speaking, widowed mothers who had had limited formal schooling."[29]

Barred by the Immigration Act of 1924, few Koreans came to the U.S. between the mid-1920s and mid-1940s. After Japan's defeat in World War II and her forced surrender of occupied lands, including Korea, American armed forces stationed there fraternized with the local population and an increasing number of marriages occurred between GIs and Korean women. The outbreak of war on the Korean peninsula in the early summer of 1950 led to the massive expansion of U.S. involvement—and to many more liaisons and marriages. With the passage of the Refugee Relief Act of 1953, a steady stream of Koreans began entering the United States. Some were classified as refugees; most were "war brides."

A further surge occurred after the passage of the Immigration Act of 1965, which not only abolished the old country-quota system but liberalized the rules regarding family reunions, accounting for the influx of hundreds of thousands of Asian petitioners. The 1970 Census indicated that there were over 200,000 Koreans in this country. By 1980 there were nearly twice that number.

Perhaps because of the disproportionate number of Korean women married to American servicemen, a higher percentage of Koreans have obtained U.S. citizenship than immigrants from other Asian countries. And, owing to the strong political and military ties between the U.S. and South Korea, and the active religious participation of many Koreans in Protestant churches here, there is considerable support for the conservative policies of the current administration within the Korean American community.

Today, as Illsoo Kim and others who have conducted extensive community studies indicate, Korean Americans are employed in a wide variety of occupations; far fewer are laborers than in the old days.[30] Excluding housewives, most of the recent immigrants were white-collar workers in Korea and seek similar employment here. Many try to enter the technical, managerial, or professional ranks upon their arrival in the U.S. A number have been successful. Others, especially those with language problems or a lack of outside contacts, have gone into small businesses, many into the selling of fresh produce in large cities such as Los Angeles, Chicago, and New York.

It was recently estimated that 900 of the 1,600 greengrocers in

New York City were from Korea.[31] In many ways their preponderance in this single industry recapitulates an old immigrant
pattern of carving out economic niches, establishing networks,
and providing work for family members and other compatriots.
(One recent study found that 80 percent of Koreans employed in
Los Angeles County worked in Korean-owned firms). One thinks
of Jews in the needle trades; Italian barbers, cobblers and construction workers; Chinese hand launderers; Greek restaurateurs; Irish barmen and policemen; and Japanese gardeners. Like
the others, Korean greengrocers have sometimes been resented by
those who see them as chauvinistic and clannish. They have also
been seen as threats to established entrepreneurs and as ex-
ploiters of other minorities (many of the Koreans' customers are
blacks and Hispanics), and, on occasion, the Koreans have run
afoul of the law for using business practices inappropriate in this
country but perfectly reasonable in their homeland. But by and
large they have proven to be hardworking, law-abiding, upwardly
mobile, and quite sensitive to maintaining good race relations in
the marginal areas where many of their shops are located.

The children of the grocers are unlikely to stay in such small
enterprises. Rather, they want to join the ranks of those who were
able to go more directly into the professions or are now active in
the expanding export-import business and in large scale manufacturing. From all indications, they are on a fast track toward such
goals and are using the educational system as a principal stepping
stone. Koreans, most of them still foreign born, now represent a
substantial percentage of the ever-increasing Asian population in
American colleges and universities and graduate schools.

The Other Asians. Aside from the Chinese, Japanese, Korean,
and Indochinese (the latter will be discussed further on)—who in
large measure share a common racial origin and a common
cultural background—there are two other major Asian immigrant groups in the United States. One is made up of the people
of the Indian sub-continent (India, Pakistan, and Bangladesh).
The other is Filipino, a category of people who share a common nationality but are of diverse racial and cultural backgrounds. To
many with little knowledge of either group, Indians and Filipinos
are sometimes lumped together in the public mind. In fact, they

are very different. The popular misconception may stem in part from the disproportionate number of foreign doctors and nurses in America who come from India and the Philippines.

The Filipinos have had a long history of residence in the United States, dating back to 1763 in New Orleans.[32] Most of the Indians, however, are quite recent arrivals. Until 1980, the Census Bureau did not account for the latter group at all.

Many of those who are of Indian origin came (or their parents came) directly from India. Others migrated from East Africa, the West Indies, Guyana, and the United Kingdom, where their families had lived, sometimes for several years, sometimes for several generations.

Some Indians came to the United States early in this century when Punjabi farm laborers settled in California. Many of them left for Canada owing to economic problems and crop failures. A few stayed to form the first Indian settlements on the West Coast. It wasn't until 1946 that Indians were allowed to own land, become citizens, or request permission to bring in relatives. All this changed when the new, liberalizing immigration bill was passed in 1965 and large numbers of Indians applied for and received permission to enter the United States.

While they represent a wide spectrum of ethnic, religious, and linguistic groups, the recently arrived Indians constitute a uniquely high-status group of immigrants. According to several reliable sources, 93 percent were already either "professional/technical workers" or "spouses and children of professional/technical workers" when they arrived.[33] Americans welcomed many to serve in American hospitals, while the exodus of doctors has contributed to the brain-drain from South Asia and, to some extent, from Britain and many former British colonies.

For many years, Indian spokesmen claimed that their official racial designation should be "Caucasian," but the federal judiciary thought otherwise and repeatedly denied their claim to "whiteness." Maxine Fisher, one of the few scholars who has studied Indians in the United States, reports that, even though they were finally permitted to be classified as they had long wished, some members of the community would now like to change back to a non-Caucasian designation. She cites "the economic benefits to be derived from being considered non-white" as a possible reason for this.[34] Despite the objections of many, there have been efforts to use the ethnic category "Asian American" to lump such diverse parties as Indians and Filipinos under the broad rubric "Asian" in order to achieve the benefits of affirmative action programs.

In his book, *Asian Americans and Pacific Islanders: Is There Such An Ethnic Group?*, Filipino Lemuel Ignacio argues for a common label under which simultaneously to counteract and emulate the successful movement of black power brokers. He wants his people to get their fair share of government funding. Because the Filipinos are, like the Indians, a highly diverse, multilingual, multi-ethnic community, they need to come together as well as to ally themselves with others who share their fate if not their history.[35] Fisher rightly states that "Ignacio is fully cognizant that Asian American ethnicity—and even Filipino ethnicity to a lesser extent—are artifacts which he has helped create."[36]

Ignacio sought to present a powerful third bloc of Asians that could make its own claims for affirmative action in competition with blacks and Hispanics. In many ways, he was to prove successful. The ostensible rationale for linking these seemingly odd bedfellows was that all had originally come to the United States from the East; all had suffered from some form of racial discrimination; and, the sentiments of some East Indians notwithstanding, none were white, nor were they black. They were a separate entity seeking their own "group rights."

That such a move should originate with a spokesman for the Filipino-American community is not surprising. Of all the large, transpacific groups that have come here, the Filipinos or "Pinoys," as they often call themselves,[37] are at once among the most marginal and most American of Asian subgroups. Their marginality *and* their Americanness are a result of their peculiar history, which has led them to be seen—and in many ways to be—"the Puerto Ricans of the Pacific."

The Philippine archipelago, situated in a strategic area of the South Pacific, was long a colony of Spain. Spanish *conquistadores, padres,* and *patrones* had left a profound imprint on the culture, religion, and character of the predominantly Malayan population by the time they were finally expelled at the end of the nineteenth century. In 1902, after but several years of independence, American forces overthrew the nationalists, took possession of the islands, and reorganized the society, its laws and, in many ways, its mores. After several hundred years of Spanish rule and "nearly fifty years of Hollywood," the people of the Philippines were subjected to yet another takeover when the Japanese conquered the country in the early days of World War II. American forces were eventually to avenge the Fall of Bataan in 1944 and, two years later, the Philippines became one of the many "independent-dependencies" of the victorious allies. It still retains strategic ties to the United States.

To some, the modern Philippines is a case study in cultural amalgamation. To others it is a highly volatile, fragmented, and schizophrenic society that, again like Puerto Rico, isn't quite sure what it is and what it wants to be. No better example of its own confusion is to be found than the practice of many Filipino patriots who, citing the absence of an "F" sound in the their native Tagalog tongue, eschew its use in the spelling of their official names. Often they say they are 'Pilipinos," not "Filipinos." Ironically, the same local boosters still render gender distinctions in the traditional Spanish manner ("Pilipino" and "Pilipina") while requiring everyone in the nation to learn English! To confound matters further, once they get to the U.S., they are sometimes classified as Hispanics owing to the preponderance of Spanish surnames.[38]

Since the first "Manilamen" jumped ship in Louisiana in the eighteenth century, Filipinos have been difficult to pigeonhole. They never quite fit into standard schemes and frequently followed their own paths toward integration. They are from the East but are not "Orientals" (save for the many "overseas Chinese" in their midst). They often have Spanish names and some Filipinos of the old, partially European elite can still speak Spanish. Nonetheless, Filipinos are not really Hispanic. They have long been a community unto themselves and yet, since the early days of their immigration to the U.S., they have had very high rates of intermarriage with non-Asian Americans.

It used to be said that many Filipinos came because "they lusted after white women."[39] There were other, less disagreeable stereotypes: Filipinos were viewed as diligent workers, ambitious students, and aggressive fighters for their rights.

By 1930 there were over 45,000 Filipinos on the American mainland (and many more in Hawaii), most of them in agricultural work.[40] After the war increasing numbers came to the United States. Many were veterans who had fought in American uniform or served as mess stewards aboard U.S. ships. Many others were the brides of American servicemen. A decade later they were to be followed by large numbers of countrymen and women who benefited from the changes in immigration legislation (some 250,000 entered the U.S. between 1966 and 1976). That last group, to which more are being added every year, includes a large percentage of highly educated physicians, lawyers, engineers, and teachers who have come for reasons quite similar to those of their forebears and most other immigrants: to benefit from job opportunities in the new society.

Filipinos still rank lowest among those now labeled "Asian American" in terms of their overall socioeconomic status, but their situation is changing, especially for the most recent arrivals. Most Filipino immigrants now come knowing English, already trained in needed skills, and sharing many of the same attitudes about making it in America that other Asians possess. In the years ahead, this enigmatic minority may be more closely identified with Asians (as Lemuel Ignacio would like) than with the other Spanish-surnamed Americans with whom they are often grouped.

The most recent census indicated that, counted according to the country of last permanent residence, some 740,000 Chinese (from China and Hong Kong), 411,000 Japanese, 431,000 Filipinos, 276,000 Koreans, 182,000 Indians, and 134,000 Vietnamese are living in the United States.[41] Not included in these figures are large numbers of American-born children and grandchildren of Asian immigrants, but estimates suggest that there were 895,000 members of the overall Chinese cohort in the country, 800,000 Japanese, 795,000 Filipinos, 377,000 Koreans, 312,000 Asian Indians, and 215,000 from Vietnam in 1980.[42] Since then the numbers of those in the last subset have increased considerably, augmented by the arrival of boat people and other Indochinese refugees, including many who had already experienced life as members of minority groups overseas.

The Newest Asian Americans

A third of all Asian Americans in the United States are Indo-chinese who have arrived in this country since 1965, a large percentage of those since the fall of Saigon in 1975. To date nearly 700,000 Indochinese have been screened, accepted for admission, and resettled in various parts of the United States. As of May 1, 1984, the heaviest concentrations were in the states of California (estimated to be 254,000), Texas (56,100), Washington (31,800), Illinois (24,600), New York (24,000), Pennsylvania (24,000), Minnesota (21,900), and Virginia (21,300).[43] Other states with anywhere from 16,600 to slightly more than 10,000 Indochinese refugees were Massachusetts, Louisiana, Florida, Colorado, Michigan, and Ohio.[44] (See Table 2.)

Those from the countries of Indochina—Vietnam, Laos, and Cambodia (Kampuchea)—while often treated as a single entity, are a mixed lot in political, ethnic, religious, and socioeconomic terms. There are former government officials and military personnel, individuals who worked for one of the many agencies of the U.S. government, "war brides," and Chinese minorities from all areas of Indochina. There are people from the major cities of Vietnam, Laos, and Cambodia; from the rural areas and from the highlands (including the Hmong, Hmien, and Laotung); "old" Khmer who had been part of Lon Nol's forces and "new" Khmer who fled Cambodia during Pol Pot's reign of terror or after his downfall, when the country was occupied by Vietnamese forces.

Within groups separated by nationality and divided by ethnicity are French-educated cosmopolites, bourgeois provincials, and dirt-poor peasants; Roman Catholics, Buddhists, Taoists, Shamanists, and Animists. There are gifted intellectuals, street-wise hustlers, and unworldly fisherfolk and farmers. There are whole families who managed somehow to escape together or to eventually bring in dispersed relatives. And there are single individuals who lost everything but their own lives crossing the "sea of heartbreak."[45]

Though the Indochinese are a variegated lot, most of those who have come to the United States since 1975 have shared a common fate and now share a common status. Unlike most other Asians in the West, they are *political refugees* rather than *economic migrants,* a status ascribed to them because they left their home-

Table 2
Southeast Asian Refugee Populations in the U.S.
(By State of Residence, 5/1/84)

State of Residence	Estimated Total	State of Residence	Estimated Total
Alabama	2,500	Nevada	2,100
Alaska	200	New Hampshire	600
Arizona	5,000	New Jersey	6,200
Arkansas	3,000	New Mexico	2,500
California	254,100	New York	24,000
Colorado	10,400	North Carolina	5,100
Connecticut	6,300	North Dakota	900
Delaware	300	Ohio	10,200
District of Columbia	1,300	Oklahoma	8,900
Florida	12,100	Oregon	16,700
Georgia	8,500	Pennsylvania	24,000
Hawaii	7,000	Rhode Island	6,500
Idaho	1,400	South Carolina	2,400
Illinois	24,600	South Dakota	1,100
Indiana	4,400	Tennessee	4,300
Iowa	8,500	Texas	56,100
Kansas	9,100	Utah	8,400
Kentucky	2,400	Vermont	600
Louisiana	13,900	Virginia	21,300
Maine	1,500	Washington	31,800
Maryland	7,900	West Virginia	500
Massachusetts	16,600	Wisconsin	9,800
Michigan	10,300	Wyoming	300
Minnesota	21,900	Guam	200
Mississippi	1,500	Other Territories	a
Missouri	6,600		
Montana	1,000		
Nebraska	2,300	Total	689,100

aFewer than 100.

Source: *The Bridge,* July, 1984, p. 9.

lands after suffering—or fearing—persecution. In other words, they were in a sense driven out rather than pulled away by the enticement of a better life on some distant shore.

Not only are the Indochinese different from other Asians who have settled—or resettled—in the country, they are different from other refugees. Unlike most of those who came to America prior to 1965 (Armenians, Jews fleeing Hitler, Czechs, Hungarians, even many of the Cubans who left after Castro's revolution), those from Vietnam, Laos, and Cambodia have been almost completely dependent on direct governmental support or on programs funded primarily if not exclusively by federal departments.[46] This unique situation is related to American response to the defeat in Vietnam.

In April 1975 the U.S. military airlifted thousands of people out of Vietnam. At transit centers in the Philippines, on Guam, and at four bases in the U.S., representatives of voluntary agencies with prior experience working with refugees were called in to facilitate processing and resettlement. Few thought that those who were being assisted would be harbingers of a massive exodus of people escaping from the newly established Democratic Republic of Vietnam. But they were. The thousands who followed bought or bribed their way on unreliable, overcrowded vessels that set out for the nearest landfall. These "boat people" hoped, eventually, to be permitted to move on to the United States or, perhaps, to France.

Resettling the Refugees. The relatively small number of Vietnamese already in the United States could hardly have been expected to house, feed, and otherwise provide for their countrymen, and certainly not for those coming from Laos or Cambodia, traditionally rival states. Something had to be done—and fast. Moreover, the growing crisis was greatly aggravated by the reluctance of those in the countries of "first asylum" to allow boat people to land, fearing they would not move on but would stay there and drain the local economies, becoming thorns in the sides of the bodies politic and potential fifth-columnists. These fears were expressed in all the countries of the area, but it was Malaysia—worried about inundation by the ethnic Chinese from Vietnam, which could upset the strategic balance between the politically dominant Malays and the economically powerful Chinese—that unintentionally provided the catalyst for a global response.

Americans and others around the world were horrified by satellite-relayed pictures of boats laden with refugees being pushed back to sea by members of the Malaysian armed forces and local militiamen. In a sort of delayed reaction, an international conference was called and an agreement was reached among Western nations and Japan: the refugees would be resettled in "third countries" in the West.

While Canada and Australia took in the largest percentage relative to the size of their populations, the United States accepted the largest number of Indochinese refugees by a factor of ten. Once again, "volags," or private voluntary agencies—the American Council of Nationalities Service, Church World Service, the Hebrew Immigrant Aid Society, the International Rescue Committee, the Lutheran Immigration and Refugee Service, the U.S. Catholic Conference, World Relief Refugee Service, and several smaller agencies—were called upon to use their expertise to assist the newcomers while the government provided funding and logistical support.

The problems that such an arrangement created were and remain complex and cumbersome, yet a remarkable feat was accomplished and close to three-quarters of a million Indochinese entered the United States to begin their lives anew.[47] Moreover, the relationship of the federal government to the voluntary agencies, a marriage of both convenience and necessity, was institutionalized within guidelines specified in the Refugee Act of 1980, the first comprehensive bill to deal with the plight of refugees as distinct from that of immigrants.

The bill called for the establishment of a coordinator (with the rank of ambassador) to oversee the foreign policy aspects of the refugee program within the Department of State and to work with those in the Immigration and Naturalization Service of the Department of Justice and the newly established Office of Refugee Resettlement (ORR) in the Department of Health and Human Services. ORR was to allocate funds through state welfare agencies and, sometimes, through direct grants to "service providers" who offered ESL (English-as-a-Second-Language) instruction, job training, and employment services. Private voluntary agencies involved in reception and placement were to be reimbursed for "core services" at a rate of $500 per capita. (This has recently been raised to $525 for Indochinese refugees.) Additional money was to be set aside to support a variety of "grass roots" mutual assistance associations. Such funding was to help the refugees to help themselves.

There were some highly successful programs; some that failed rather dramatically; and many that are still struggling to deal with the problems of initial resettlement, first contacts with the wider community, and acculturation. Nonetheless, one thing is quite clear: without the substantial financial assistance of the federal government, the Indochinese would have had a much more difficult time once they arrived in America. And without the assurance that aid would be forthcoming, it is doubtful that many American communities would have been as receptive to the influx as they have proven to be—even against the predictions of many that there would be echoes of the cries of a hundred years ago of the "threat from the East."

The American Hosts. A Harris Poll conducted in May of 1975, immediately after the communist victory in Vietnam, indicated that only 36 percent of the American people thought Indochinese should be allowed to enter the U.S. More than 50 percent favored keeping them out, and many seemed to agree with Congressman Burt Talcott (R.-Ca.), who vehemently opposed their admission because "Damn it, we have too many Orientals." They came anyway. Not just a few, but hundreds of thousands. Yet, unlike most who came before, the newest Asian candidates for American citizenship were greeted with surprisingly little hostility. To be sure, there were instances of difficulties, some of them quite ugly. Nevertheless, considering that the Indochinese refugees constitute the largest non-white, non-Western, non-English-speaking group of people ever to enter the country at one time, and to arrive moreover during a period of economic turmoil, their reception has been quite remarkable. So, too, has their readjustment.

The reception was eased by governmental assurance that the Indochinese would not become financial burdens on American society. But even this cannot explain the unprecedented willingness on the part of thousands to serve as sponsors, guides, and go-betweens for those with whom they had no ethnic ties and did not know. The Indochinese were war victims, and this fact offers a most important clue to American response. As I have hypothesized elsewhere the willingness to help or, at least, to minimize opposition to the Indochinese, is directly connected to the sense of responsibility felt by many in the political establishment and many private citizens.[48]

A number of those who supported America's war effort in Southeast Asia argue that since "we" failed to stop the communists, allowed them to overrun the countries of Indochina, and forced many to flee for their lives, "we owe them something." Many who opposed the war believe that Americans destroyed the countries of Indochina and that it is our duty to provide those who suffered with protection and assistance. The entire situation represents a fascinating example of converging commitments from heretofore rather incompatible bedfellows, both now recognizing that there was a debt that needed to be paid.

It would be naive and wrong to say that all who supported the war and all who opposed it are now as one. Support means (and meant) many things; so does opposition. Many who actually fought in Vietnam are angry, especially draftees who reluctantly went to war and then came home only to be seen as embarassing reminders of a debacle rather than as heroes of a glorious campaign. They believe that refugees get more favored treatment than they, that increasing benefits are given to those from Indochina while their own are being cut. Most of the bitterness has been contained but occasionally it breaks out in spontaneous acts of violence and, in rare instances, of calculated vigilanteeism. One recent episode occurred in western Massachusetts: a small group of disturbed and disgruntled veterans on a weekend pass from a Veterans' Administration hospital burned a Buddhist temple to indicate their displeasure with the present state of affairs. The nationwide response, especially from Vietnam veterans' groups, was a clear indication that many vehemently disavowed the vandalism. Not only did local branches of major veterans' organizations disclaim any support for such acts, but many offered to contribute money and manpower to help rebuild the religious edifice. (They also used the occasion to remind the nation that the thing that triggers such unfortunate outbursts is the failure to adequately deal with the plight of the veterans themselves—especially those suffering from the malady called "post-traumatic stress syndrome.")

In addition to the troubled veterans, there are two other sources of opposition to the presence of large numbers of Indochinese. Those who might be called "old nativists" and those who are appropriately labeled "neo-nativists." The former are quite familiar to students of North American immigration, those like Burt Talcott and Clare Booth Luce who see outsiders, especially those who are quite different from themselves, as unassimilable aliens who could potentially undermine the Anglo-American way of life. Those in the second category are not so well known. They are often members of non-white (and, usually, non-Asian) minority groups who have come to claim that scarce funds for welfare and job training are being squandered on foreigners while Americans like themselves are still being discriminated against and suffering in a depressed economy. They are concerned with what they see as the differential and favored treatment of the refugees and their publicly supported encroachment on their turf.

Voluntary agencies frequently place refugees in the least expensive areas of town. There they represent an alien force to many who least understand who they are and why they came. They are also convenient scapegoats for poor blacks and Hispanics. The fact that many landlords seem to prefer the Indochinese, who, they claim, are less apt to make trouble, exacerbates the potentially explosive situation. Sometimes the seething hostilities burst forth in racial conflict.

Crossing the Threshold. Still, the record overall is quite impressive. Even in the worst of the urban areas, the number of serious confrontations has been relatively few. Perhaps it is because "they don't make waves." Perhaps it is related to the fact that, to the authorities, they are "good" minorities rather than troublemakers and therefore deserve more protection. Or perhaps it is because of the widespread publicity given to those who seem to be moving into the wider society with such determination and success.[49]

The rapid movement from barely peripheral involvement to extensive participation that has occurred has been quite exceptional, especially when we are reminded that the people under consideration here are those who were rather suddenly uprooted and dispossessed, who came from highly stratified societies with world views quite different from those of the West, and who had little preparation for what they were to find.

Not surprisingly, given the socioeconomic heterogeneity of the Indochinese who came, some have had an easier time of it than others. The "first wave" Vietnamese, many of whom are two-time refugees, having fled from the North to the South in the mid-1950s and then from the new communist state to the U.S. in the late 1970s, have had some decided advantages. These have included marketable skills, English language capability, a trove of cash, a number of American contacts made during the war, or a combination of these. Likewise, many of the ethnic Chinese, sometimes called the "Jews of the East," have also fared better than many of the others. Some argue that, having always been "marginal men" who often lived in their own separate areas, spoke their own languages or dialects, and maintained their sense of ethnic identity even while serving economic and professional needs of others, the Chinese from Indochina are more adaptive than those who had been members of the majority groups of the nations of the region.

This is not to say that prior minority status is, *ipso facto,* a boon to adjustment in new situations. It depends very much on the placement of the minority in the home society. Thus, while the ethnic Chinese were prospering as "middleman minorities" in Indochina, others were placed far lower in the social order and were often far less worldly. The 60,000 to 70,000 Hmong and members of other hilltribes from the Laotian highlands now in the U.S. are good cases in point. Along with the Khmer from Cambodia, they have had a far more difficult time adjusting to their new environs.[50]

Between those advantaged because of their place in the status hierarchies or because of their functional marginality, and those who are most culturally estranged, is the majority, the Vietnamese "boat people." The latter have been here only a few years, but they are already beginning to take on the characteristics of a truly American ethnic community replete with national and local leaders, political organizations, business associations, blocs of solid citizens, and gangs of troubled youth.

Although most Vietnamese left on slow boats and languished for a time in the limbo of the refugee camps, once they boarded the jumbo-jets from transit centers in Bangkok, Kuala Lumpur, Hong Kong, or Manila, they were on a fast-moving treadmill. In twenty-four hours they moved 10,000 miles into the hurlyburly of life in the land of the Big PX. They haven't stopped. Encouraged by sponsors, mesmerized by TV, enticed by the desire to fit in, Vietnamese seem on the whole to be accelerating the pace of acculturation.

In the well-known pattern the first generation, the immigrants, remain in their enclaves living in the past and trying to maintain a semblance of old ways in the alien setting. The second generation, the infants they bring and their American-born children, become the bridges between the world of their fathers and the new society. While often eager to escape the confines of the ghetto and partake of the opportunities seeming to abound beyond it, they are often plagued with uncertainty and anxiety about who they really are. The grandchildren become the new Americans, some abandoning their heritages altogether. However, owing to their appearance if not their aspirations, Asians, including Southeast Asians, are rarely able to be fully assimilated or absorbed. They are now and will remain hyphenates. In this they are unlike many Europeans.

For many Vietnamese families, especially those ensconced in such places as Orange County and San Jose, California; in Versailles outside of New Orleans; or in Alexandria, Virginia, it all seems to be happening at once. The older people still "stay behind." Older children, while far from babes-in-arms, often go through a rapid course in resocialization, learning to assume new responsibilities and to walk the tightrope between the two worlds. Younger children, even some of those born in Indochina or in the camps in the ASEAN countries, take on the dress, manners, and—to the chagrin of their parents—many of the mores of the new society. Yet, even those in the last group (the "third generation") seem to maintain some sense of identity, though it is hardly one their relatives back home would comprehend. They are a new breed, Vietnamese Americans—or Vietnamericans.[51]

It is never easy to make such momentous adjustments or to create what Nathan Glazer once called "a new social form."[52] Ironically, given the strong support provided to the Indochinese, some predicted it would be *harder* for them than it was in the old days when widespread discrimination forced earlier groups from Asia to rely almost entirely upon their kith and kin, when such defensive insulation led to an even greater sense of interdependence and fellow-feeling among members of the same group. Perhaps. But it is also true that that sort of argument sounds strikingly like the one that says that every time Jews find they are about to be fully accepted in the host societies where they have settled, some new wave of anti-Semitism "saves them" from disappearing. Surely the liability of acceptance is far less damaging than the scourge of exclusion. In this, the Indochinese are fortunate to be in a special situation.

While they will continue to face unexpected obstacles, the newcomers have several decided advantages having to do with *who* they are, with *why* they came, and especially with *when* they arrived—a time of philo-Asianism unprecedented in American history. Like other Asians, those from Indochina are coming to be seen by many not merely as "model minorities," but as "model Americans": hardworking, achievement-oriented, and, for the most part, anti-communist.

The Future of Asian Ethnic Groups in America

In his final essay in *Ethnic Dilemmas: 1964–1982,* Nathan Glazer discusses "The Politics of a Multiethnic Society." He begins by summarizing what he and Daniel Patrick Moynihan said in the revised edition of *Beyond the Melting Pot* about what they saw as two alternative paradigms of intergroup relations in the United States circa 1970. One was southern (and rural), the other, northern (and urban). While in both patterns total assimilation did not occur, the patterns were quite different from each other. The southern alternative was, essentially, a dichotomous black-white model in which "'separate but equal' [was] an ideology if not a reality."[53] The northern scheme was closer to the old notion of the multiethnic spectrum and the idea of *e pluribus unum* (in many, one).

Glazer and Moynihan were quite prescient. While one could quibble with some of their specific predictions, their major failing was that they did not see or acknowledge *other* paradigms based on other circumstances. Their views of the North and South were largely limited to what was going on—and would go on—from Memphis to Manhattan but not from Seattle to San Diego.

Perhaps it was because it was an extension of their study of New York's ethnic minorities that their perspective had such an East Coast bias. Glazer clearly acknowledges this in the new volume in which he offers a third alternative, a western one, which takes into account the experiences and encounters of those large minority groups whose heritage is neither African nor European.

In contrast to the Mexicans, by far the largest of the newer groups, others are more alien to us culturally. As Glazer notes:

[The] newer groups are more distant in culture, language and religion from white Americans, whether of the old or new immigration, than these were from each other. We now have groups that are in American terms more exotic than any before. Added to the Chinese and Japanese are now Filipinos, Koreans, Asian Indians, Vietnamese, Cambodians, Laotians, Pacific Islanders, many of them speaking languages unconnected to the languages of Europe, many practicing religions that have very few representatives in this country (though there are many Christians among them), and most [are] of racial or ethnic stocks distant from the European.[54]

A western alternative—or what Lemuel Ignacio might have called a "third bloc approach"[55]—could have been advanced a decade ago because the trends were already being established then. Today it is even more applicable, for the main sources of immigration are not Europe and Canada, but Latin America and Asia. The third alternative is a complex one, not nearly so paradigmatically pure as either of the earlier models. While different from both, it contains elements of each.

Importantly, any new "western" model must address the matter of the offering of government protection and benefits to an array of officially designated "minorities" regardless of their actual need. At present, poor Mexicans and wealthy Chinese can both take advantage of "affirmative action." Any new model must also consider the still viable practice of carving a niche and entering specialized trades, engaging in bloc power, and learning to form coalitions of convenience as well as interest. This leads to the conclusion that there may well be *two* sub-types within the western alternative, or, more accurately put, two divergent paths that will be followed by those minorities living mainly in the western states. One, ostensibly "blackward," will be signposted with phrases like "institutional racism," "second-class citizenship," and by demands that whites be made to recognize the bicultural (meaning in this instance the Latin/Anglo) character of the country to give deprived individuals their just due. Hispanics, who place greater emphasis on power politics, voter registration, and direct appeals for governmental assistance, will take this course of action far more often than will the Asians (with the possible exception of the anomalous Filipinos).

Most Asians, despite their own continuing encounters with prejudice, will follow the other path. They will do what they have
generally done in the past: that is, they will use communal action
less for raising the consciences of their own peoples or those in the
controlling sectors than for the aggrandizement of kin and clans-
men *within* the different and still distinctive ethnic groups. In this
they are on a repaved road toward European-type assimilation.

Most Asians—newcomers as well as oldtimers—have had ambivalent attitudes about capitalizing on inherited "disadvantages." To most, meritocratic principles are the norms by which
their lives in the United States have been organized in the past
and ought to be in the future. It is this ethos—and the publicity
their achievements have received—that causes many to look to
them (but rarely to the Hispanics) as archetypes of acculturation.

And, yet, the paradox remains. While more and more Asian
Americans have come to represent the best of what those who pro-
mulgate "Americanization" would like to create, as stated earlier,
they are not and will not be fully assimilated, at least not in the
foreseeable future. It will be a long time in Californ' or in any
other part of the country before they are simply absorbed (for that
is what assimilation is). Rather, like the Jews to whom they are so
often compared, they will retain their marginal status.

No matter how adaptive in values and aspirations, no matter
how similar to whites in mannerisms and actions, Asian Americans cannot be members of the majority. They can become
"Bananas," but they will remain yellow in the eyes of their
beholders. Some, like the Japanese of Los Angeles County, will
intermarry, thus reducing the issue of racial difference or, more
likely, giving it greater subtlety. Most however, will remain
relatively endogamous, clearly conspicuous, and fully conscious of
their double identities.[56]

10

NATHAN GLAZER

Immigrants and Education

Anyone growing up in the school systems of our large northern and midwestern cities in the 1920s and 1930s would have experienced schools in which the overwhelming majority of the children were the children of immigrants. That situation had prevailed almost without variation since the 1840s and 1850s, when the public school systems of those cities were being founded. One would think that if any schools were adapted to the education of vast numbers of immigrant children it would be American urban schools. But when, after a period of forty years in which immigration, radically reduced by immigration restriction acts, depression, war, and continued restriction in the postwar period, began to rise in the mid-1960s (in 1966 immigration passed 300,000 for the first time since 1924), a great number of things had changed. The education of immigrants today is as controversial as it ever has been, indeed more controversial than it was during the great age of mass immigration that ended in 1924.

For in the decades before 1924, despite almost continuous battles over such questions as the use of the languages of immigrants in education,[1] or the control of schools, whether by decentralized wards with considerable immigrant input, or by centralized school boards, a consensus was forged, and it had reduced almost all opposition to silence by the 1920s.[2] American public schools were for the purpose of Americanizing the immigrant, which meant to teach him or her English and the superiority of American ways in all respects: from diet, hygiene, and sports, to attitudes and ideas. He would salute the flag, recite the pledge of allegiance, be taught that he should have orange juice and milk in the morning rather than coffee, that he should not wear a cap or a *yarmulk*, that he should believe in the almost inherent decadence of all foreign nations and the god-given rightness of American government.

Dissident voices were scarcely to be heard. Catholics objected only to the Protestantism of the schools, hardly anything else, and taught the same attitudes in their schools. Jews had just about no parochial schools, and tried to add their supplements to American education in afternoon schools, and this was true of every other group. The immigrant child's culture, language, religion, was ignored as if it did not exist. His forebears played no role in American history, and he was left to be confused as to why in school he learned about George Washington, and in his afternoon schools about heroes and nations that played no part in the first. .

Did it work? Asking this question with reference to the 1910s or 1920s was rather different from what it was to mean in the 1980s. In the earlier period the school leaving age was twelve or fourteen, only a minority of Americans attended high school, and a small minority attended college. Many jobs were available for the illiterate, and the failure to gain a high school diploma did not raise a question as to employability.

If we had been making studies of average income by ethnic group or by immigrant and native status at the time, we might well have decided that it did not work; that the immigrant Italian, Jew, Pole, was much poorer than the native, and his children were not that much better off. But an epoch's problems are determined by its perspectives: neither immigrant nor native raised such questions. It was taken for granted by the first that he would begin at the bottom and have a hard life and hope for a better life for his children. It was taken for granted by the latter that all this would take a long time, and that it was only proper that it should.

By other measures, it worked. America raised armies on a mass scale, filled with immigrants and their children, that fought for their adopted nation against its enemies—including their home countries—without any evidence that the immigrant and his children fulfilled their duties with any less commitment or enthusiasm than the native. Immigrant languages declined rapidly in favor of English.[3] And despite the severity of the Great Depression, even economic adaptation and equality were not far behind: by the 1960s it was hard to see any evidence that those who had come in the great European immigration and their children were any worse off than long-established native groups, and some of them were indeed better off.

There is much argument as to whether the schools had much to do with this. If the measure of success was political, social, and economic assimilation, and if one grants a sufficient length of time (two generations or forty years), it is hard to demonstrate that the schools hurt.

But by the time immigration began to rise again, and began to fill the schools of the great cities of the North and West again with the children of immigrants speaking foreign languages, a number of things had happened. The situation was transformed.

We have indicated one thing that changed the situation: education was now seen as far more crucial for economic fate. By the 1960s the failure of everyone to complete high school (still only three-quarters do) was seen as a national crisis, demanding national action.

The second thing that changed the situation was that the schools were already dealing with the consequence of a mass inflow of the poor, unskilled, and poorly educated; but we do not call this inflow an "immigration" because it was an internal migration of blacks from Southern states to Northern and Western states. Fierce battles were already in course as to how they should be, could be, educated.

The third was that a new armature of federal law was being forged in the 1960s and 1970s, originally designed to protect blacks from segregation and discrimination, but almost immediately applied to other groups, in particular Mexican American and Puerto Rican. There were assumptions and biases built into these laws that were to dominate the argument over the education of immigrants.

The fourth thing that changed was that by the late 1960s, American self-confidence was severely shaken by internal riots in the cities, overseas failure in Vietnam, the disillusion of the highly educated and intellectuals with American decency and capacity in dealing with domestic and foreign problems.

As a result of the facts that the schools were mired in the problems of black education and governed by a structure of federal law, invoked by minority defense organizations with resources and power that were unimaginable in the previous periods of immigration, the problems of the education of immigrant children became immediately assimilated to the problems of the education of poor, minority, and Spanish-speaking children.

Because of this historical context, we hardly have seen any discussion of the education of immigrant children as such. Rather, that issue has become part of a number of other issues that somewhat overlap it. What do we do about the education of poor children? Of minority children? Of foreign-language children? The new rise of immigration occurred while the United States was struggling over these questions, concurrently with the period of great expansion of civil rights for minority groups represented by the major civil rights legislation of 1964, 1965, 1968, and 1972, and with the period of civil disturbances in American cities during the summers of the late 1960s. This was a period in which the theme of "black power"—increasing the independent power of the black minority—was prominent and expressed in heightened rhetoric; and this rhetoric inspired or was echoed by similar rhetoric from Chicano (Mexican American), Puerto Rican, American Indian, and Asian American militants.

The chief repercussion of these demands was in the field of education. Ironically, the demand for minority power had few effects in the political realm, the realm of government, local, state, or national. The impact on institutions of higher education was particularly marked. Hundreds of programs of black studies, Chicano studies, Puerto Rican studies, Native American (American Indian) studies, Asian studies, were launched. The character of these programs was, in the context of American higher education, exceptional. They were programs that emphasized advocacy (of group maintenance, of group values, of group power) more than analysis of group history, culture, and problems. Their faculties were drawn in large measure from persons without traditional scholarly or scientific education; their students often formed a separate enclave on campuses. Also, the objectives of these programs were unique for higher education since they aimed at neither occupational nor professional qualification, nor were they well-linked with traditional fields of scholarship for which their students could be prepared as researchers or teachers. It was not therefore surprising that these fields, after the early 1970s, lost their appeal to students who were increasingly concerned with occupational futures, declined in number, and were in many places transformed, insofar as they survived, into departments with a more traditional academic flavor.

Higher education thus bore the brunt of early demands for minority group recognition. A rather steadier presence was forged in the elementary and secondary schools, but there the social dynamics were very different. In the higher schools, the argument was that enclaves of power and recognition had to be created in the form of free-standing and independent departments and programs. In the elementary and secondary schools, which are more oriented toward skills than content-laden studies, the argument was that the recognition of culture—and, for those of foreign-language background, language—and the use of culture and language in teaching was essential for the academic progress of children of minority background. The recognition of culture, the use of language, would show that these children were respected by the larger culture. This respect would lead to heightened self-image. Heightened self-image would lead to greater academic achievement, and would close gaps in achievement evident between minority children and "majority"—white—children.

The argument was made for all groups that were considered minority—blacks, Mexican Americans, Puerto Ricans, other Latin Americans, American Indians, and Asians—despite the enormous differences among these groups, the great differences in their experiences, and, one would think, differences in their educational needs. But an argument was forged, and for a while had considerable force. It applied to blacks, whose native language was English, and whose forbears had been resident in the United States for three centuries; to Mexican Americans, some of whom were descended from ancestors who had settled in the territory of the United States as long or longer ago than blacks, but most of whom were recent immigrants and their children, and who were identified by foreign language rather than different race; to American Indians, whose presence on the continent preceded the first two groups and the majority, and who, it could be argued, differed more from the dominant society in culture than any other group; to Asian Americans, themselves diverse, and who, in contrast to all the other minority groups—despite severe prejudice and discrimination to which they had been subjected from the time of their arrival to the 1950s or so—showed educational and economic achievement superior to that of the white majority.

It was always doubtful whether similar claims could be raised effectively for all these groups, and whether similar programs would meet their demands and their needs. In particular, there were striking differences between the demands of black political leadership and Hispanic political leadership. The first, owing to the long history of segregation, against which they had fought, demanded that black children be widely distributed through the schools and that they nowhere be allowed to form a majority, for that would indicate segregation. The Hispanics were less concerned about concentration, and indeed demanded programs in the Spanish language that could only be effective if there was some substantial degree of concentration. Since desegregation was a major demand of the black community, leading to many extended constitutional cases and programs designed to break up these concentrations, black and Hispanic leaders were often at odds. Blacks were willing to go to the trouble that desegregation required: very often this meant long bus rides for black children into distant areas. Since redistribution of one group required redistribution of others, these programs also meant long bus rides for Hispanic children, and Hispanic parents and leaders could not see the reason for that.

These differences however did not overwhelm all efforts to form a common alliance educationally and politically. Politically we have seen as recently as the 1984 presidential primary campaign of Jesse Jackson an effort to forge what he called a "rainbow coalition" of all minorities—attractive among blacks, more doubtfully so among Hispanics, not at all among Asians. But educationally a common analysis was forged to explain the educational difficulties of minorities. To some extent even a common program was forged, leading to such an anomaly as the demand in at least one case for the recognition of "Black English" as a separate language.[4] In this case black claimants made use of civil rights protections that had been designed primarily for Hispanics from non-English-speaking homes; more commonly, Mexican Americans and Puerto Ricans made use of the legal techniques first used by blacks, and the legal remedies originally designed for their protection, to press their own demands. As we have indicated, these tended not to be demands for desegregation but for special programs—which some blacks also demanded.

The basis of a common educational program, insofar as one existed, was to be found in the work of social scientists and scholars of education in the 1960s. They argued that minorities were treated differently by teachers; that teachers expected less from them, therefore providing less direct teaching for them; that in effect the racism so common in American society affected teachers and administrators too, and this was the explanation of educational failure. An explanation as total as this offers difficulty: how does one deal with a racism so pervasive that it changes the school experience for the minority child? Law had gone just about as far as it could. But anti-discrimination law, it was argued, could be supplemented by independent power for minorities. That independent power would consist of programs run by members of a minority, for members of a minority, using the culture and the language of that minority. Their culture would be maintained, their respect enhanced. With this kind of analysis all minorities, despite differential legal status, educational achievement, and educational need, could forge a common program. And to some extent they did.

The underlying rationale for this approach owed much to the work of social scientists in education. The Coleman report of 1966, and its reanalyses in Mosteller and Moynihan, suggested the importance of self-image for achievement,[5] though it was not at all clear whether self-image contributed to achievement, or achievement contributed to self-image, or whether any part of self-image was shaped by respect for a minority's ethnic or racial heritage. The rationale, insofar as it affected children from foreign-language homes, was in any case incorporated into legislation—

tentatively in 1968, more fully in 1974.[6] The Congress asserted that a full-bodied bilingual education was valuable for children from homes speaking a language other than English. This legislation and subsequent appropriations also provided funds for such programs to local school districts.

The legislation did not affect blacks, despite the black English case referred to. But if power was essential to self-respect, and self-respect essential to education, blacks did not need much recourse after the early 1970s to federal legislation: blacks were becoming dominant demographically in city after city. First their children became majorities in big-city school districts,[7] and not long thereafter blacks were able to become mayors of major American cities: Atlanta, Washington, Los Angeles, Detroit, Chicago, Philadelphia. This political dominance, which now extends to the public school systems, may be expected to last a long time.

Thus if the black community truly wanted a black component in education, it had the power to implement that component increasingly, without recourse to federal power or to judicial intervention, in the late 1970s and 1980s. But power has strange effects. It might have been expected that black-run school systems would have greater concern for black culture, and in measure they do. They certainly take Martin Luther King Day more seriously than do other school systems. Their textbooks may reflect this concern. But power meant responsibility. It was easy to demand black culture when blacks were out of power. Once in power, the constituents of black educational and political leaders insisted on educational achievement, and couldn't care less, it seemed, about black English, black history, black mathematics, or black science. They wanted the kind of achievement that led to competence to take jobs and to enter higher education. The weight of black demands, now addressed to school systems often run by blacks, was no longer for a distinctive culture, but for achievement in the common culture.

The situation for Hispanic Americans was somewhat different. Their numbers were fewer, and they less often controlled cities and school systems (though Cubans controlled Miami, Mexican Americans San Antonio). Further, many spoke Spanish, and were committed to the maintenance of Spanish for their children. Thus education that contained a substantial amount of Spanish was desired, and in some measure achieved, largely through federal legislation, administration, and court decisions. Hispanic Americans also made advances—not without effort—in the states in which they were numerous, such as California and Texas and New York, in putting a bilingual component into education.

But the major struggle was at the federal level. This was less a struggle for funds than for regulations to impose programs—and the costs for them—on local school systems. The federal government has the power to defend the civil rights of students in schools, under legislation of 1964 and 1972, and this defense reaches not only to children identified by race, but to children marked by foreign language. Regulatory power can do more than the simple contribution of federal funds; together they can do a great deal. The federal regulatory role expanded, particularly after the key *Lau* decision of the Supreme Court in 1974, which ruled, on the basis of a claim made for Chinese immigrant children in San Francisco, that a local school district must make special provision for children with a foreign-language background. Other cases filed in other jurisdictions—perhaps the most important was the *Aspira* case in New York City—also guaranteed that there would be extensive programs of bilingual education. And these continue.[8]

Despite these early victories, I believe the demand for maintenance of culture and language has weakened and is no longer the dominant element of language minority groups. The hard economic times of the 1970s and the increasing strength of conservative and nationalist political forces in the United States, as indicated by the successive victories of Ronald Reagan in 1980 and 1984, have changed the emphases in discussions of the education of minority and immigrant children. Educators may still be concerned about children's self-image and minority culture. Ethnic and racial nationalists and militants are of course concerned with the maintenance of culture, and in particular with control of the political and social content of the education of minorities, in order to encourage identity and militancy. However, they have lost power in their communities. On the other hand, ethnic and racial minorities are concerned—as they have always been—with jobs for their people, and this is perhaps now the sturdiest support for special programs using foreign language: that they enable members of the community to get jobs. But the dominant emphasis in education now, among majorities and minorities, is for traditional achievement, on the assumption that this is crucial for raising the economic level of minority communities.

The cultural component in education for minorities has lost power: fewer among minorities demand it, and hardly anyone but professional educators among majorities accede to it or consider it important. The language component is considered important by the majority and legislators only if it provides a base for academic achievement so as to enhance future economic performance. In law and opinion, the objective of maintaining competence in a foreign, native language declines and the objective of transition to competence in English predominates. And if the objective is competence in English, the argument that some preliminary years of learning in one's native language are necessary becomes subject to pragmatic test—and may fail.[9]

The pragmatic test may still be argued about: a great deal of research is under way on various kinds of programs for children of foreign-language background. The political test is a different one. It may be affected by research but is more decisively affected by power and opinion. By that test bilingual education in its strongest form—use of foreign language for as long a period as possible— has already, it would appear, reached its high point and is in recession. Before the term of office of the Carter administration came to an end, the Secretary of Education announced new regulations on bilingual education. These gave the advocates of the strongest form not everything they wanted, but a great deal. Federal regulations, supplementing federal law, are extremely powerful. They not only govern the distribution of federal funds for bilingual education, but also embody the federal government's position as to what is illegal discrimination in the treatment of such children, and they have great weight in federal court decisions as to what is the statutory requirement for the education of these children. One of the first actions of the new Reagan administration in 1981 was to withdraw these regulations. The announcement of these regulations, and their withdrawal, was the high tide of influence of the advocates of bilingual education in a strong form.

Why the United States is Different

The United States is no longer unique as a country of immigration. All the developed countries of Europe now have large immigrant communities, and issues of immigrant education are high on the agendas of these countries. They are now dealing with the degree to which they should differentiate educational programs for immigrant children on the basis of their language and culture. There is considerable support—among educators, among ethnic group leaders, among radical educationists—for such a response to the needs of immigrant children, and the programs are being developed. After the period of militancy of the 1970s, support for them in the United States has declined. The United States is different. Why?

1. *European minorities settle predominantly in communities created by migrant laborers or guestworkers who still maintain citizenship in their native countries.* (The only exception on a major scale is the United Kingdom, with its West Indians, Pakistanis, and Indians, who are British citizens.) As such, the question of language and culture must be important for them. It would infringe on the rights of resident foreigners if the nations in which they are perhaps temporarily residents were to undertake a forceful assimilatory policy, as was typical in the United States during the period of the great migration. Such policies have much stronger support in the United States than equivalent policies on the continent. The question of the language in which Turkish children in Germany or Algerians in France should be educated is a meaningful one, even if it turns out, as most believe, that they will remain permanently in France and Germany.

This question of language of education is less meaningful in the United States. No one here would dream of educating the masses of new immigrant children stemming from Mexico, Nicaragua, Colombia, and other Latin American countries in Spanish to prepare them for a return to those countries, or of educating the almost equally large numbers of Asian immigrants in their native tongues. The reason is simple: the United States is a country of immigration, expects immigrants to become citizens, and makes it easy for them to do so. The fact may be—it is—that great numbers of immigrants to the United States do return to their home countries, and many villages in Italy and Greece have substantial populations of returned immigrants, but this return process plays no role in American policy-making. American immigration policy assumes permanent immigration, makes no allowance for temporary workers. It once did in the "bracero" program, and it is often proposed that it should again, to deal with the enormous problem of illegal immigrants, particularly from Mexico. There is great resistance to such a policy, and since the bracero program was ended in 1964 it has not been resumed.

2. At the same time, Europe is acquainted with regional differences of dialect or of language. These dialects and languages are not considered a matter of indifference by those who use them, but are often culturally valued, and the population of the region that uses them does not want to give them up. *There is thus a model in Europe, despite the history of centralization and the creation of a single national dialect taught in all the schools, for allowing or acceding to the maintenance of distinctive language and culture in the schools.* There is nothing like this in the United States. Southerners may speak with an accent that often makes it hard for northerners to understand them but there has never been a claim set forward that Southern English should be enshrined in the schools, that the dialectal variation should lead to a different spelling of English words, that a separate cultural curriculum should be taught and encouraged. The curricula of southern schools, despite their pride in their heritage, and despite local control which permits local variation, is identical today to that of northern and western schools. The United States has not experienced the kind of regional difference which might be used to support the idea of maintaining immigrant and minority group culture in the schools.

3. Finally, one must point to the fact that *the scale of immigration to the United States, and the resultant size of American minorities, is so huge in contrast to that of Europe that it is considered a threat to national unity to encourage the maintenance of linguistic and cultural difference.* A former Senator from California, S.I. Hayakawa, himself of Japanese origin, is one of the strongest opponents of giving legal recognition to non-English languages, and has helped create an organization, "U.S. English," which fights against bilingual education and calls for a constitu-

tional amendment declaring English the national language of the United States. (Despite the fact that the Constitution was written in English for an overwhelmingly English-speaking nation, there is no such provision in it, and never has been. A knowledge of English is required for naturalization, but this is waived for old persons, and paradoxically no knowledge of English is required to vote. Indeed, those who speak Spanish, Chinese or Japanese, or American Indian languages, must by federal law get special assistance in voting. For example, ballots must carry translations into their languages of state referenda, proposed state constitutional amendments, etc.)

These three factors—that the United States is and expects to be a country of permanent immigrants who become citizens, that its history is not of growth through accretion of territories with a different culture and language (with the one exception of the Mexican American settlements in the Southwest territories annexed from Mexico in 1845),[10] and that as a country of immigration it is committed to the forging of people of many linguistic backgrounds and races into a common American people with a common loyalty and a common language and culture—all serve to mitigate against demands for a culturally distinctive education that maintains home language.

What Targets Groups for Public Policy?

The terms we have used somewhat interchangeably up to now— "minorities," "immigrants," "children from non-English-speaking homes,"—are not of course identical. Indeed, the question of what target groups one defines for public policy is no simple matter in the United States. One senses that the situation in Europe is simpler: there, the decisive line is between *natives* and *immigrants*—immigrants including the children of immigrants—a line which tends to coincide closely with the line between citizen and non-citizen, the line between native-language speaker and non-native-language speaker, and the line between those whose school career does or does not raise difficult problems of what kind of curriculum and approach to use. It is true of course that in the native-born, citizen, and native-language speaking majority there are substantial differences in educational achievement by class, and much concern over raising educational achievement in Europe has focused on this class gap. The problems raised by the new immigrants and their children are seen as both similar and different: similar in that the immigrants are themselves overwhelmingly lower-working-class socially, and different in that differences of language and culture (and not simply "working-class culture") complicate the educational question.

The difference in the situation in the United States is that it is not so easy to define the target groups, or even find words for them. The term "minority" is the most common: it is "minority" children about whom we are concerned. But the conception of "minority" is so muddled that there is considerable dispute over just who we mean.

There is no category of "official minorities" in the United States, if one considers official status to be one recorded in personal documents, or defined by law, and definable in courts of law. There are citizens and non-citizens, legally or illegally immigrant, and the only ethnic or racial category that has a definition in law beyond that is that of the American Indian, the original native inhabitant of the territory that became the United States. Nevertheless, public policy does define various categories as minorities deserving some special protection or attention. Four categories are so defined: American Indians, blacks, Hispanic Americans, and Asian Americans. In addition, there are, particularly for educational policy, categories known as "limited-English-proficient," and of "non-English-language background," which both overlap with some of the four defined minority groups and include many others not in any of these minority groups.

The number of categories that are actual and potential targets for educational policies directed toward some cultural and linguistic features of a student group are numerous indeed: immigrant children in general, immigrant children of non-English background, immigrant children of this background deficient in knowledge of English, the four somewhat official minority groups, and yet other groups. Hence, European-origin ethnic groups originating in the mass immigration from Europe of the late nineteenth and early twentieth centuries raise claims for the recognition of their cultural and linguistic background in the teaching of their children. The situation is thus enormously complex. The complexity is reflected in many arguments over just who is eligible or should be eligible for programs taking account of language and cultural background. The major target groups and their relationships to the education of immigrant children are:

1. Native Americans or American Indians. If there is anything like an officially-defined minority in the United States, it is American Indians. They are the only group that is defined in law: blood descent defines an Indian as a member of a tribe. This definition does not serve to deprive the Indian of any rights. It serves rather to give him certain rights in the governing of Indian reservation territory, rights sometimes of substantial worth since there are valuable resources of timber and minerals on many reservations. In addition to the legal definition, there is also a self-definition, and by self-definition the number of Indians in the United States has been increasing at a phenomenal rate, from 800,000 in 1970 to 1.4 million in 1980. Undoubtedly this is owing to many individuals redefining themselves as Indians when responding to the census.

Indians were once educated almost entirely on reservations in schools maintained by the U.S. federal government—a rarity in American life. Concerning these schools, there has been endless dispute as to what account should be taken of Indian languages and culture. In the past they tried forcefully to assimilate Indian children. In recent decades, as Indian political power has increased, in part because the majority accepts more than it did the legitimacy of minority interests, these schools have incorporated a greater degree of acceptance of Indian culture and language. But these schools play a steadily declining role in educating American Indian children: two-thirds of American Indians now live outside of reservations. Four-fifths of Indian children attend local schools. Indians have participated in the movement to increase the amount of specific cultural content in their education, but their current interest, along with that of other American minority groups, is to improve educational achievement defined in traditional terms and to increase the numbers of Indians who attend college and professional school.

Indians are of course neither an immigrant community nor (except for small numbers) a community defined by non-English-language background—most Indians today are raised speaking English. They nevertheless exhibit problems of educational backwardness. This raises the question, what kind of educational policy to use?

2. Blacks. Blacks, at 12 percent of the population, are by far the largest American minority. By many measures they are the minority that in general exhibits the most severe educational problems. They are politically the most powerful and effective. Many programs that now benefit other minorities (or at least are applied to them) were originally launched to aid blacks. Their progress or lack of it is still the chief touchstone used to test the success of efforts to provide equal opportunity.

Blacks are neither an immigrant nor a foreign-language background group, though in recent decades there has been substantial immigration of blacks (whose native language is English) from the British West Indies, and more recently a substantial immigration of Creole-French Haitians. Only 12 per cent of the total population, blacks make up a much larger percentage of the population in the central cities of the large metropolitan areas. They constitute an even larger percentage of the school-age population of these cities owing to a population distribution skewed toward younger age groups, and a still larger proportion of the public-school population of these cities owing to a lesser participation of black children in private, Catholic, and non-Catholic education. This leads to school systems with a majority of blacks in many large American cities (Boston; Detroit; Cleveland; Chicago; Baltimore; Washington, D.C.; St. Louis; New Orleans; and many others). Thus the processes of concentration lead to a relatively small minority becoming in many social settings a majority, indeed an overwhelming majority.

The major thrust of black political leadership for thirty years or more has been for desegregation; a lesser but substantial thrust has been for more recognition of black culture and history, and perhaps its greatest success has been the declaration of Martin Luther King Day as a national holiday (the only other individuals whose birthdays are marked as national holidays are George Washington and Abraham Lincoln). Both thrusts, it was hoped, would improve levels of educational achievement, but that was by no means the only motive that led blacks to support desegregation and recognition of black culture and history. On the whole the improvement in educational achievement among blacks in the past twenty years has been disappointing, which is perhaps the principal reason black efforts, particularly at the local level, are now concentrated on measures to improve educational achievement directly.

3. Hispanic Americans. If one thinks of educational programs addressing problems of immigrants, it is the Spanish-speaking groups in the United States that are inevitably the principal target group. Arguments over bilingual and bicultural programs, even though they may (and do) involve more than a hundred different language groups, are overwhelmingly programs for Spanish-speaking children: for Mexican Americans in the southwestern states from California to Texas; for Puerto Ricans in New York and other northeastern states; for Cubans in Florida; for Dominicans, Colombians, Nicaraguans, Salvadorans and other Latin Americans in the chief immigrant-attracting parts of the country (California and New York, predominantly). Despite the great differences among and within these groups, in class and occupational background, in recency of migration, in legal status (citizenship, immigration status), they are lumped together as a minority deserving special protection in education, occupation, and voting rights. They form almost one-half of current American immigration (probably more than that, if one takes account of illegal immigration), and are the most rapidly growing group in the American population, through immigration and rapid natural growth. Hispanic Americans raise an exceptionally complicated question as to how American educational policy should respond to their needs.

The overall Hispanic population increased between the census of 1970 and that of 1980 from 9.1 to 14.6 million—6.4 percent of the population—and was estimated by 1983 to have increased to 15.9 million. In the decade of the 1970s, while the American population aside from those of Spanish origin showed an increase of 9 percent, the Spanish-origin population increased 61 percent and, within that, the Mexican-origin population almost doubled. But these increases probably reflected the fact that the 1980 Census made a more intense effort to count Hispanic Americans and perhaps that, as with American Indians, there was more incentive for individuals to declare Hispanic origin.[11]

The foreign-language population of the United States is today preeminently the Spanish-language population. This group has come to dominate all arguments on the need or suitability of bilingual and bicultural education in the United States. In 1980 a question on the usual language spoken at home showed 11 million persons reporting Spanish, three-quarters of whom said they also spoke English well or very well. More people responded that they spoke other languages at home, but these were divided among many language groups and the largest of them—Italian, German, French, and so on—do not make a strong demand for an education responsive to language and culture.[12]

4. Asian Americans. This element of the population is growing more rapidly through immigration than Hispanic Americans, but from a much smaller base. The category includes Chinese, Filipinos, Japanese, Asian Indians, Koreans, Vietnamese, Laotians, Cambodians, and others. It is a more varied mix than even the Hispanic American group. The overall population of Asian Americans was 3.5 million in 1980, and had doubled since 1970.[13] Next to Hispanic Americans, it is Asian Americans who provide the largest numbers for bicultural and bilingual programs, in particular the recent immigrants from Indochina—Vietnamese, Laotian, and Cambodian. Asians show on the whole greater educational achievement than Americans in general, and generally do not present a problem of educational deficiency. However, as the class and occupational sources of immigration change, in particular those from Indochina, this condition will probably not be maintained for all groups.

5. Others. Finally, we must say something about "all the others," ethnic groups of European origin, even if they are not considered minorities and are no longer numerous among immigrants. They nevertheless consider themselves in some degree distinctive, and their cultural and linguistic demands sometimes impinge on the educational system. But who are "all the others"? The United States is a country of immigrants, but it is also a country that radically changes immigrants and their children: they lose their native tongue and begin to speak English, lose aspects of culture, change their religions in form if not in name, intermarry. Is it still necessary to make a count of these assimilated Europeans by ethnic background? In the past, the Bureau of the Census did not think so. It counted the foreign born and the children

of the foreign born. As the period of mass immigration faded, a count of foreign born and their children did not give an adequate measure of the size of the various European immigrant groups. The demand then arose that a question on ethnicity be incorporated in the 1980 Census.

Leaders of ethnic and racial groups in the United States want to see larger numbers of their own in official statistics—this provides a large denominator on the basis of which it can be claimed that whatever the group's educational and occupational achievements, they are not proportional to the size of the group. There are also social psychological and political reasons for wanting to maximize one's numbers. The argument over numbers is not meaningless because it is on the basis of numbers—if they come out right—that one can claim the group is discriminated against or does not get enough services.

In the 1980 Census, European ethnic groups, alarmed at the degree to which numbers were being used as a basis for policy in favor of the old minority groups and recent immigrant groups (blacks, Hispanic American, American Indian, Asian), fought for a question on "ancestry." It is perhaps not an accident that this question almost by design had the effect of maximizing the number of persons of each ancestry, since the question permitted, and many gave, multiple ancestries. Thus 50 million gave English ancestry, 49 million German, 40 million Irish, 13 million French, 12 million Italian, 10 million Scottish, 8 million Polish, 6 million Dutch, 4 million Swedish, 3.5 million Norwegian, etc. Many gave multiple ancestries; only 17 percent answered "American" or gave no ancestry.[14] Hispanic Americans were the beneficiaries of two questions trying to get their numbers. One, already discussed, asked "is this person of Spanish/Hispanic origin or descent?" The second was the general ancestry question, to which 7.7 million responded Mexican, 2.7 million Spanish/Hispanic, 1.4 million Puerto Rican (on the American mainland), .6 million Cuban, and smaller numbers of Dominican, Colombian, and others.

6. Children without English. What is to be made of the ancestry question in terms of education? Not much. For educational purposes, the most crucial factors are what languages are spoken in the home and to what degree children come to school with problems with English. There have been substantial efforts to document how many of these there are.

Owing to the entitlement of those of foreign-language background to some kind of special program and the preference in
federal (and in some state) laws for a bilingual program, this estimate is affected by political considerations. There are competing
interests at work in making such estimates: proponents of
bilingual education want to show that the numbers who need
bilingual language instruction are great; school administrators
who have to provide such instruction and federal authorities who
(now) want to downplay bilingual instruction want to see the
number small. These interests are fought out in the census
and in special surveys, and the figures available are something of
a compromise.

"Language-Minority" children between five and fourteen years
old ("members of households where the usual or second, often
spoken household language is other than English") increased
from 3.5 to 4.5 million between 1976 and 1982, or 27 percent. As a
percent of total population of their age group, they increased from
9.4 to 13.3 percent. Within this group, "limited-English-proficient"
children ("scoring below the 25th percentile on a special test of
English proficiency") were estimated to have increased from 2
million in 1978 to 2.4 million in 1982. (All children between five
and fourteen years old numbered 34 million in 1982.) As would be
expected, the numbers in certain states that are the traditional
and new magnets for immigrants were much higher. A somewhat
different measure, of children who speak a non-English language
at home, showed a national average of 9.6 percent in 1980—but
this figure rose to 23 percent in California, 25.6 percent in Texas,
17.2 percent in New York. Of course the percentages rose much
higher in certain metropolitan areas and school districts—in the
Los Angeles school district, a majority of children are now of
Spanish-language background.[15]

What Programs?

Having reviewed this area of diversity, it will become immediately
apparent that there is no such thing—nor should there be—as a
uniform response to children of such varied backgrounds, abilities,
and statuses. Basically, we have seen three responses to the problems posed by children of different racial, ethnic, cultural, and
linguistic background.

The first has been desegregation: mix the children. This policy becomes very significant because in so much of American history, and so large a part of the United States, the effort had been made to segregate the children: blacks in the South, Chinese and Japanese in the West, Mexican Americans in the Southwest. If this was the evil, the response was desegregation, or integration, and in the most concrete sense, mixing. This is not the place to tell the complex story of the effort to mix, which continues, by means of busing programs, to move children out of schools in which their race or group would be dominant into other areas in which they could form part of a representative mix. During the Reagan administration, federal efforts to expand mixing in the face of the steady opposition by white majorities, opposition or indifference among minorities other than black, and split opinion among blacks themselves, ceased. Busing programs already instituted have continued, and minority-group litigators have tried to institute more. I have indicated that improved achievement was one objective of this enterprise. Whether it followed has been much disputed. Recent research suggests that there is a modest improvement in black achievement as a result of desegregation.[16]

The second policy has been compensatory education for all poor children. This would effectively reach the blacks, the Puerto Ricans, the Mexican Americans, and would be proportionately less effective in reaching groups (some Asian groups) that did not have large numbers of children in poverty. This is, from a financial point of view, by far the greatest effort mounted by the federal government. It includes "Head Start," begun in the middle 1960s, which provides pre-school for poor children, reaches over 400,000 children a year, and spends almost one billion dollars a year, at a cost of $2,200 a child. Even larger is Compensatory Education for the Disadvantaged, begun in 1965 and continuing at a rate of $3.5 billion a year, reaching 5 million children a year. Pre-school programs are run by community groups and may well be conducted in foreign languages and have a strong cultural component. Compensatory education is conducted by school districts, concentrates on reading and arithmetic, and although programs vary from district to district and school to school, pays on the whole no attention to culture and background. The effects of such programs have been much disputed; recent studies suggest modest positive effects.

This is indicated most convincingly by the National Assessment of Education Progress, which tests large national samples of 9-, 13-, and 17-year-olds. Black 9- and 13-year-olds showed a better rate of improvement than whites on reading performance between 1971 and 1980. In mathematics, between 1973 and 1978, there was a decline for white 9-year-olds, and an improvement for blacks of that age; a small improvement for black 13-year-olds, a small decline for white 13-year-olds. For 17-year-olds, there were declines for both groups, but less for blacks than whites.[17]

The third kind of programs relevant to our discussion are those that directly take into account language and culture— bilingual programs. The federal government provides funds (about $150 million a year) for such programs to local school districts; the states spend much more. School districts are required to have such programs on the basis of the Supreme Court *Lau* decision in 1974, which asserted that account must be taken of weakness in English. Until the Reagan administration came to power, the Civil Rights Office of the Department of Education insisted, as did the legislation that provided funds, that these programs must make use of native language.

There is enormous controversy over these programs, a controversy that can only be understood in the light of American history. The United States has taken in tens of millions of immigrants of foreign language; their children have attended public schools, and whatever their early backwardness on the basis of language, by the 1970s it had been forgotten. Jews, Italians, Poles, and Germans no longer recalled that their parents or grandparents once had had problems in attending or sending their children into English-language public schools. What they now remembered was their success in adapting to English and to the United States. And what they feared was that, by acknowledging in schools the need for education in a foreign language, this process would be delayed. The fear was all the greater because the great majority of children speaking a foreign language entering the public schools were Mexican American and other Spanish speakers, and they were concentrated in certain areas in the Southwest that are adjacent to their country of origin. The process of assimilation, which from the perspective of the 1970s had been so successful with European immigrants, was to many Americans now threatened by the new bilingual and bicultural policies introduced as a result of political action by Mexican American and other Hispanic groups, action which coincided with the dominance of liberal attitudes in education.

These programs continue, despite the coolness of the Reagan administration. They are also sustained by many state laws that permit or require them. Federal programs reached in 1983 about 200,000 children, state-funded services almost a million. (These figures may be compared with the estimates of target groups above.)[18]

The most severe controversy rages around the effectiveness of bilingual education in terms of educational achievement. While there seems to be a consensus as to a small moderate achievement effect for desegregation and a small modest achievement effect for compensatory education, there seems to be no such consensus regarding bilingual education. It is understandable that gauging the effect of programs whose major dimensions are set by political considerations, as well as educational ones, and whose actual concrete character differs greatly from school district to school district, school to school, and even teacher to teacher, would be very difficult. Why should very diverse approaches unified only by the term "bilingual education" and the regulations, variously and imperfectly satisfied, that define it bureaucratically, be expected to have a uniform effect? Such a uniform effect indeed has been detected for desegregation and compensatory education, which are also divisive; not so for bilingual education.

It is of course a serious question whether a positivistic research orientation should dominate political and social judgments in determining the kind of education minority children should receive. In fact, judgements are often made on other bases. Some researchers will be influenced by the best-designed research, others less so. Parents may simply make an experience-based judgment that they want their children to move rapidly into English, whatever the psychological costs. If less achievement-oriented, they may be indifferent to what kind of education the children receive. If proud of their heritage, they may want more native language and culture. Political leaders and school personnel will make their own decisions based on their situations. There is no decisive answer in the research. The fact that there is no decisive answer is important, because it means that political and social judgments, which will in any case tend to prevail, should prevail.

The weight of these judgments, among minority and majority, now leads to an insistence on achievement as a basis for economic mobility and social and political integration into American society. This becomes the dominant consideration affecting judgment on education for minority-group children and outweighs all other considerations: preservation of culture and language, independent power in the educational sector, reduction of psychological stress for the students, jobs for minority group members, superiority of native over American culture, or any other consideration that can be set forward.

Achievement and Minorities

It is because the United States is a country of immigration that the issue of the economic integration of immigrants and minorities becomes so urgent. The fact is that all American opinion, left and right, business and labor, conservative and liberal, not only knows that the American people is made up of many peoples of very different races and original languages, but also *expects this process to continue.* Immigration to the United States— legal—runs to 600,000 a year, more than four-fifths of which is considered "minority" (that is, not European) in American law. Illegal immigration runs at a substantial volume, most of it "minority."

The majority not only expects this process to continue: it expects and wants these immigrants to become citizens. The nativist resistance to immigrants different from the majority in culture, language, religion, and race has never been weaker. A public that expects mass immigration to continue and immigrants to become citizens must also be concerned with their economic adaptation to society; it must be concerned to overcome the differences in income and occupation that separate "majorities" from "minorities," and that separate immigrants from natives. Not all "minorities" show an economic status inferior to that of the majority (this is particularly the case with Asian immigrants, among whom Chinese, Japanese, and Asian Indians do better than the "majority"). Nor is this uniformly the case with immigrants: immigrants from Asia tend to arrive fairly highly educated, and it is therefore no surprise that they do well. But there is surprising evidence that immigrants in general do well, better than the "native majority," after a few years.[19]

The expectation of permanence also affects the attitude of the American immigrants and determines how much they feel they *should* demand from educational institutions in acknowledgment of their special culture and language. Historically, they have asked very little and have been content to maintain ethnicity and language through voluntary organizations, generally religious in nature. In the late 1960s and 1970s they demanded more from educational institutions, less I believe because they truly wanted to or hoped to maintain ethnic culture and language in a full-bodied way in the United States, than because this was a means of insisting upon respect and equal treatment. The terms on which respect and equal achievement are now demanded have changed even in the minds of militant ethnic leaders: they realize academic achievement and economic achievement are crucial in their own right, and that respect for culture will do little to forward these. National holidays for ethnic leaders and respect for language, as such, do not grant achievement.

The key questions then become how to measure—and in light of the measurements, increase—achievement. In the United States there is enormous concentration on—and great dispute over—achievement as measured by standardized tests; rates of graduation from high school; entry into community college, college, and university. New measures are being set as a result of the educational reform movement, in particular tests for high school diplomas, tests for teachers, higher requirements for academic subjects that must be taken in high school, and higher requirements for entry into public and private colleges. There is no question that blacks, despite the improvements indicated above, do poorly. Hispanic Americans do poorly, but there is variation among the major groups of Hispanic Americans: Puerto Ricans do worst, Cubans do fairly well. Though there is great difference among Asian Americans, on the average they perform better than white Americans, who may be taken as the norm. For example, in one of these measures of achievement, "dropout rates"—failure to complete high school measured by the percentage of second-year high school students who had left school by the spring of 1982, and therefore would not graduate that year—the white non-Hispanic rate was 17 percent, the black rate 12 percent, the Hispanic rate 18 percent, the Asian rate, 3 percent.[20] Other measures suggest this is representative. These figures understate overall dropout rates: on the whole only about three-quarters of American youth gain high school diplomas.

The statistics vary greatly by region: the South, despite improvement, still does worse than the other sections in general and for the black minority. Of course the measures correlate with class position. But it would be an error to simply see these variations as an expression of class. A differential ethnic factor plays an independent role in achievement. Sociologists emphasize class as the key determinant in educational achievement. It explains much, but it explains rather less in the United States. Here we see that some groups of low socioeconomic position, measured by parental income, education, and occupation, have done well in school. Nor does class alone explain the poorer achievement of blacks: class held constant, they still do worse on the average. These ethnic and racial differences stand out boldly in the American mind. They substitute, in American thinking, for the class differences that in Europe have often been a driving force for educational reform.

But even if ethnic and racial factors—we can substitute for this term the somewhat vague notion of "culture" as anthropologists understand it—explain a great deal in the differential educational achievement of racial and ethnic groups, they cannot be used in devising the programs that may overcome these differences. I make this bald statement on the basis of the experience of both the recent and more distant past. Historical experience tells us that groups have done well educationally in the absence of any recognition of their culture or language. The cases of the Japanese and the Jews are particularly noteworthy: not only was there a total absence of their culture and language in school curricula, they also were doing well at a time when they were subjected to severe discrimination in the 1920s and 1930s.[21] Recent experience, on the other hand, tells us that the effort we have made to introduce racial and ethnic curricular materials, particularly for black and Hispanic groups, into reading materials, social science, literature, and the like, seems to have been without any discernible effect in dealing with *their* educational problems. This is not to say the effort should not have been made: a curriculum is not only determined by effects on achievement measures, but also by political and social decisions as to what should be taught and learned. From that point of view, to learn that the United States is a multi-racial and multi-ethnic country is necessary.

Of course an argument can be made to justify even more such content. If, as some (but fewer and fewer) ethnic militants argue, the life of immigrants and minorities has been and is being shaped by exploitation, cultural and economic, then they will insist on a revolutionary style of education that incorporates more and more of the material demonstrating this exploitation and calling for the need for revolutionary change. But this rings increasingly hollow in a society in which groups that have been subject to severe discrimination as outsiders nevertheless find themselves today fully integrated into the society.

Thus one major conclusion seems to result from our distinctive experience: culture explains some part of differences in educational achievement. But approaches to overcome them cannot easily make use of the cultural differences themselves. In a society where all aspire to equal participation, all must undergo education in the same modes: the language in use in the society, literacy suitable for fulfilling jobs in that society, the methods of calculation that have universal validity, the science that is everywhere the same. This conclusion, self-evident as it may seem, is not unchallenged. In the middle 1970s national policy favored the use of native languages and even of distinctive approaches making use of the distinctive culture of each group. But the results of our efforts to overcome differences in educational achievement using such methods are not encouraging. Majority and minority alike, in part for different reasons, in part for shared reasons, now come together in agreement on traditional educational methods deemed to be the most effective means for raising the educational achievement of minority groups and groups of different language and cultural background.

11

PETER SKERRY

The Ambiguity of Mexican American Politics

"Some of us have been here for three hundred years, and some of us for three days." I heard this over and over during more than a year of observing and interviewing Mexican American politicians and community leaders. More than most over-circulated fragments of conventional wisdom, this one bears attention. For its enormous diversity is the most striking aspect of the Mexican American community today. This is underscored by the continuing discussion within that community as to what to call itself: "Chicano" came into vogue during the 1960s and is still popular among activists and their sympathizers; "Latino" is popular in Los Angeles, where it links Mexican Americans to the growing but still silent Central American communities there; "Hispanic" is a generic term tolerated by a few and seen by most as an ill-conceived label concocted by government bureaucrats; "Mexicano" is often used interchangeably with "Mexican" and is typically heard in South Texas, where the bonds of community and tradition remain strong; and finally, "Mexican American," the most widely used and least controversial term, is popular among the middle-aged and more acculturated members of the group. This is the form I will use here in a broad sociological sense to include ethnic Mexicans who are American citizens and Mexican nationals who, in whatever status, live and work in the United States.

But more than diversity, this babel of names reflects the ambiguity of the Mexican American's place in our history and society. Is this a minority group that has been oppressed by Anglo society just as blacks and Indians have been? Or is this merely another immigrant ethnic group that will be absorbed into the mainstream? Interpretations of Mexican American politics typically rest on either point of view. And though both have important things to say, neither perspective is by itself fully satisfactory. Actually, these constitute the two poles of a continuum depicting ethnic relations in the United States, and in my view the Mexican American experience lies somewhere in between. What I attempt here, based on field work primarily in San Antonio and Los Angeles, is to begin carving out that space between the two extremes.

The Mexican American Mosaic

Mexican American political leaders repeatedly express dismay at their ethnic group's lack of cohesiveness. To many the political discipline of blacks and Jews, for example, is an embarrassing foil to what they see as Mexican American infighting. It is certainly no accident, say such leaders, that there is no serious Mexican American counterpart to the NAACP—no membership-based, national advocacy organization. The irony, however, is that while such "factionalism" may sometimes reflect lack of political sophistication and experience, it also reflects—much more than Mexican American leaders seem to realize—a healthy diversity within the Mexican American community.

After all, there are Mexican Americans descended from the families of the Spanish colonial elites in New Mexico and California, and Mexican Americans descended from the middle-class refugees who left Mexico during the revolutionary upheavals at the beginning of this century. Then there are the descendants of campesinos who came here at various times either to avoid political instability or economic hardship—or more likely, both. And for many, of course, the story has been a less simple one of moving back and forth between Mexico and the United States.

Then, too, there has been much migration within the United States. There are Mexican Americans for whom the mining areas of Southern Arizona or the ranches of New Mexico were home, but who then moved to California. For others the journey was from South Texas to Chicago. There has also been much movement between rural and urban areas, as families who could not make it in one place would move to the other. Today, most Mexican Americans live in our cities and are eager to leave their rural image behind. Indeed, this sentiment is a contributing factor in the declining stature of the United Farm Worker Union in the Mexican American community.

There are also distinctions to be drawn between established Mexican Americans—citizens or non-citizens, legals or illegals— who have been here long enough to put down roots and raise families, and the hundreds of undocumented aliens arriving daily. As the newcomers crowd into rented houses in modest but once-stable neighborhoods, they bring with them old habits and new problems. Those from rural areas of Mexico may see no harm in relieving themselves at the curb. Eager entrepreneurs may open a vegetable stand on the front porch. Others may solve parking problems by leaving their cars on the front lawn. Meanwhile, neighborhood schools are increasingly overcrowded. Under such circumstances it is hardly surprising that Mexican American homeowners in working- and lower-middle-class neighborhoods feel under seige by the newcomers. To other Mexican Americans, of course, the recent arrivals may represent a source of income as renters or customers. And to securely situated upper-middle-class Mexican Americans, they may be not much more than a curiosity or a minor source of embarrassment.

Still another piece of the Mexican American mosaic is the new generation of university-educated young people. With much more education than their parents, they are much less conservative and much more impatient. This is hardly surprising. What is intriguing is that these Mexican Americans today are the products of a university culture that has itself changed markedly in the last few decades. One result is that these young people, many influenced by or products of Chicano studies programs, have a sense of mission about their cultural heritage and its maintenance that ethnic elites of previous generations lacked.

Some Mexican Americans have endured near caste-like status in the small towns of the Southwest. Others have suffered much less severe but nevertheless hurtful discrimination. Still others have been able, without much apparent difficulty, to disappear into middle-class America. Yet despite this diversity of backgrounds and interests, there is something that binds Mexican Americans as a group together. But what it is remains elusive.

The Internal Colony Model

Perhaps the loudest response to this question has come from young Mexican American academics who have elaborated what they call "the internal colony model." Based on historical researches of the Southwest, this perspective sees Chicanos as a conquered people, whose alienation from their lands, language, and culture gives them much in common with American Indians and blacks.

For some it is tempting to dismiss the internal colony perspective as a hot-house theory developed in the shelter of the university. But much of the sad history this perspective draws upon is undeniable. And perhaps for this reason fragments of it resonate clearly with what I hear from Mexican Americans outside the university.

In the most general terms, the internal colony perspective can be discerned in the views of Mexican Americans who continually pointed out to me that, unlike European immigrants, "we did not have to cross an ocean to get here." Those who say this seem to think that migrants from Mexico have come to this country with more ambivalence than those from Europe. In light of what historians tell us about the numbers of recent immigrants leaving the United States for their homelands around the turn of the century, this seems problematic. But my point here is that there is a pervasive sense of exceptionalism among Mexican Americans, that in some fundamental way they are different from other ethnic groups in America. Of course, whether this means they identify with minorities such as blacks and Indians is another question, which will be taken up shortly.

Another indication of this Mexican American exceptionalism is the sense of turf that Mexican Americans have about the southwestern United States. Once again the internal colony approach is suggestive, for it focuses attention on the fact that Mexican Americans today predominate where their Indian and Spanish forebears once lived and ruled. And though historians such as T.R. Fehrenbach remind us that this Mexican culture was not as deeprooted or as extensive in the region as is sometimes claimed, it is undeniably true that Mexican Americans in the Southwest feel at home there in a way that cannot be said, say, of the Irish in Chicago. This becomes evident when, after discussing the immigration question with even the most moderate Mexican American, one is invariably reminded that "we were here first," or "this was our land and you stole it from us."

The internal colony perspective also highlights the persistent legacy of United States–Mexico relations. Certainly, if wars against Japan and Germany adversely affected ethnic Japanese and Germans living in the United States, it should not surprise us that generations of tensions and outright hostilities with Mexico have left their mark on Mexican Americans. Nevertheless, Americans tend to overlook this history. As one Mexican saying has it, "Americans never remember, and Mexicans never forget." And what Mexicans never forget is that theirs is a country conquered first by American military forces and then by American social and economic forces. How this sense of national humiliation vis-à-vis the United States has affected Mexicans who have settled here is difficult to say. But it seems undeniable that being Mexican in this country has long carried the stigma of being poor and backward. This, of course, is a problem most immigrant groups have had to deal with. But it is particularly pressing for Mexican Americans, whose homeland and its problems stand in such stark and proximate contrast to the United States.

But the legacy of the past is hardly just embarrassment on the part of Mexican Americans. There is also profound resentment at the way their people have been treated by Americans. Along the border at McAllen, Texas I was told how the Texas Rangers terrorized the local Mexicans in the early 1920s by riding around

town with a dead Mexican heaped on either fender. Echoes from
the same period are heard in Los Angeles today, from Mexican
Americans whose grandparents lived in El Paso and suffered at
the hands of the "gabachos" during the border hostilities there.
From the more recent past, in the Rio Grande Valley, I heard
numerous accounts of Mexican Americans up until a generation
or so ago being assigned to "the Mexican school" in town. Or in Los
Angeles one hears from middle-aged Mexican Americans how
they were allowed to swim in municipal pools only on assigned
days; or how after World War II, returning Mexican American servicemen were kept from buying houses in various Los Angeles
suburbs. Such accounts of course often get exaggerated and blown
out of proportion, but they are heard in the Southwest with such
consistency and regularity that I take them to be essentially accurate. More importantly, such stories are now clearly part of
Mexican American folklore.

That such fragments and variants of the internal colony
perspective can be heard among ordinary Mexican Americans is
plain enough. Less clear is their relation to political behavior.
After all, all ethnic groups have their horror stories about early
experiences in this country. These serve to define the collective
identity of the group and to remind its members of the gains they
have made. In the hands of politicians such stories can bolster
group identity and cohesiveness, but they seldom result in fundamental challenges to the status quo. In this regard Chicano consciousness among Mexican Americans is analogous to latent class
consciousness among American workers. For in both instances extremely negative views of American society can be elicited, but
they are typically deflected as the group is further absorbed into
the mainstream.

A deeper problem with the internal colony model is that the
boundaries around the presumed "colony" have proved to be
rather permeable. A good example is the experience of migrant
farmworkers moving north with the crop cycle. On such journeys
Mexican Americans learned that when they got out of Texas, their
lot improved a bit. They discovered that not all Anglos were the
same. As one San Antonio housewife and community activist in
her forties explained to me, the Oregon farmer her family worked
for every season provided them with better housing than they had

back home in Texas. In this way she learned "there were good Anglos and bad Anglos."

For other Mexican Americans, military service offered similar opportunities. Unlike blacks, Mexicans did not serve in segregated units during World War II. As a result Mexican Americans raised in the small towns and cities of the Southwest realized, as a small businessman from San Antonio put it, "we were just another ethnic group ... and we were just as good as and could compete with Italians from Philadelphia and Irish from New York."

I don't mean to say that military service or migrant farm work were entirely positive experiences for Mexican Americans. I do mean to suggest that for many Mexican Americans there were opportunities to escape the restrictive and harsh environment of the Southwest. It is precisely such opportunities that the internal colony perspective overlooks.

Indeed, the internal colony perspective in no way prepares us for the gains being made today by Mexican Americans. Emerging from what was for many near caste-like status a few decades ago, Mexican Americans today are moving into the middle and professional classes to an unprecedented extent. Perhaps the most crippling blow to the internal colony model is the degree of intermarriage today between Mexican Americans and Anglos. In the late 1970s more than one-third of all Mexican Americans marrying in California chose partners outside their group. And even in the much more traditional context of San Antonio, about one-sixth of Mexican Americans marry outside their group.

Mexican Americans and Blacks

Despite these trends the internal colony model persists. And one of its more pervasive, albeit diluted, variants is the tendency to identify Mexican Americans as another minority group that shares common experiences and interests with black Americans. This popularization of the internal colony model lacks the self-conscious neo-Marxist theorizing of the academic version. It is especially evident in Los Angeles, where Anglo liberals and Mexican American activists take their cues from highly successful black politicians. A homely example of this is the ethnic argot of Southern California. Whereas in Texas Mexican Americans refer to "Anglos," in California they refer to "whites." Obfuscating the self-evident fact that many Mexican Americans are as "white" as Anglos, this term is typically used to put "whites" on the defensive, and to remind them they are dealing with a "people of color" whose history entitles them to special consideration. In such a milieu it is not surprising that Jesse Jackson captured some 15 percent of the Mexican American vote in California's 1984 presidential primary—a much higher percentage than he received in Texas, for example.

Elsewhere in the Southwest, relations between blacks and Mexicans are hardly as positive. In cities such as Corpus Christi and San Antonio, for example, the two groups eye one another with a good deal of distrust. But it is in the neighborhoods of south-central Los Angeles itself where the divergence of interests between blacks and Mexicans is most in evidence. It is there that recent arrivals from Mexico are displacing blacks from their neighborhoods and, it is felt, from their jobs. And from areas such as Compton one hears reports, despite the best efforts of authorities to quiet them, of violent confrontations between blacks and thugs hired by Mexican American proprietors trying to protect their fledgling businesses. Thus, the close cooperation one observes between blacks and Mexican political leaders in Los Angeles is really quite illusory. What it reveals more than anything is the special lack of accountability enjoyed by California politicians representing poor and unorganized constituents.

The issue that most vividly highlights the divergence of interests between Mexican Americans and blacks is busing. In Los Angeles, at the height of the busing controversy in the late 1970s, many Mexican American leaders supported their black allies and paid lip service to busing. But many others did not. Regardless of the positions taken by the leaders, it was obvious to all that the vast majority of Mexican American parents were opposed to busing their children—either to Anglo or black schools. Today, busing in Los Angeles is a moot issue, but the preference of Mexican Americans for neighborhood schools is still evident as their leaders press for new schools in the overcrowded barrios, while others argue that this will further segregate the Los Angeles system.

In a city such as San Antonio, the dynamics of the busing issue have been different from Los Angeles, but nevertheless instructive. In San Antonio the Mexican American leadership decided early on not to pursue busing as a remedy to overcome the problems of majority Mexican schools. They focused their efforts instead on school finance issues. Out of this emerged litigation challenging Texas's system for funding public education, culminating in the 1973 *San Antonio vs. Rodriguez* case, in which the Supreme Court ruled against the Mexican American plaintiffs. Undaunted, activists continued their efforts, and in 1984 succeeded in pushing through the Texas legislature a major increase in state funding of property-poor school districts.

It is clear that Mexican American leaders in San Antonio did not turn to busing because the city is carved up into many small independent school districts that have traditionally been patronage bases for local politicians. In the early 1970s Mexican Americans began taking over school boards that had long been dominated by Anglos. Any efforts to disperse concentrations of Mexican American students would therefore have undercut these emergent power bases.

In Los Angeles no such political calculations have entered into the Mexican American position on busing. Over the past fifteen years there has been at most only one Mexican on the seven-person board governing the huge Los Angeles Unified School District. Rather it would seem that in Los Angeles, Mexican American opposition to busing reflects fundamental community values—values which also underlie anti-busing sentiment in San Antonio.

At the core of these values is an intensely and self-consciously close-knit family life. Perhaps because they have had relatively little experience with other ethnic groups with similar values, Mexican Americans take considerable, often exaggerated, pride in their families. Whatever its origins, this focus on the primary bonds of kinship translates among Mexicans, as it does among similarly oriented groups, into a distrust or uneasiness toward individuals and institutions outside the family orbit. The evidence suggests, for example, that Mexican Americans turn to child care institutions less than one would predict given their socioeconomic characteristics. And while the school symbolizes the aspirations that drew Mexicans to this country, it may also represent new and fearsome values intruding from the dominant culture. Especially for recent arrivals from Mexico, but also for Mexican Americans still accustomed to rural or small town life, it is sometimes tempting to solve their ambivalence toward the American mainstream by letting their kids stay home from school. After all, among families struggling to get by, there are always lots of chores at home that girls can help with and many ways for boys to earn a little money. As a school superintendent in San Antonio explained to me, truancy is a real problem among the children of lower- and working-class Mexican Americans. But his response must be subtle, I was told, for if he pushes parents too hard on the point, he will—even though himself a Mexican American—be told to mind his own business.

Even, or perhaps especially, among more secure working- and lower-middle-class families, Mexican American parents see busing as just one more threat to the ties that bind them to their children. In the Mexican American neighborhoods of Los Angeles, mothers can be seen at mid-day bringing their children's lunches to the schoolyards. Is it any wonder that such mothers, typically left at home without the family's one car, which the father takes to work, do not want their children sent to the other side of the sprawling metropolis? In such families the question about busing that gets raised over and over is, what would I do if my child gets sick at school? How would I get to him?

Black parents who send their children off on school buses no doubt have similar concerns. But the fact is that as a group blacks have struck a very different bargain with American schools than have Mexicans. As the educational attainment statistics for the two groups suggest, Mexican Americans, with much lower education levels, have simply not turned to the schools the way blacks have. But beneath such attitudes, the Mexican American view of busing is sustained by an acceptance of ethnic neighborhoods and institutions that is always highly problematic for blacks. For Mexican Americans, most of whom are not that far removed from some kind of disruptive migratory experience, moving to a new place and settling in a neighborhood where Spanish is spoken, and local businesses cater to your tastes, is a given. To be sure, for some the barrio and its ways may be a source of embarrassment; for others it may be a source of pride; for many more probably a mix of the two. However these feelings sort themselves out, it is clear that the barrio does not bear the stigma for Mexicans that the ghetto does for blacks, for whom the history of segregation inevitably taints the natural tendency of like to associate with like.

Busing, then, directs us back toward the immigrant perspective. One does observe in Mexican American communities dynamics that are reminiscent of the experiences of European immigrant groups. I have just discussed the tensions between strong family ties and the demands of the wider society. But these same family bonds often provide Mexican Americans, as they have other ethnic groups, with the means—both manpower and money—to sustain a high level of small business activity in sheltered markets created by language and culture.

Traditionalism and Religion

Like the classic immigrant communities, the barrio exhibits a high degree of traditionalism, a high degree of respect for the old ways, that derives from peasant distrust of change. In a relatively traditional community such as San Antonio, a young man returning from the University at Austin to teach school who wants to get involved in church and community affairs has a hard time getting himself taken seriously by his elders. And even in cosmopolitan Los Angeles, young Mexican American politicians typically rely on their parents to legitimize their appeals to the community.

The nexus of family and traditional values so evident among Mexican Americans is nurtured, as it has been for many immigrants to America, by Roman Catholicism. Yet Mexican Americans are Catholics in the mold of Italian Americans more than, for example, of Irish Americans. Mexicans in the United States have brought with them from their homeland an intense religiosity that many clergy complain verges on superstition. Mexicans have also brought an intense distrust of the institutional Church that reflects its identification with the ruling elites back home. Among other problems this has made it difficult to recruit clergy. And with relatively limited manpower to minister to the vast populations there, the Church in Mexico, indeed in all of Latin America, has been physically as well as emotionally remote from the people. Unlike its role in Ireland and Poland, the Church in Mexico has never gained the status of defender of the nation against an alien oppressor.

Circumstances in the United States have not been propitious for changing these Mexican habits of indifference and even hostility to the Church. The American Southwest was for a long time mission territory for the Catholic Church. This meant that there were no formally organized parishes, and clergy were scattered widely to serve a dispersed population. Just as at home, Mexicans in the United States have found the Church to be a remote institution. Perhaps more to the point, they have found a Church controlled by clerics, typically Irish, who do not share their history and culture.

With this record it is hardly surprising that the Catholic Church in the Mexican American community is today a rather embattled institution. One indication of this is the presence of fundamentalist evangelical churches in barrios across the Southwest. One can sit in the rectory of a Catholic Church on San Antonio's Westside and hear the latest gossip about who has joined the new storefront church around the corner, and who has forbade her children to associate with Catholics. Mainstream Protestant denominations have long maintained mission efforts among Mexican Americans, but the aggressive anti-Catholicism of these fundamentalist groups has the Catholic hierarchy concerned.

Other signs of the Church's weak hold on the Mexican American community are perhaps less obvious. Walking with a young Mexican American priest through a housing project in San Antonio, I noticed the indifference his cheerful greetings earned him from the young men hanging out on the corner. Or in one of the poorest parishes on Los Angeles's Eastside I was surprised to see a priest, for fear of being robbed by local gang members, collect the proceeds from the various booths at the parish carnival accompanied by an armed guard. A less dramatic sign of what the Church is up against is the frequent complaint from clergy that Mexicans come to them only when they need something, especially at the crucial junctures in Mexican family life—baptisms, weddings, and funerals. At other times, the complaint goes, attendance at mass and contributions to the parish, financial or otherwise, are infrequent.

Perhaps this will begin to change as Mexican American clergy, though few in number, rise in the hierarchy. Foremost among these has been Archbishop Patricio Flores of San Antonio. The son of a Texas farmworker family, Archbishop Flores has encouraged the development of new liturgies drawing on Mexican folkloric traditions. He has also been a champion of Alinsky-inspired community organizing efforts in Mexican American communities throughout Texas. Brought together under the banner of the Texas Interfaith Network, these organizations played an important role in the passage of the Texas school finance reform mentioned earlier. The most powerful of these is the San Antonio-based Communities Organized for Public Service (COPS). The success of COPS is directly attributable to the Archbishop's open support, which permits the organization to recruit members and collect dues—in many cases, right off the top of each Sunday's collections—from some thirty member parishes. With this kind of base COPS is, not surprisingly, a key actor in San Antonio politics.

The efforts of Archbishop Flores and his colleagues have been directed at the great mass of working- and lower-middle-class Mexican Americans who have been left out of the mainstream in places like San Antonio, El Paso, and the Rio Grande Valley. And while they have undoubtedly given many a greater sense of belonging in the Church, they have just as surely alienated many others who recall the fruits of Church meddling in politics back in Mexico. Generations of ambivalence and outright hostility toward the Church are not easily turned around, especially among Mexican Americans who are sufficiently well off and assimilated that they don't feel in need of its help in economic or political matters. Indeed, a likely scenario would be that the weak attachments of Mexican Americans to the Catholic Church will grow even weaker as they assimilate.

Just such a tendency is discernible in Los Angeles, where Mexican American parishes are not the vital social institutions they are in San Antonio. This seems most directly attributable to the extraordinary fluidity of the populace there. While San Antonio's Mexican American community is rather rooted and traditional, Los Angeles' is marked by the constant comings and goings of recent arrivals from Mexico, and the movement out to the suburbs of the upwardly mobile.

Yet another consideration is the stance of the hierarchy in Los Angeles. Timothy Cardinal Manning, following in the steps of his predecessor, arch-conservative Cardinal MacIntyre, has set a tone quite different from that of Archbishop Flores in Texas. Though some gestures toward the Mexican American community have been made, the Los Angeles hierarchy has definitely not reached out aggressively to the Mexican population in the metropolitan area. And while Cardinal Manning has tolerated a community-organizing effort in the East Los Angeles barrio similar to COPS in San Antonio, he would never be accused of encouraging the political development of the Mexican American community. Indeed, the hierarchy has long drawn a sharp line between religion and politics in Los Angeles. As a result, politicians, Mexican and Anglo alike, do not turn to the parishes as political bases. This again is in contrast to San Antonio, where politicians have long worked the parishes for votes.

Any consideration of the relationship between the Catholic Church and Mexican Americans must appreciate that "the Church" is hardly a monolith, for its responses vary greatly from community to community. But because of the weakness of other institutions in the Southwest, especially unions and political parties, the Church must in general be seen as a key factor in Mexican American politics. Thus, even in Los Angeles the Church, by virtue of the community organization it only halfheartedly supports, sustains a relatively strong voice in the Mexican American community.

As I mentioned earlier, there are certain parallels between the place of the Catholic Church among Mexican Americans and among Italian Americans, at least Italian Americans of an earlier generation. Like Italians, Mexicans have roots in peasant cultures where the primary-group bonds of the family are much stronger than the bonds to formal organizations or societal institutions, including the Church. This reliance on the ties of blood is of course evident in peasant cultures generally, but it is undoubtedly reinforced in nations such as Italy and Mexico that have experienced periods of political incapacity and societal breakdown.

But my larger point here is that the emphasis on family values among both Mexicans and Italians persists in the United States, even as acculturation proceeds. As I have already indicated with regard to Mexican American educational attainment, strong family ties can be dysfunctional. But they can also provide the basis for the entrepreneurial activity so evident in the Mexican American community today. Indeed, among both Italian Americans and Mexican Americans one can discern the transformation of peasant cynicism toward the outside world into small-business, petty-bourgeois shrewdness.

Opportunities for Republicans

In politics these same values lead to conservative positions on the divisive social issues. Foremost among these is abortion, of which Mexican Americans take a rather dim view. And while many Mexican American political leaders today adopt the liberal stance on these issues, they do so mainly out of pragmatic deference to their liberal allies in the Democratic Party. Few Mexican American leaders delude themselves that such positions are popular with their constituents. Indeed, it is difficult to find a Mexican American politician who doesn't admit having a brother, mother, or some other relative who is more conservative than he on such issues. Keenly aware of the volatility of this social conservatism, the Mexican American politician relies heavily on the fact that bread-and-butter economic issues, especially among the less affluent Mexican Americans, are more salient.

Yet entrepreneurial and social conservatism do motivate the politics of many Mexican Americans. And it is among these that the Republican Party has made gains. And here again the situation of Mexican Americans today is reminiscent of Italian Americans a few generations back. In his classic study of New Haven politics, *Who Governs?*, Robert Dahl describes how many Italians shut out of the Democratic Party's patronage moved over into the Republican column. Democratic politicians don't have much patronage to distribute these days, but many Mexican Americans are not pleased with the treatment they have received in the Party and have, as a result, changed affiliation. As one young Mexican American lawyer with a degree from Harvard told me, "The line is shorter in the Republican Party." Ambitious Italian Americans a few generations ago in New Haven presumably felt the same way.

It remains to be seen, of course, how substantial Republican gains among Mexican Americans will be. Exit polls do show that President Reagan got about 30 percent of the Mexican vote in California. But it is one thing to vote for a Republican President and quite another to identify oneself as a Republican. And yet there are numbers of Mexican Americans who are willing to do just that. But the story does not end there. My evidence indicates that the ambitious Mexican Americans from business and professional backgrounds who are typical Republican converts are motivated not by ideology or principle so much as personal advancement. One interesting implication of this unremarkable fact is that few Mexican American Republicans are eager to run for office. For many, public office would mean an unacceptable cut in income. And among those for whom the opposite would be true, the goal is not elective office, but the relative ease and security of an appointed position. But the best way for a recent Mexican American convert to prove oneself to Party stalwarts is to declare one's candidacy. As a result, some Mexican American Republicans run, but few expect to win. And given the still considerable allegiance of Mexican American voters to the Democratic Party, and the demonstrated reluctance of Republican activists to enthusiastically support Mexican American Johnnies-come-lately, not winning is a reasonable expectation. But without serious candidates who can win elections, it is unclear how Republicans will sustain a vital presence among Mexican Americans.

This kind of comparison can of course be overdrawn. My point here is not to equate the experience of Mexican Americans with that of Italian Americans. It is merely to suggest how much the immigrant perspective can contribute to an understanding of Mexican Americans. At the same time, this perspective does have its limitations. For while there may be certain sociological similarities between Mexicans and the classic American ethnic groups, there are important differences. I have already mentioned the unique situation of the Mexican in the American Southwest. It is also significant that Mexican Americans today are dealing with a political and social system vastly different from that confronting European immigrants several generations ago. Mexican American politicians today, for example, lack the patronage resources that earlier ethnic politicians used to lure their countrymen into the political arena. Then, too, Mexican Americans are raising questions about ethnic politics and cultural pluralism at a time when the old rules and understandings are challenged and changing.

Conclusion

But does this throw us back upon the minority group perspective? As I have already demonstrated, this too has its shortcomings. Yet enough of its insights resonate among Mexican Americans to make it difficult to dismiss. This is particularly true now that the perspective has been institutionalized in many universities, and in advocacy groups such as the Mexican American Legal Defense and Education Fund (MALDEF) and the League of United Latin American Citizens (LULAC), both of which played key roles in defeating the Simpson-Mazzoli immigration reform.

In the hands of politicians the subtleties and nuances of the Mexican American experience are, not surprisingly, eliminated. In their place is utter confusion. At least this is what I make of politicians who one day declare their group to be just like any other immigrant people, and the next declare it to be an oppressed minority in need of affirmative-action protections. The politicians, of course, are not to be blamed. They work with what they have; and besides, it makes good sense to store new and potentially bitter wine in old bottles. But the rest of us have a bit more room to maneuver, and within it we must reconcile ourselves to the ambiguity with which the Mexican American experience is imbued.

V

Portents of the Future

12

MICHAEL S. TEITELBAUM

Forced Migration: The Tragedy of Mass Expulsions

The mass expulsion of hundreds of thousands of people can no longer be viewed as the aberrational behavior of mad political leaders. To the contrary, such actions have become quite deliberate instruments of both domestic and foreign policy for various sovereign nations. In the past decade alone, literally millions have been coerced—often by their own governments—to flee their homes, sometimes onto the high seas in unseaworthy boats. Obvious examples include those of Vietnam, Uganda, and Cuba, discussed in greater detail below, but other expulsions have also occurred or loom as future possibilities.

Such actions present uniquely difficult dilemmas for other nations. In extreme cases, they are faced with the unacceptable alternatives of unwillingly providing temporary safe haven or permanent asylum, or watching passively as thousands die. As they contemplate their decision, often under severe pressures of time, they must simultaneously consider the odious possibility that an extremist government might resort to genocidal policies if the mass expulsion option is precluded. As they grope for a decision, there is little if any guidance provided by existing norms of international behavior, and few effective measures available with which to deter the would-be expellers.

The disturbing mass expulsion experiences of the past decade seem unlikely to be the last. Similar mass expulsions are plausible outcomes in many of the world's troublespots, especially in developing countries faced with political and economic instability, inter-ethnic antagonisms, or violent insurrections. Such a situation is substantially a new one on the world scene, as a multitude of new or revolutionary nation-states undergo convulsive change, or as their present leaders seek to prevent change by coercive consolidation of their rule. The prospects of expulsions arising from such situations are heightened by the common circumstance of arbitrary, disputed, or unclear national boundaries, often established by colonial powers without reference to the homelands of antagonistic ethnic, religious, and tribal groupings. Finally, the sheer numbers of potential expellees is now of unprecedented magnitude, due to the extraordinary growth in populations that has occurred in only the past twenty years.

No one can predict if, when, or where the unhappy events of the past decade may be repeated in the coming years. By their very nature, mass expulsions are convulsive events, dependent upon an unpredictable confluence of political, economic, and social forces. Yet at any given time, developing situations that *could* lead to such expulsions may be identified and followed with appropriate concern. At the time of this writing (January 1985), such examples include the Bahais in Iran, the Kurds in Iran and Iraq, the Miskito Indians in Central America, various groups in Kampuchea and Lebanon, Palestinian Arabs in the West Bank, and perhaps very large numbers of blacks and/or whites in southern Africa over the longer term.

The phenomenon of mass expulsion is largely uncharted territory for foreign policy. Such expulsions clearly are disruptive of the established order of affairs among states, yet foreign-policy responses to the past decade's expulsions have been *ad hoc,* in the absence of agreed political instruments able to cope. The severely negative political consequences of recent expulsions, the serious humanitarian concerns they have raised, and the prospects for their future replication suggest that the time is ripe for dispassionate analysis of what now appears to be a phenomenon on the rise, and largely unconstrained by international norms.

Aliens, Conquerees, Citizens

Webster's defines "expulsion" as "a driving or forcing out; summary removal," though in international law the term is usually applied more narrowly to the removal of aliens only.[1] Using the broader definition, three relevant categories of expulsion may be distinguished:

- the expulsion of aliens, whether legally or illegally resident;
- the expulsion of residents of conquered territory over which sovereignty is claimed;
- the expulsion of nationals or citizens.

The expulsion of aliens has many postwar examples, including Operation Wetback in the United States in 1954 (in which over one million Mexican illegal aliens were apprehended and returned to Mexico in a paramilitary operation), the 1983 expulsion of one to two million Ghanaians and others from Nigeria, and the earlier Ghanaian expulsion of Nigerians and others in 1969. The expulsion of Bangladeshi nationals from the Indian state of Assam is a fundamental demand of the Assamese National Movement.

There also have been many examples of forcible expulsions of conquered peoples. Generally the goal of such actions is to establish sovereignty and effective control over conquered territories by removing the local population and repopulating with nationals,[2] or to dispose of conquered populations deemed somehow "inferior." Such expulsions had been practiced in territories conquered by Nazi Germany, before it settled upon mass extermination. After World War II, the realignment of Eastern Europe's borders by the victorious Soviet Union led to massive forced movements of millions of German and Polish nationals. It is at least arguable (and it would surely be argued on both sides) that some of the departures of Afghanistanis, Cambodians, Greek Cypriots, Lebanese, and others from their homelands resulted from such military conquests by neighboring states.

The third category, mass expulsion of citizens, presents the most difficult problems in both theoretical and practical terms. Expulsions of this type have occurred recently in at least three countries: Uganda in 1972, Vietnam in 1978–79, and Cuba in 1980. Since much can be learned from a detailed discussion of the circumstances and rationales in each of these cases, they are described in some detail below.

Uganda. On August 9, 1972, President-for-life Idi Amin Dada issued a decree ordering the expulsion from Uganda of all Asians holding nationality in Great Britain, India, Pakistan, and Bangladesh. He charged the Asians with sabotaging the Ugandan economy, "practicing and encouraging corruption," and "frustrating attempts by Ugandan Africans to participate in the economic and business life of their country."[3] A week later, on August 16, Amin extended this decree to include those Asians who held Ugandan citizenship, in accordance with what he claimed was a long-standing Ugandan policy of Africanization.

These two edicts affected approximately 74,000 people: 27,000 were British passport holders; another 11,000 were under British protection without passports; 2,000 held Indian, Pakistani, or Bangladeshi passports; and over 23,000 claimed Ugandan citizenship. On the advice of Ugandan legal counselors, Amin later rescinded the amendment expelling Ugandan Asian citizens, but the authenticity of many of their citizenship claims was then challenged. Through bureaucratic manipulation (and allegedly through prudent use of a paper shredder), about 7,000 Asians were found to have acquired Ugandan citizenship through fraudulent means.

Meanwhile, the British government was less than eager to accept all of the British subjects who had been expelled. Recent British law changes had restricted the immigration of Commonwealth citizens unless they were "assured employment or had adequate means of support," and as one British Minister commented about British Asians without passports, "No British subject has a legal right to a passport. The grant of a United Kingdom passport is a Royal prerogative. . ."[4]

In the end, after many diplomatic exchanges and negotiations involving Uganda, Britain, India, and other countries, the expulsion program went largely according to both of Amin's expulsion orders. Almost all of the 74,000 Asians, whether Ugandan nationals or not, departed before the November deadline, and each carried out little more than the $100 per family that Amin had allowed them to extract from the Ugandan assets. The rest of the departing Asians' businesses were expropriated and distributed to political supporters of the Amin regime. Britain accepted a good percentage of the expellees with British passports, India took back its citizens. Those who were stateless or Ugandan citizens went to transit camps sponsored by the U.N. High Commissioner for Refugees (UNHCR), and finally to twenty-five countries for permanent resettlement.

It seems clear enough that these actions by the Ugandan government breached international legal norms by coercing its own citizens to leave. Although the expulsion order against Ugandan citizens was rescinded, many in this category found their citizenship claims rejected, and it was made clear to all that it would be wise for them to depart "willingly."

Ugandan law may also have been violated. The Ugandan Constitution allows the de-nationalization of those citizens who had been naturalized, but not of native-born citizens.[5] Nonetheless, native-born Asians found their citizenships declared "obtained in a fraudulent manner," and the reportedly widespread destruction of citizenship records renders suspect the Ugandan government's determinations.

Such actions by the Ugandan government have been justified by some African lawyers by reference to the behavior of the former colonial power, Great Britain.

Many of the problems that have risen in East Africa can be regarded as those of decolonialization and they all stem from Britain's unwillingness to discharge the obligations it incurred at the time of the establishment of the empire. Governments in East Africa have been saddled with problems that really belong to Britain. The fairness of holding these governments to rigid international standards of nonracial treatment in the face of Britain's behavior may well be questioned.[6]

In retrospect, of course, the expelled Asians may now feel fortunate to have been expelled (though many are still seeking financial compensation from the post-Amin Ugandan government), given the evidence of large-scale killings in Uganda implemented by Amin's notorious State Research Bureau and elements of the military. The Uganda experience therefore provides a useful example of the profound ethical dilemmas posed by mass expulsions when compared to possible alternatives in totalitarian states.

Vietnam. It became evident in early 1978 that a mass exodus of close to half a million people was taking place from the Socialist Republic of Vietnam. Over 60 percent of the so-called "boat people" were ethnic Chinese, and it is now reasonably clear that the government in Hanoi was applying a policy of coerced emigration or expulsion against Vietnam's ethnic Chinese population. In the words of the *Far Eastern Economic Review,* "Hanoi actively encourages departures, and has the power to turn the refugee flow on or off at will."[7] The motivations behind these actions will be discussed after a brief review of the history which led to this situation.

In March 1978 the Vietnamese government suddenly abolished all "bourgeois trade" in Ho Chi Minh City (formerly Saigon). Thirty thousand businesses, 80 percent of which were owned by ethnic Chinese, were closed down and their assets confiscated, and a new currency was issued by the Hanoi government. These actions of "socialist transformation" were directed mainly against the Chinese population of the south, who had previously made their living as commercial middlemen in the southern non-socialist economy. The combination of the loss of their businesses and savings, along with the previously introduced new economic zones[8] and re-education camps initiated by the government, were the proximate causes of the forced flight from Vietnam. There were no formal proclamations, legal decrees, or mass denationalizations. In effect there were no formal expulsions (or at least none were acknowledged) but the policies followed provided powerful coercion toward departure, as evidenced by the truly desperate character of the boat peoples' flight.

Vietnamese prejudice against ethnic Chinese, coupled with their concentration in "bourgeois" middlemen occupations, was undoubtedly an important part of the explanation for the Vietnam government's pressure upon Vietnamese nationals of Chinese ethnicity. But there may have been other reasons as well. Most member-states of the Association of Southeast Asian Nations (ASEAN) believed that an important Vietnamese goal was to destabilize their societies. Most of these nations, which were the countries of first asylum for the bulk of the Vietnamese boat people, already had ethnic problems between their Chinese minorities and their majority populations, and these were aggravated by the introduction of thousands of ethnic Chinese refugees.[9] Most ASEAN nations were also low-income countries whose economic problems were exacerbated by the introduction of the Vietnamese expellees.

It was also asserted that the expulsion was intended to introduce espionage agents and spies into the ASEAN countries. For example, Malaysian Home Minister Safie described the expulsions in a 1978 speech as a Vietnamese effort

to plant their workers and agents among these so-called refugees, with the purpose of slipping away into thin air on arrival at Malaysian shores ... Malaysia cannot rule out the possibility of a Vietnam now planning for immediate contingencies or a long-term objective."[10]

Similar remarks were also made by Malaysian Prime Minister Hussein, by Singapore's Prime Minister Lee Kuan Yew, by several Thai officials, and even by the Chinese Communist Party's official newspaper *Peoples' Daily*, which explicitly mentioned the infiltration of communist agents as a goal of Vietnam's expulsion policy.[11] It is, of course, impossible to assess the validity of such claims.

Another apparent reason for the Vietnamese expulsion of ethnic Chinese was the government's desire for hard currency and gold. According to journalistic reports based on interviews with boat organizers and former Communist military officers, the Ministries of Interior and Finance participated in and regulated the trade in boat people, and reported on their efforts directly to the Politburo.[12] Ten *taels* of gold, the equivalent of U.S. $2,670 per boat-person, was paid to middlemen who were granted government permission to organize boat departures. These middlemen were required to remit half of these fees to the Hanoi government. In addition, travel documents needed for travel across provincial lines to the port of departure had to be bought from Vietnam government officials, at a further cost of about $2,000 per person for those not living near ports of departure. The total hard-currency receipts from the refugee trade taken in by Hanoi as of June 1979 were estimated at $115 million per year.[13] This figure, if true, would have amounted to approximately 2.5 percent of Vietnam's GNP, and perhaps half of its hard currency earnings in that year. Such earnings would have been a considerable help in financing essential imports at a time of poor harvests, very low hard-currency reserves, and economic and political ostracism by much of the rest of the world.

Finally, the Hanoi government's actions may also be attributed in part to the utility of the Chinese minority as scapegoats for the floundering economy,[14] coupled with the poor state of Sino-Vietnamese relations. There apparently was great concern in the Vietnamese government that its Chinese population might provide covert aid to China should there be any major conflict between the two nations, such as occurred during the border war of 1979.

The Vietnam government has continually denied all reports of governmental involvement in the refugee trade. This position was stated in the government-published pamphlet *Those Who Leave*, which said that although Hanoi recognized the fact that there was a mass exodus in progress, this was due to "counter-revolutionary" elements. But Wain poses an unanswerable question as to the government's involvement: "Does anyone seriously believe that in a totalitarian state 50,000 people a month can be organized, ticketed, transported to departure points, and allocated boats—a major logistical exercise—without the government's knowledge or involvement?"[15]

Various legal justifications for its actions were offered by the Vietnamese government. One was that the southern Chinese population had not been naturalized in 1965, as had the entire population of the north, because the southern Chinese population had not undertaken military service required by the Constitution of the Socialist Republic of Vietnam: "Citizens are obliged to do military service and to take part in building a national defense of the whole population." This conflicted with a July 1978 Vietnamese pronouncement directed toward the People's Republic of China, which stated that "it is an historical fact that the Chinese residents in south Vietnam took Vietnamese citizenship and became Vietnamese of Chinese origin 20 years ago."[16]

Cuba. The case of Cuba may be a partial exception to the rule in these case studies of mass expulsion, for it is arguable that most of the 125,000 migrants entering the United States from the Cuban port of Mariel in the spring of 1980 were not expelled against their will. The Cuban government holds that it simply withdrew "protection from the Florida Corridor," allowing those who wished to emigrate to go to any country that would accept them. The immediate catalyst was an incident in which a small number of Cubans forced their way past Cuban police guards into the Peruvian Embassy in Havana. The Cuban government's response was to remove police control over entry to the Embassy compound. Eventually 10,000 persons entered and camped out under unsanitary conditions, awaiting action by the governments of Peru, Cuba, and other countries. After a series of negotiations among the governments involved, the Cuban government broadcast an invitation to Cuban-Americans to send boats to Mariel Harbor to pick up their friends and family members, and by the time Cuba closed down the flow over 125,000 Cubans had departed.

The 1980 migration from Cuba had its origins in economic factors,[17] coupled with desires to reunite families separated by earlier migrations to the United States. The faltering of the Cuban economy in the 1970s was a blow to public morale, for the 1960s had been austere, and the government had promised that the 1970s would be years of prosperity. This economic dissatisfaction was exacerbated when in 1979, President Carter and Premier Castro agreed to loosen travel restrictions between Cuba and the United States. Within a year, over 100,000 Cuban exiles returned to visit their relatives and friends in Cuba, bringing with them often-exaggerated stories of luxury and physical proof of a greater affluence in the United States. Some reports indicated that Cuban-Americans took out loans to buy luxury items to be shown off in Cuba.

Much has been made of the social characteristics of the 1980 migrants, with distortions from all sides. Premier Castro described the "Marielitos" as "anti-social scum," and openly admitted emptying jails and mental institutions to enlarge the exodus. The U.S. government was notably ambivalent in its response to the influx, vacillating between welcoming the migrants as refugees from Communism and discouraging them as illegal aliens. In May of 1980, President Carter announced that the Cuban migrants would be welcomed under the terms of political asylum, but also promised that those with criminal records would immediately face exclusion proceedings. Meanwhile, some accounts in the American press concentrated heavily upon the serious criminals and mental patients arriving in the boats, thereby tending to exaggerate the proportion of the flow these represented.

It could be argued that the Cuban government did not act illegally in allowing the departure of the bulk of the Cuban migrants, most of whom appear to have departed willingly, primarily for economic or family reunification reasons. The willingness of the United States, Peru, and Costa Rica to grant them entry, even if under duress, might support this claim to some extent.

However, those cases (a minority that still may number in the tens of thousands) in which organs of the Cuban state coerced or "encouraged" criminals and seriously-ill persons to join the "freedom flotilla" do raise serious questions of international relations. There is ample testimony of such coercion from boat-lift participants: prisoners and former prisoners given the option of continued imprisonment or departure for the U.S., psychiatric inmates moved en masse by bus to Mariel, and so on. President Carter, by refusing to accept persons with proven criminal records, was properly exercising a State's right to define an acceptable refugee; and Cuba, by organizing the outflow of such excludable persons, was almost surely violating the territorial supremacy of the United States. Moreover, although the Cuban government has never claimed to have denationalized the departed Cubans, in negotiations since 1980 it reportedly has refused to readmit those Cuban citizens excluded by the United States, although it has agreed to accept some on a discretionary basis. (Recent news reports suggest that bilateral agreement in principle may now have been achieved on this issue, but we shall have to wait and see how such agreement is implemented, given both the nature of past Cuban actions and the intervention in the matter by a federal judge in Atlanta.)

By almost universal agreement, one of the clearest effects of the 1980 Cuban migration was to inflict severe damage on U.S. willingness to assist and resettle *bona fide* refugees. The expulsion of violent criminals (more than a thousand of whom are still detained in federal penitentiaries), seriously-ill persons, and others seen as highly undesirable immigrants served to crystallize latent public opposition to the Carter administration's policies of large-scale refugee resettlement. Some believe that the issue was an important latent factor in the 1980 electoral defeat suffered by President Carter. In these (probably unintended) ways, the actions of the Cuban government may be said to have had dramatic impacts on domestic U.S. politics and policies.

Prospects for Future Expulsions

Future mass expulsion policies are possible in other countries, though in the nature of things such actions are unpredictable in the extreme. What we can say is that circumstances of political or economic instability coupled with racial, ethnic, or religious tensions provide fertile ground for political decisions to expel significant numbers of people. The following examples are worthy of attention.

The West Bank. The issue of expulsion now is arising in discussions of the status of the West Bank, so central to Middle East peace negotiations. The Israeli claim to sovereignty over the West Bank raises difficult domestic issues for the Israeli government, since the incorporation of Arab residents of the West Bank could substantially change the population composition of the Israeli state were the West Bank to be annexed.[18] A 1983 newspaper account quoted the then-Deputy Speaker of the Israeli Parliament, Mr. Meir Cohen, as stating that Israel had made a mistake by not expelling 200,000 to 300,000 Arabs from the West Bank after capturing the territory from Jordan in the 1967 War.[19] Such expulsion is an explicit campaign promise of the extremist Kach Party led by Meir Kahane, which won a parliamentary seat for the first time in the 1984 elections.

This situation has led to considerable speculation. For example, Henry Kissinger has argued that annexation of the West Bank:

is not even in the interest of Israel however narrowly conceived. . . . the incorporation of Gaza and the West Bank into Israel will sooner or later produce an Arab majority that will destroy the essence of the Jewish state. And if Israel seeks to escape this dilemma by expelling all the

Arabs it will lose the moral support of even its best friends. Over an historical period, Israel would not be able to withstand the crisis that would result.[20]

In August 1983, a Palestinian lawyer associated with the International Commission of Jurists wrote that such a mass expulsion, which he admits "sounds farfetched," is seen by extremist groups within Israel as a "radical solution to the demographic problem." He concludes:

The extremist plan to expel us from the territories may seem incredible, but to us it looks more plausible every day. The longer Israel retains the territories and denies our national aspirations, the quicker such horrible plans will become not only possible but inevitable.[21]

These speculations may prove to be excessive, since the West Bank situation is highly volatile and unpredictable. But the demographic realities do seem to clash with the geopolitical situation faced by the government of Israel.

Africa. The national boundaries of modern African states are notorious for their poorness of fit with ethnic/tribal boundaries. Although they are vestiges of colonialism, existing boundaries have been firmly supported by most African states and by the Organization of African Unity. However, when political and/or economic problems arise in African states, they are often linked to the longstanding divisions of tribe and ethnicity. Past instabilities and crises have led to tribe-based repression, expulsion, and even genocide. Examples over the past decade include those involving the Hutus of Burundi; the Matabeles in Zimbabwe; various tribal groups in Uganda; and the Somali, Eritrean, and other tribal groups in Ethiopia.

Looking to the future, Angola may someday join this unhappy list. Its long civil war is heavily tribal, and the nature of its resolution will determine whether tribe-based repressions or expulsions will occur. Similar comments may be in order about countries such as Ethiopia and Uganda, depending upon the outcomes of their long internal crises.

Another obviously threatening situation is that in South Africa. In a sense the South African government's ethnic "homelands" policy may be described as a form of "internal expulsion." The government has described each "homeland" as an independent or prospectively independent state, has designated persons of its ethnic group to be its citizens and not of the Republic of South Africa, and has forcibly removed such persons to the "homeland" territory. As political, economic, and demographic stresses have arisen for the *apartheid* policy, the South African government has been buffeted by conflicting forces favoring repression or gradual liberalization. No one can predict what direction future policy movements will take. However, the development of either a more extreme white nationalist movement or a successful black nationalist movement could result in largescale expulsions of blacks or whites.

Asia. The most obvious potentials for mass expulsions in Asia are in Iran and Afghanistan. In Iran, non-Islamic minorities such as Bahais are threatened by the ascendancy of militant Islamic revivalism. In Afghanistan the five year old civil war and Soviet intervention has not resolved fundamental political problems, many of which have a tribal component. More than 15 percent of the Afghanistani population has already fled to neighboring Pakistan and Iran; if the current Kabul regime proves able to consolidate its control over the countryside, more could be expected to depart voluntarily or under coercion.

Other Asian nations with at least a hypothetical potential for mass expulsions are Sri Lanka (with regard to its Tamil minority) and perhaps even India, depending on developments in Assam and in the Sikh militancy that has already led to military intervention in the Punjab and the assassination of Indira Gandhi. Fortunately, both Sri Lanka and India have long traditions of relatively stable and humane governments, hence mass expulsions seem unlikely unless traumatic political changes were to occur.

Meanwhile, there are real prospects for mass expulsions from Kampuchea resulting from the civil war and the related Vietnamese military intervention. Moreover, on the basis of past behavior further expulsions from Vietnam are possible, depending upon political and economic developments in that country.

Latin America. In several Latin American countries, Indian tribal groups have been seen as threats to ruling regimes and have been subjected to repressive actions stimulating mass departures. Current examples include the Miskitos from Nicaragua and various groups from Guatemala. The prospects for similar events elsewhere depend upon political developments in the many unstable countries in the region.

The general message seems clear enough: in various parts of the globe there are numerous situations with the basic ingredients that can lead to mass expulsions. While prediction is impossible for such traumatic and draconian actions by governments, the possibility cannot be ignored.

Mass Expulsion and International Norms

While expulsions are traumatic and disruptive for those expelled, most are by no means violations of international norms. To the contrary, expulsion is generally agreed to be a legitimate, and indeed fundamental, right of sovereign states, so long as international obligations are not contravened.

Expelling Aliens. Most expulsions of aliens are consistent with agreed norms of international behavior. States have assured themselves wide latitude to determine whether such expulsion is appropriate and desirable, as long as such actions do not violate treaty obligations and are not arbitrary[22]—though it is unclear who would decide the latter question. The most important such obligations are those relating to *bona fide* refugees, which prohibit forcible expulsion to the refugee's home country (*refoulement*), although expulsion to a third country willing to provide admittance is allowable.

In cases involving legal entry by non-refugee aliens, expulsion should be effected only "in accordance with law,"[23] typically through the operation of normal deportation proceedings. Such actions usually involve case-by-case adjudications, and hence would not normally result in mass expulsions in any case.

Finally, in cases of illegal entry or other violations of immigration law, mass expulsion without benefit of formal deportation proceedings is an available legal option. The only limitation under international human rights law appears to be the ambiguous prohibition in the American Convention on Human Rights against the "collective expulsion of aliens."

Expelling Citizens. It is generally agreed that mass expulsions may not be applied to nationals or citizens unless another country is willing to admit them.[24] This is not because expulsion *per se* is unacceptable, but instead because each sovereign state may legitimately refuse to admit citizens of another. In contrast, all states have a well-established international obligation to admit their own citizens ("No one shall be arbitrarily deprived of the right to enter his own country.")[25] Hence, according to the leading academic interpretations, a state's expulsion of its own nationals into another state unwilling to admit them constitutes a violation of the fundamental international principle of territorial supremacy,[26] and also creates potential duties for other states and encroaches upon their jurisdiction without an internationally valid reason.[27]

One may therefore conclude that *expulsion of its own citizens is not an option for a state unless another state can be found that is willing to admit them.* But this rather legalistic conclusion begs many real-world issues. Two categories of expulsion are worth separate consideration here. The first occurs when states deny the validity of expellees' nationality claims, or strip them of nationality before expelling them. The second type of expulsion is more flagrant, with no such legal niceties observed.

As to the first, it is obvious that the legality of an expulsion depends heavily upon a determination of who is a "national" or "citizen" and who an "alien." A national or citizen is best defined as an individual who is *recognized by a sovereign government* as an inhabitant of that country and therefore the holder of certain privileges, protections, and duties. Conversely, an alien is an individual who resides, works, or visits in a state of which he is not a national. The important element of these definitions is that they are largely controlled by each state's national law. Not surprisingly, ambiguity and confusion can result when international and national codes intersect.

An extreme case of such ambiguity arises when one state annexes territory claimed or previously controlled by a second state. If the residents in the annexed territory are recognized as citizens by the second state, it may have an obligation to admit them if they are expelled by the first state. The situation becomes even murkier if the second state contests the act of annexation.

Moreover, nation-states have preserved remarkably wide discretion in denationalizing their nationals. Weis lists five common, but by no means universal, categories for the deprivation of nationality through state action:[28]

1. Entry into foreign civil or military service or acceptance of foreign distinctions.

2. Departure or sojourn abroad.

3. Conviction for certain crimes.

4. Political attitudes or activities . . . Such grounds as disloyalty or disaffection, acts prejudicial to the state or its interests, collaboration with the enemy, advocacy of subversive activities, etc., are frequently stipulated in municipal legislation as grounds for deprivation of nationality.

5. Racial and national grounds.

There are limits to such enormous discretion, such as when states revoke nationality solely to legitimize arbitrary mass expulsions and thereby to avoid international obligations, and some authorities argue that even denationalization cannot justify expulsion of those to which it is applied.[29] But arguments that denationalization is implicitly inadmissable on the basis of the international accords on human rights, statelessness, and refugees are viewed skeptically by leading scholars of the subject.[30] Hence, while it is generally agreed that deprivation of nationality should not be "arbitrary," the above list of acceptable reasons for such actions should be sufficient for almost any authoritarian state to denationalize almost anyone it wishes.

Thus, ironically, traditional international law may provide fewer protections from expulsion for citizens than for some categories of aliens, especially refugees. This is the case although the entire structure of such international law rests on the rights and obligations of sovereign states in relation to other states and to their nationals. If the body of international law relating to human rights is considered, the protections for citizens are more secure, but significant gaps remain.

The second category, that of flagrant expulsion of acknowledged nationals into another state without its consent, represents a clear violation of the fundamental principle of territorial supremacy.

Unhappily, in the real world such principles are enforceable primarily through force, via police or military actions. This suggests the unattractive conclusion that such flagrant mass expulsions constitute hostile acts, to which the only effective responses may need to be equally hostile. Hence the expulsion of nationals poses special—perhaps unique—problems both for international law and for peaceful relations among states.

What Might We Learn from the Above Discussion and Case Studies of Recent Expulsions?

First, the motivations of expelling nations vary broadly, but often combine domestic goals of disposing of a despised or threatening minority with foreign policy goals of embarrassing or even destabilizing foreign adversaries. In the Cuban case, the target adversary was clearly the United States; in the Vietnam case, targets probably included ASEAN countries along with the United States; and in the Ugandan case, Great Britain was the foreign focus.

Second, all three cases involved totalitarian states, two of a Marxist-Leninist variety and one of a more eclectic Third World totalitarian nationalism. Future mass expulsions of citizens can be expected to come primarily from totalitarian regimes of the right or left, or from states in chaos (e.g., Lebanon). However, non-totalitarian and non-chaotic nations may be prepared to adopt policies of mass expulsion for aliens, especially when they are unlawfully resident and/or are perceived as threats to national security or domestic tranquility (e.g., Nigeria in 1983 and perhaps Assam in the future).

Third, a mass expulsion may form a component of a larger migration stream of more conventional immigrants and/or refugees. The recent mass movements out of Vietnam and Cuba were of this type, with expellees forming only a part of a larger outmigration. Hence all future mass exoduses deserve careful scrutiny, with a view to determining whether a mass expulsion also is in progress.

Fourth, the three cases demonstrate that a variety of alternative outcomes might have occurred had the expulsions been deterred. These range from severe persecution, even mass killings, in the case of Uganda, through severe hardship and possible persecution in Vietnam, to little likelihood of persecution (except for political prisoners) in the Cuban case.

What Is To Be Done?

Expulsions of Aliens. As indicated earlier, there are few agreed prohibitions upon sovereign states in expelling aliens *en masse*. Despite the criticism from some governments and in the Western media of Nigeria's 1983 mass expulsion, few were prepared to argue that Nigeria was violating its international obligations by deciding upon the expulsion. Instead, the criticism was aimed at the precipitous nature of the expulsion, and the suffering caused the expellees. In response, the Government of Nigeria stated that substantial warnings had been given to affected governments (this matter continues to be in dispute) and that the suffering was caused by the decision of the Ghanian government to close its borders to its own citizens.

While mass expulsion of aliens may be a legal prerogative of nation-states, other states can—and should —insist that the nations of the expellees' nationality be given fair warning to provide adequately for the influx of large numbers of people. It may also be possible to agree on minimal standards of decency for those expelled, so as to minimize hardship and physical risk. For the same reasons, the expellees' states of nationality should be required to fulfill their international obligations to admit them without delay.

Expulsion of Citizens. Mass expulsions of citizens violate fundamental principles of territorial supremacy and numerous instruments of international law. They also pose horrific humanitarian problems, in which the lives of tens or hundreds of thousands are placed in jeopardy. Finally, they raise a clear and present danger to future international willingness to provide assistance and resettlement to future refugees. As such, threatened mass expulsions of citizens warrant the strongest feasible measures of deterrence by other states and by the international community.

One of the perverse dilemmas posed by such expulsions is that in some extreme settings they may represent the lesser evil when compared to prospects of mass killings or even genocide. Observers of recent history cannot lightly dismiss the possibility of such actions by nation-states against despised groups among their own citizenry. Even in such stark cases, mass expulsions pose serious threats to peace and to international receptivity to refugees.

Fortunately, most cases of impending mass expulsion are not likely to pose such desperate dilemmas and it is clearly desirable to deter the would-be expellers from their actions. Yet in such cases the available modes for international response are severely limited, for both practical and ethical reasons. Possible measures include: formulations of new limitations in international law; direct police actions or military responses; bilateral economic and political sanctions; and multilateral initiatives.

There is little doubt that mass expulsions of citizens violate existing international law, but there may still be some merit in further specification of the rights and obligations of states in this area. Such a resolution might reaffirm that states may not expel their citizens without agreement from the receiving state, and that they must re-admit their own citizens. It might also further codify the prohibition of mass denationalization for purposes of expulsion, and point to appropriate sanctions to be imposed upon those offending against such basic international norms. An unadorned resolution in this area might prove popular in the United Nations General Assembly, in view of the centrality of concerns about national sovereignty among a large majority of member-states from all regions and blocs. However, proponents would have to anticipate efforts to politicize such a resolution through now-standard attacks upon imperialism, colonialism, hegemonism, zionism, apartheid, transnational corporations, etc., and expeditious action does not seem likely. Moreover, the provisions of such a resolution would be no more enforceable than existing international law that already prohibits most mass expulsions of citizens; hence the effect would be more exhortatory than directive.

If mass expulsions of citizens constitute violations of territorial supremacy analagous to military invasion, police or military actions may be seen as appropriate responses. Most states are prepared to employ military means against another state only in response to serious threats to their national security, and hence each government would have to determine for itself the level of threat presented by a mass expulsion. Of course, those expelled are hardly suitable targets for such military actions, as they are usually themselves innocent victims and deserving of protection. Hence such responses would have to be directed against targets other than the expellees.

Despite their limitations, military and police measures are by no means useless in deterring governments bent upon mass expulsions, especially in those cases where they can be employed without jeopardizing the peace or the lives of innocent victims. For example, it is at least arguable that military intervention in Uganda by Tanzania and in Kampuchea by Vietnam had positive humanitarian consequences over the short term, although these were hardly a principal concern of the intervening states.

The 1980 Cuban boatlift provides another example. The boats involved were mostly American, and hence prompt police action by the U.S. government to prevent their departure for Cuba might have raised the cost of the expulsion for the Cuban government and thereby reduced its size. Once the boats had been allowed to go to Cuba and were returning full of people, police and military options were sharply constrained. Of course it is easy to say this with the 20/20 vision of hindsight; the circumstances were far less clear for the policymakers involved. Nonetheless, in the future police and military deterrents should not be dismissed without consideration of their potential—and their risks.

Bilateral economic and political sanctions against expelling states have clear attractions when compared to military actions, although sanctions are subject to well-known limitations. One possibility would be to re-direct any foreign assistance intended for the expelling country toward relief of those it is expelling. However, while such actions might have some deterrent effects, they might also lead to further deterioration within the expelling nation and thereby to even more drastic actions directed against the groups subject to expulsion. This has led some Western critics to argue that positive economic and political *assistance* rather than punitive sanctions should have been offered to expelling states such as Vietnam and Cuba. Others would see such assistance as ransom to be paid to unscrupulous governments prepared to threaten mass expulsion as a form of international blackmail.

However this rather theological debate is resolved, we know from more than a decade's experience that bilateral sanctions are unlikely to be effective unless bolstered by additional multilateral measures.

Given the palpable limitations of legal, military, and bilateral sanctions, multilateral initiatives seem to hold the most promise of deterring future expellers. To be effective, early warning of impending mass expulsions must be available, and contingency plans for diplomatic initiatives must be formulated well in advance. Interested nations would have to establish their own "early warning" systems, perhaps by requiring periodic reporting on such issues by their embassy personnel or through the auspices of private voluntary organizations concerned with human rights issues.

An impending mass expulsion might then evoke such actions as: direct bilateral diplomatic representation from several countries in concert; indirect pressures via third countries maintaining good relations with the potential expeller; initiatives within relevant regional groups (such as the Organization of African Unity, the Organization of American States, the Arab League, or the Group of 77); and/or calls for emergency consideration by the Security Council. Flagrant expellers might be denied certain important benefits of the international system, such as access to the facilities of the International Monetary Fund and the World Bank. Of course, skepticism is appropriate as to the likely effectiveness of such measures in cases of extreme instability or repression. Nonetheless they do seem likely to have some moderating influence upon non-extremist governments that are in control of events and have some concern for their international standing.

As suggested earlier, efforts to deter mass expulsions may pose serious ethical dilemmas in those special cases in which gross persecution or even genocide might result. Hence a special burden rests upon nations seeking effective deterrents to continue to monitor closely all such situations, and in extremes to be prepared to initiate "orderly departure" arrangements for those most threatened.

An initiative in the U.N. General Assembly offers some promise of increasing the effectiveness of efforts to deter mass expulsions. In 1981, the Human Rights Commission appointed the former High Commissioner for Refugees, Prince Sadruddin Aga Khan, as

Special Rapporteur on Human Rights and Mass Exoduses. The report and recommendations produced by this effort ranged widely over all forms of mass exodus, as required by its mandate. But one of its major recommendations might be of special use in deterring mass expulsions: that the Secretary General appoint a Special Representative for Humanitarian Questions, whose tasks concerning mass expulsions would be:

(a) to forewarn; (b) to monitor; (c) to de-politicize humanitarian situations; (d) to carry out those functions which humanitarian agencies cannot assume because of institutional/mandatory constraints; (e) to serve as an intermediary of goodwill between the concerned parties.[31]

Thus, such an office would serve simultaneously to provide a multinational early warning system for future mass expulsions, and to employ the good offices of the Secretary General to avert them. Such a multilateral instrument would emphasize the international scope and portent of mass expulsions, and would also provide neutral auspices for convening multinational discussions of impending crises before they occur.

There is, of course, an understandable reluctance to contribute to further growth of the international bureaucracy. Yet such an office would fill an important gap in existing international institutions, which lack an explicitly political instrument focussed on averting mass expulsions and other mass exoduses. The principal international agency concerned with refugees, the UN High Commissioner for Refugees (UNHCR) believes that it must maintain a strictly nonpolitical posture in order to fulfill its mandate of protecting its vulnerable charges. Moreover, the main functions of the UNHCR involve refugees who have already been generated, whereas the proposed Special Representative would focus upon the prevention of future flows. For these reasons, this recommendation deserves careful scrutiny by states concerned about the prospects of future mass expulsions. Those who regard the United Nations system as an unattractive setting for such activities should consider other institutional alternatives that could serve similar purposes.

There need be no illusions as to the prospects of success for such initiatives. An authoritarian and insular government intent upon expelling a despised segment of its population would be unlikely to be deterred even by concerted multilateral measures. What such efforts could do, however, is to raise the international visibility and the political cost of such state actions, which for some might represent a significant deterrent. Even in cases in which the only effective deterrent would be direct military or police action, such initiatives would at least provide advance warning of impending mass exoduses, thereby allowing for better preparation of humanitarian relief for the victims.

Whatever approach is taken, it seems clear enough from the experiences of the past decade that mass expulsions of citizens pose serious threats to peaceful relations among the states involved, and to the human rights of the victims. The prospects for future state actions of this type are disturbingly real, and as such the matter deserves attention at the highest levels of governments and international institutions.

13

PETER H. SCHUCK

Immigration Law
and the Problem
of Community

If the idea of community is "the central concept of politics," as
Carl Friedrich believed,[1] it follows that immigration law is one of
the polity's chief architects. Immigration law prescribes the composition and shape of the political community, and its design inevitably influences future generations. Immigration law seeks to
answer the very first questions that any society must put to itself:
What are we? What do we wish to become? Which individuals can
help us to reach that goal? And most fundamentally: Which in-

This article builds upon an earlier, more comprehensive article, "The Transformation of Immigration Law," 84 *Columbia Law Review* 1 (1984). The author wishes to acknowledge the financial support of the John Simon Guggenheim Memorial Foundation and the useful comments of Owen Fiss, Anthony Kronman, Steve Legomsky, Eugene Rostow, Rogers Smith, and
Judith Thomson on an earlier draft.

dividuals constitute the "we" who shall decide these questions? In the course of answering them, the American community is defined.

A polity like ours asks these questions with an especially intense self-consciousness. We cannot answer them by invoking divine revelation or settled tradition, or by resort to some immanent, organic social principle. Our social ethos demands instead that these questions be addressed through rational argument, felt loyalties, and political choice. Because these are open-ended processes, American society has never satisfactorily or finally answered the questions. Because our values and reality are constantly evolving, it probably never will.

The Conception of Community

The American tradition, deeply rooted in a commitment to individual rights and equal opportunity, properly regards any fixed or exclusive definition of community with profound suspicion. A nation of immigrants cannot easily justify a restrictive immigration policy. Criteria of inclusion and exclusion based upon geographical accidents of birth, contingent events that arbitrarily and inexorably label some individuals as insiders and others as outsiders, run against our grain. To restrict an individual's access to economic opportunity, physical security, and freedom on such grounds is difficult to justify, especially in a world in which the initial distribution of those goods is so unequal.[2] Instead, a thoroughgoing individualism would invite persons to come and go, form attachments, and live according to their own aspirations, respecting the equal right of others to do likewise.

In essence, this conception of community—one embracing all who wish to come and remain here—prevailed in America until the 1880s. Of course, persistent efforts to restrict immigration and even to expel some immigrants who were already here testify to the acidulous nativism that punctuated the Republic's first century. Yet for reasons that were perhaps as much economic as ideological, these efforts ultimately failed. American society was busy populating an empty continent and exploiting its vast, untapped wealth. Immigration meant cheap labor, increased land values, and mass markets for goods. Attracting immigrants to

America became a big business. And in 1886, just as America's borders were beginning to close, the Supreme Court created a permanent constitutional foundation for the individualistic ideal by extending constitutional protection beyond the citizenry to embrace and succor all aliens in the United States.[3]

But the American frontier was closing. The nation turned from agrarian expansion to urban and industrial development, supplanting the social and spatial milieu in which the individualistic ethos had flourished by a set of conditions and attitudes far less congenial to it. An array of exclusionary impulses—class-based opposition to foreign labor, racist animosity toward Asiatics, xenophobic hysteria, religious bigotry, and repression of radical movements in which new immigrants from exotic cultural backgrounds were prominent—challenged this ethos. Industrial America was emerging as a world power with a far-flung empire. Strong, interventionist presidents from McKinley through Wilson mobilized these forces to fashion a burgeoning, aggressive ideology of national dominance.

Immigration law implemented this ideology. In the 1880s, it began for the first time to define a restrictive, *national* community.[4] This definition was at first a dynamic one, as the flood of "new immigrants" prior to World War I attests. But it gradually constricted that community, transforming it from an essentially universalistic one into a kind of close corporation self-consciously molded by Congress. America was now obliged to develop criteria of exclusion.

Predictably, the idea of a community based not upon universal, individualistic values but upon contingent national preferences and interests proved very hard for many to swallow. Earlier idealizations of community—the intimacy of participation in the Greek *polis* or the spiritual unity of a universal religion, for example—were obviously irrelevant to conditions in America. And traditional liberal theory, so closely-linked to American political values, provided no satisfying answers. As articulated by Hobbes and Locke, it essentially viewed society as an artificial contrivance driven by individuals' self-interest, by their need for protection from strangers and from each other. It denied the natural sociability and shared public philosophy that the ancients took to be the fundamental motive and basis of political life.

Indeed, traditional liberalism articulated no real theory of community at all. Its vision of the good society was privatistic not solidaristic; it emphasized acquisitiveness, not common purpose. Unable to stake out a middle ground between the utopian community of all mankind and the ahistorical community of atomized individuals freely contracting in a state of nature, liberalism could not furnish immigration law with a coherent, politically-relevant definition of community. Nativism, never far beneath the surface of American politics, rushed in to fill the vacuum. By the end of World War I, immigration law had acquired a decidedly illiberal, nationalistic character; the exclusion of Asiatics, the national origins quota, and extremely stringent deportation provisions are examples. The latter feature persists in current law.

As America's third century begins, the struggle over the dominant conception of community continues, but it is now being waged in a new legal and political context. Today, large numbers of migrants easily enter United States territory surreptitiously. Once here, they quickly form social and economic attachments that the government cannot readily sever. Open borders, easy citizenship, and equal rights, which raised no special difficulties when government played no significant role in promoting distributional justice, seem more problematic in a society in which politics and public law entitlements are central. When government allocates almost as much wealth—often in the form of public benefits and legal statuses—as the market, when courts have interpreted the Constitution to constrain government's power to pick and choose who shall receive its largesse, and when the duties that most individuals owe to government are (apart from taxation) minimal, the stakes in the definition of community—in inclusion and exclusion—increase markedly.

Finally, aliens find here a legal order whose premises are slowly and subtly shifting from individualistic values, which emphasized the government's conditional consent to entry as the sole source and measure of its legal obligations to aliens, to more open-textured, "communitarian" values, which derive those obligations—and aliens' rights—from more diffuse conditions, such as social relationships, interdependencies, and expectations. Given the tattered state of INS law enforcement, aliens who are here illegally usually cannot be detected and apprehended, much less deported, until they have had a chance to form the kinds of attachments that make it very difficult for the government ever to expel them. The Simpson-Mazzoli legislation, especially the legalization provisions, would ratify this development and might even strengthen the deportable alien's hand.[5]

America, then, faces a poignant predicament. Committed to the rule of law but confronted by millions of individuals who, sociologically and legally speaking, have found community here only after flouting that law, American society cannot easily legitimate their presence. Committed to the moral primacy of mutual consent, a liberal ethos cannot comfortably embrace those who enter and remain by stealth. Committed to universal human rights, liberalism can only secure those rights in the real world through political institutions that can actually implement its values, institutions that for the foreseeable future are those of the *nation*.

But even a liberal nation has powerful propensities to exclude. The very idea of nationhood implies a coherence of shared tradition, experiences, and values—a national community. This community defines itself in ways that are often parochial, exclusionary, and inward-turning; by affirming a core of common commitments, it sets the nation apart from, if not above, the rest of humanity. I am inclined to agree with Michael Walzer's suggestion that this tendency toward closure and boundary-setting is inevitable.[6]

It is also, on balance, desirable. Despite the aggressive, destructive jingoism to which national closure can occasionally lead, the idea of a national community makes the triumph of social justice and individual freedom more likely. Having ordained an activist welfare state that increasingly defines liberty in terms of positive, government-created legal entitlements to at least minimal levels of individual security and well-being, the nation cannot possibly extend these ever-expanding claims against itself to mankind in general. Instead, it must restrict its primary concerns to those for whom it has undertaken a special political responsibility of protection and nourishment, most particularly those who reside within its territorial jurisdiction.[7] Even this more limited task becomes impossible if masses of destitute people, many ill-equipped to live and work in a postindustrial society, may acquire legally enforceable claims against it merely by reaching its borders.

In addition, the nation must often mobilize its people's passions and energies against real or imagined threats, as in wartime or domestic crisis. To accomplish this, powerful emotional appeals to national unity and sacrifice are often necessary. Whether the goal is to implement universal values (e.g., "making the world safe for democracy") or more parochial ones (e.g., "manifest destiny," "the great society"), individual wills must frequently be merged into an almost mystical embodiment of national character and purpose. Paradoxically, then, the nation turns out to be instrumental (though of course not always sufficient) to attaining cherished humanitarian goals. It may even be a *sine qua non*. Certainly, no more effective one has yet been devised.

But there is, of course, a price to be paid. By investing the distinction between insiders and outsiders with moral and political significance, nationalism—the ideal of national community—rejects (or at least subordinates) the humanitarian vision of global community and universal individual rights. The nation represents a competing conception of community that threatens liberal values even as it promises to actualize them (albeit for only a limited portion of humanity).

This tension seems inescapable. Both the universal brotherhood of man enjoying natural rights and the society of strangers linked by little more than the market are too impractical and alienating, and represent too impoverished a view of what our social, psychological, and political natures require, to fully realize our humanity. Both ignore our basic need for what Walzer has called "communities of character, historically stable, ongoing associations of men and women with some special commitment to one another and some special sense of their common life."[8] For the liberal welfare state to enlist the active public support necessary to do its affirmative, individuality-enhancing work, some community that affirms its distinctive nature by excluding at least some individuals for at least some purposes seems essential. The relevant questions for immigration law, then, are how much exclusion this sense of community requires, and upon what basis exclusion can best be justified.

The Changing Character of Immigration Law

Today, unlike in the past, American values rule out certain answers to these questions—exclusion based upon race, for example. In practice and probably in principle, however, these values also permit many possible answers. In immigration law as in other areas of social policy, Congress, the administrative agency, and the federal courts are busy narrowing the range of possibilities, enhancing some while foreclosing others. This transformation of immigration law (as I have elsewhere called it[9]) is tentative and fragmentary but is well worth pondering. It may presage a crucial change, a paradigm shift, in the way in which American society conceives of itself.

From the inception of restrictive immigration law in the 1880s to the early 1980s, American law defined individual and governmental sovereignty very broadly. Individuals' sovereignty was protected through an array of private property rights, including the right to exclude trespassers and those who had entered upon the owner's property with his permission but had then violated the conditions under which the permission was originally granted. Moreover, the owner owed no duty to trespassers, except to refrain from willfully injuring them or using unreasonable force in their expulsion. The owner was ruler over his domain; his home, as the saying goes, was his castle. Governments, for their part, were protected by analogous public property rights, as well as by immunity doctrines that severely limited the claims that could be asserted against them. Tort law imposed few affirmative legal duties toward strangers on either governments or private individuals; in general, their only obligations were those that they had voluntarily undertaken.

Control over which strangers might enter, under what conditions, and with what effect, was viewed as the most fundamental expression of the nation's sovereignty. It was immaterial how desperate strangers were to enter, how much they had invested in getting here, or what reasons prompted the government to refuse them admittance. The government simply owed no legal obligation to those who sought to enter or remain without its explicit consent. Sovereignty thus implied a relationship between government and alien that resembled the relationship that private law then established between landowner and trespasser. The essential purpose of immigration law, like that of property law, was to preserve and enhance this sovereignty.

But the individualistic premises of the legal order did not necessarily require either a restrictive immigration policy or a denial of all alien claims to legal protection. A laissez-faire economy implied a policy of free, unimpeded immigration, essentially the policy maintained in America from the colonial period until the 1880s. American individualism did not merely affirm the primacy of consent as the bedrock of political and juridical relationships, but also located universal human rights in individuals without regard to contingencies of status or condition. Just as the sweeping legal rights of landowners against trespassers recognized an exception for "attractive nuisances," so public international law recognized competing principles that emphasized the state's obligation to protect strangers who were drawn to it.

Immigration law sought to resolve these tensions through a number of overlapping legal doctrines. First, the law excluded certain racial groups; after 1917, it strictly limited admission to those of certain national-ethnic backgrounds. On the other hand, citizenship remained easy to acquire (albeit some citizens—blacks, women, Japanese, and residents of the territories, for example— turned out to be less equal legally and politically than others).[10]

Second, aliens' ability to participate in American life was severely limited. Although they were still entitled to constitutional protection, the Supreme Court construed the Equal Protection Clause to permit governments at all levels to bar lawful resident aliens from public employment, public works jobs, ownership of real property, and many other activities through which political and legal communities customarily express their essential character and unity.[11] The Court held that although the Due Process Clause applied to deportable aliens deprived of liberty, the process that was constitutionally due did not even include a right to a judicial hearing (unless the individual claimed that he or she was an American citizen).[12]

A third legal precept was that in immigration cases, judges should be seen (if absolutely necessary) but not heard. Justice Field penned the classic statement of this position in the infamous *Chinese Exclusion Case:* "If Congress considers the presence of foreigners of a different race in this country, who will not assimilate with us, to be dangerous to its peace and security, . . . its determination is conclusive upon the judiciary."[13] To the contemporary reader, accustomed to lusty assertions of judicial machismo, such self-abnegation may seem a bit fainthearted, especially when applied (as it was in that case) to a measure that combined blatant racism, ex post facto effect, and flagrant denials of due process. Moreover, the Court extended this "special judicial deference" in immigration matters to administrative officials as well as to Congress.[14]

Judicial rhetoric about deference to the "political branches" and to "administrative expertise," of course, is a common, venerable aspect of the courts' protective coloration; ordinarily, it should not be taken too seriously. What is so striking about this rhetoric in immigration cases until very recently, however, is that courts almost invariably meant what they said. With few exceptions, the Supreme Court reflexively confirmed the deference principle by ruling for the government rather than using that principle, as is now commonplace, merely as a disarming prelude to judicial self-assertion. Although the reasons for this extraordinary deference are not altogether clear,[15] I suspect that the ideal of a unified national sovereignty in matters touching upon foreign affairs, an ideal that lay at the heart of classical immigration law, exerted a powerful gravitational force, a compelling metaphorical symbolism, in a constitutional system marked by pronounced political, institutional, and social fragmentation.

Another axiom of classical immigration law was the extra-constitutional status of the exclusion process—the process for determining which aliens may enter the United States for the first time; which ones, having entered previously, may reenter after a significant absence; and which ones may remain after having been "paroled" into the country. Concerning aliens not yet admitted, "the decisions of . . . administrative officers, acting within powers expressly conferred by Congress, are due process of law."[16] Here, at least, the Constitution, not just politics, seemed to stop at the water's edge. Supporting the extra-constitutional exclusion power was the broad authority of the government to detain (i.e., imprison) aliens pending exclusion on the basis of an administrative order and subject to only narrow judicial review.

Together, these two principles have encouraged and legitimated some of the shabbiest governmental conduct toward both aliens and American citizens ever recorded in the annals of the Supreme Court. In one notorious case, the Court allowed the wife of an American citizen who had served in the United States Army and been honorably discharged to be permanently excluded from the United States without *any* administrative hearing. Her exclusion followed an administrative finding that admission would be "prejudicial to the interests of the United States," a finding that was in turn based upon confidential information (unreliable, as it turned out) disclosed neither to the wife, her husband, nor the trial court.[17] In an even more infamous case, the Supreme Court upheld the exclusion and two-year incarceration of one who had been a lawful United States resident for twenty-five years solely on the basis of this same vague standard and extraordinary procedure.[18] (The government having refused to reveal its evidence even to the court, there was of course little for the court to review or say.) All of this was quite consistent with immigration law's traditional view of national sovereignty, which held that the nation could not be obliged against its will to enter into a continuing relationship with anyone but a citizen, except on conditions prescribed by Congress.

Classical immigration law has proved remarkably durable; these McCarthy-era decisions and the *Chinese Exclusion Case,* for example, are still cited with apparent approval by the Supreme Court. Nevertheless, pressures have begun to impinge upon these hoary principles of immigration law, influencing the behavior of courts in important ways. Because other chapters in this book address these pressures at some length, I shall only briefly summarize them, noting their implications for immigration law and America's conception of community.

First, the United States today operates on the world stage with less autonomy than we have enjoyed since becoming a world power. This adjustment in the international balance of power inevitably constrains our immigration policy. Perceptions of interdependence have begun to alter courts' views about national sovereignty and community in subtle ways. In particular, some courts seem to regard the interdependence among nations as a justification for a more permissive stance toward aliens, softening the sharp boundary between government and alien, "us" and "them," that characterized classical immigration law.

Second, economic and political changes in the world have created a more intricate pattern of effects of immigration upon the domestic economy than ever before. The massive illegal migration of recent years from Mexico, Central America, and the Caribbean most dramatically exemplifies the complex relationships between immigration and economic factors. Although these relationships are extremely opaque and controversial, the courts nonetheless are influenced by them in deciding the terms and procedures under which aliens' claims to admission should be determined.

Third, the presence here of an immense population of aliens— conservative estimates place the number at 3.5 million in 1980, with an annual increase of 200,000—who entered or remain illegally undermines classical immigration law on grounds even more fundamental than economics. The central social fact about illegal aliens is this: once they enter, and especially if they decide to remain more or less permanently, they quickly begin to establish significant relationships with individuals and institutions in the locales to which they gravitate. Some bring or are joined by their spouses, others marry here. If they bring children, those children usually attend local schools and acquire American customs; if their children are born here, the children are automatically United States citizens.[19] Virtually all find employment, pay taxes, and have access to certain public benefits. Many establish ties with churches and other voluntary associations. And a substantial proportion will continue to reside in the United States, albeit illegally, for the rest of their lives.

This development poses a monumental challenge to the continued coherence and integrity of classical immigration law. Just as hopelessly porous borders demand a new understanding of national sovereignty, so the steady integration of illegal aliens into our communal life calls into question some traditional legal conceptions. New "social contracts" between these aliens and American society are being negotiated each day and cannot easily be abrogated with invocations of sovereignty, as classically defined. These "contracts" often represent commitments valued not only by aliens who seek legal status but also by the many Americans who benefit from aliens' contributions to our society. On the other

hand, most undocumented aliens have come here illegally or remain in knowing violation of our laws. Their claims on our com-
passion must be assessed in the light of their intentional illegality,
and must also be compared to those of the numerous would-be
immigrants and refugees who wait abroad patiently, often at great
personal cost, for admission through normal legal procedures.
Conventional notions of morality and community, then, simply
cannot adequately capture the complex, ambiguous relationship
between undocumented aliens and American society.

A fourth change concerns the geometric increase in asylum
claims in recent years. Today, the world is teeming with refugees—individuals displaced from their homes and countries by
civil war, persecution, natural disaster, and unimaginable destitu-
tion. There have always been refugees, of course, but the brutality
of modern warfare, the ferocity of political struggle, and the con-
vulsiveness of social and economic changes have vastly enlarged
the scale of displacement and devastation. There were some ten
million refugees in 1982 and the number is probably increasing.
What is truly unprecedented, however, is the number of refugees
who manage to reach American shores to claim asylum, and the
cultures from which they have come.

The flood of asylum claimants, many from pre-modern, agrarian societies, presents immense problems for immigration policy,
revealing in stark terms the conflict between our humanitarian
values and the realpolitik that seems necessary to function in a
dangerous world. The incentives for aliens to claim asylum are
powerful, often overwhelming. The legal standard for asylum is
ambiguous, and the benefits to the alien of the inevitable delay
associated with asylum adjudications are often great (even imprisonment may be preferable to being deported). Filing a claim is
essentially costless to the alien, who thus has much to gain and little to lose by doing so. The social costs, however, are high. The
policies of interdiction and return of potential asylum claimants
on the high seas, and the mass incarceration of asylum claimants
who arrive here—policies that reverse a long-standing, judicially-
ratified preference for admission under parole—raise urgent
legal, moral, and policy issues. They grimly contrast the abstract,
traditional principles of sovereignty, consent-based obligation,
and restrictive national community with palpable, poignant, com-

pelling human claims for protection, the kinds of claims that bureaucracies can usually resist but courts often cannot.

Fifth, far-reaching shifts have occurred in demographic patterns, public attitudes, and political power. Three of these shifts—the rise of Hispanic and Asian Americans as formidable political forces, the concentration of aliens in a small number of politically important states, and the growing public consensus on the need for fundamental change in the immigration system—seem especially significant. As we shall see below, these developments are already affecting legislative and judicial decisions.

In addition to these structural changes, a profound ideological transformation has begun to undermine the individualistic foundations of classical immigration law, especially its core notion that the government owes no legal obligation to aliens apart from those flowing from the terms and conditions upon which it consented to their entry. By conceiving of entry as only a *privilege,* conditioned on an alien's acceptance of the limited claims and inferior status offered by the government, traditional courts hoped to reconcile restrictive nationalism with individualistic values. This "right-privilege" distinction, so familiar to the constitutional lawyers of an earlier day, was a seductive principle through which courts thought to vindicate the dominant ideals of consent, sovereignty and national community.

During the 1960s and 1970s, however, the American legal system outside the immigration field experienced a tidal wave of change, one that is now beginning to wash over immigration law, traditionally a most insular specialty. Elsewhere,[20] I have described this as an incipient movement toward a "communitarian" legal order whose central idea is that legal obligation grows not only out of consensual, willed undertakings, but also out of the larger social and moral contexts in which interactions occur.

In contract law, this idea has led courts to subordinate individualistic liberal values of autonomy and self-determination to communitarian values emphasizing state paternalism and distributive justice. For example, courts now commonly refuse to enforce contracts of adhesion, and often relieve promisors of the consequences of their mistakes. In tort law, an analogous evolution has occurred. Instead of the quite limited duties to strangers imposed by traditional tort law, the entire matrix of social relationships—the expectations, dependencies, and nonmarket values that they generate—has become relevant to the scope and content of legal obligations. Ideals of distributive justice, economic efficiency, social equality, and human dignity have increasingly become explicit criteria of decision. Landlords must now compensate tenants for losses due to crimes perpetuated by third parties on their property. Property owners are obliged to protect trespassers against certain injuries sustained on their premises. Psychiatrists have a duty to protect strangers from assaults by their patients. Novel fiduciary obligations are being extended to new groups, such as insurers, which previously were relatively free to pursue their self-interest in the market.

The same moral ideas and legal consciousness that in private law have narrowed individual sovereignty and expanded duties to strangers have begun to constrict governmental autonomy in public law as well. Two developments are particularly relevant to immigration. In constitutional law, courts have abandoned the old "right-privilege" distinction and now emphasize procedural fairness and equal treatment, precisely the values that classical immigration law tended to depreciate. More generally, courts have expanded the legal rights of many groups, including criminal defendants and convicted prisoners, which are arguably less deserving and needful of special judicial protection than aliens.

As the legal order has increasingly assimilated these communitarian values, immigration law has begun to do so as well. It is important to emphasize at the outset that communitarianism in immigration law is as yet only embryonic, tentative, and fragmentary. Important centers of resistance exist, even within the judiciary.[21] Its ultimate triumph is by no means assured, but it is a development well worth attending to. A number of court cases decided only within the last few years reveal its essential character. Two of the most interesting, both Supreme Court decisions, involve the legal status of undocumented aliens. The first, *Plyler v. Doe*,[22] may ultimately come to have the same epochal significance for those aliens as *Brown v. Board of Education* has had for black and other minority citizens. In *Plyler*, the Court held that by denying undocumented alien children the public education that it extends to legal resident aliens and citizens, Texas violated the Equal Protection Clause. (Lower courts have since extended the

Court's reasoning to subsidized day care and other public services.) And in *Sure-Tan, Inc.* v. *N.L.R.B.*,[23] a case decided in 1984, the Court held that an employer committed an unfair labor practice when it notified the immigration authorities that some of its employees were illegals, thereby weakening a union's organizing efforts. Both decisions, of course, appeal to one's humane instincts; children should not be condemned to blighted lives because of their parents' illegal status, nor should even illegal workers be denied the protection of unions. Moreover, both decisions can be read narrowly—*Plyler* as a federal pre-exemption case; *Sure-Tan* as a case involving simple union-busting tactics.

The Court's approach in these cases, however, may have more far-reaching implications. Most notable is its refusal in either case to take seriously the government's interest—a state in *Plyler,* the federal authorities in *Sure-Tan*—in discouraging illegal immigration. Compared to the strong humanitarian claims of illegal aliens who work, live, and pay taxes here and who seek only the simple justice that legal aliens and citizens take for granted, the government's law enforcement interest would not be given great weight, the Court reasoned, so long as immigration law fails to punish employers of illegal aliens and is ineffectively enforced.

This reasoning has considerable appeal; the "Texas proviso," which now shields employers of illegal aliens from any legal responsibility, is hypocritical and morally indefensible. The Court's reasoning seems less persuasive, however, when one considers the labyrinthine complexity of immigration politics and the diminishing probability that the Court's policy preferences can be implemented. It took thirty-two years for Congress to muster the political will to bring a comprehensive immigration reform bill to a vote; when the extremely fragile, painstakingly-constructed coalition favoring Simpson-Mazzoli failed to win enactment in October 1984, the prospects for effective enforcement largely evaporated. If so, the practical effect of the Court's demanding political standard will have been to admit illegal aliens to the American community, creating a specially-protected group of lawbreakers for the foreseeable future. That they are lawbreakers whose ambition and industry most Americans admire is an irony that only adds to the enforcement problem.

A second constellation of Supreme Court decisions has sub-

stantially obliterated the traditional distinctions, discussed earlier, between the rights of citizens and those of legal resident
aliens—at least under state law. The principal case, *Graham v.
Richardson*,[24] invalidated state laws excluding aliens from welfare
benefits. The Court's theory was that aliens, like blacks, were a
"discrete and insular minority" entitled to special judicial protection. Except for a small, Court-created category of state jobs
that are thought to reflect the state's political self-definition,[25]
Graham's marked solicitude for aliens remains quite sweeping. It
has so defined the American community that the rights of citizens
and non-citizens now differ in only a few respects: the franchise,
access to the narrow category of state jobs described above, and
immunity from deportation. In that sense, the currency of citizenship has been somewhat debased, with consequences for immigration and community that remain uncertain.

A third group of "communitarian" cases, confined thus far to
the lower courts, involves the procedural rights of excludable, undocumented aliens who wish to receive asylum under the Refugee
Act of 1980 but who, because of administrative and judicial delays
in processing their claims, may languish in prison for months or
even years. They have argued that the Due Process Clause and the
Refugee Act guarantee them release from detention and extensive
procedural protections, including advance notice of the right to apply for asylum. Some lower courts, noting that an alien's interest
in personal freedom and in protection against persecution in the
home country are very great, have responded sympathetically to
these arguments, sometimes conferring rights (e.g., to free legal
counsel) that even exceed those enjoyed by American citizens and
legal resident aliens.[26] Although some appellate courts are resist-
ing this trend and the law remains in flux,[27] such cases create
enormous pressures on courts and on public opinion to enlarge the
community to include these aliens.

Finally, some of the Simpson-Mazzoli compromise bill's provisions, if enacted by a future Congress, will further propel the
slowly-gathering movement toward judicially-defined communitarian values. This is most obviously true of the legalization
provisions, but it applies as well to the doubling of immigration
quotas for Mexico and Canada, the improvement of asylum procedures, and some other changes. If adopted, the legalization pro-

gram will probably not attract most illegal aliens and in any event will be extremely difficult to administer effectively. Nevertheless, its unmistakeable premise is that the traditional legal concept of community should be redefined to conform to the far broader sociological idea of community, based upon the reality of existing relationships, interdependencies, and expectations. To be sure, other provisions of Simpson-Mazzoli, most notably employer sanctions and summary exclusion procedures, point in the opposite direction; the former, however, probably cannot be effectively enforced while the latter, when coupled with the Refugee Act and the constitutional guarantee of habeas corpus, will provide courts with ample opportunities to expand those procedures in the interest of a more communitarian legal order.

The Emerging Ideal of Community: Some Hard Questions and Uncertain Answers

A more communitarian immigration law promises to more closely align our practice in defining the American community with our rhetoric and humanitarian ideals. To recognize that our duties to strangers can arise out of social interactions, understandings, and expectations that are not yet, and may never be, codified in the Immigration and Nationality Act is only to acknowledge that social attitudes and legal doctrine are perpetually in flux. As a society, our views on immigration and the nature of American community have changed before; one thinks immediately of the end of open immigration in the 1880s and the abandonment of the national origins quota system in 1965. Those views may now be changing again. The same social and external forces that have weakened the hold of individualistic values on American law in so many other areas can be expected to alter the ideology of immigration and community formation as well. If so, these changes may be nothing more than way-stations on the continuing, creative journey of American self-definition.

Still, a communitarian immigration law provides some grounds for concern. The notions of social relationship, expectation, and interdependency that will be increasingly invoked to modulate, if not define, a more communitarian society's obligations to strangers are, to say the very least, exceedingly vague. (The troublesome legal standard for deciding asylum cases—"well-founded fear of persecution"—is crystal clear by comparison.) These notions are also perilously circular; the idea of "social expectation" surely imports some idea of *legitimate* expectation, which merely raises anew the question of how one can legitimately expect relief that the law does not now grant. Similarly, relationships forged in defiance of the law may not be entitled to the same respect as others. Once society's duty to aliens is no longer moored to the traditional norms of consent by the government and compliance by the alien with established legal procedures, the legal order is cast adrift upon a sea whose ungovernable tides may carry it to realms unknown, unimagined, and fraught with dangers.

The problem is not simply one of a limited American capacity to assimilate newcomers. Our history, including the recent and largely successful absorption of almost one million Vietnamese refugees, testifies eloquently to the greatness and durability of that assimilative capacity, but it is not inexhaustible. Moreover, the conditions of a postindustrial society may make the effort to assimilate masses of migrants from premodern (sometimes, as in the case of the Hmong tribesmen, preliterate) societies far more problematic that it has been in the past.

On the other hand, it is important to recall that by historical standards, the number of new immigrants that even the more generous proposals for expanded admissions envision is quite small as a proportion of the population. (The effects of expanded admissions on the incentives for additional migration is a separate, more difficult question.) More than 14 percent of the United States population in 1910 was foreign born compared to less than 5 percent in 1970. (Although these figures do not count illegal migrants, their inclusion would raise the total by only 1 or 2 percentage points.) In 1980, eight other industrialized countries had a higher percentage of foreign born than the United States did.[28] Moreover, our population is aging rapidly, current fertility rates are quite low, and labor shortages loom. In short, the prospect of even several million more immigrants joining a nation of 236 million people should be cause for eager celebration, not alarm.

Although the number of new immigrants under discussion is unlikely in itself to create serious difficulties (again, setting aside the question of the future incentive effects of easier entry), four other risks of a more communitarian immigration law cannot be so easily dismissed. First, there is a danger that it will encourage further social and cultural fragmentation, intergroup hostility, and political conflict, and that these developments may impair at some point the quality of American democracy. To endure and flourish, a polity as pluralistic as ours must maintain a core of common values, public symbols, and social commitments; it must develop and preserve a communal memory and vision of the future that can contain the chaotic centrifugal force exerted by new pressures and events; it must be able to guide that force into politically-creative channels.

A common public language is an extremely valuable, though perhaps not indispensable, instrument for sustaining the necessary political and cultural cohesion. Linguistic diversity has always characterized American life but perhaps never so much as now when the ethnic mix of immigrants is far greater than under the old national origins quota system. School systems in California and New York must now offer instruction in literally dozens of languages. Some forms of bilingual education are said to retard English acquisition by Hispanic students, although this claim is extremely controversial.[29] Ease of transportation between the United States and many countries of origin may have reduced somewhat the incentives for aliens to learn English and to commit themselves irreversibly to American society. The effects of all this on social and political cohesion must remain in the realm of speculation but the question clearly is of the utmost importance. The chronic, corrosive discord between English-speaking and French-speaking Canadians, while different in important respects from the American situation, is a haunting reminder of the power of language to fragment, as well as fuse, a people.[30]

A more open, communitarian immigration policy might also intensify political conflict between ethnic groups, as each jockeyed for a larger share of the increased quota. In some cases, such as the Cubans in Miami, large concentrations of aliens may stretch racial tensions to the breaking point, yet a self-conscious policy of dispersion would surely be morally objectionable and prove ineffective due to uncontrollable secondary migration. (An estimated 60 percent of the refugees who have come from Southeast Asia since 1970 live in only forty counties.[31]) These concentrations can place severe burdens on local public services, especially hospitals, exacerbating conflict between needy groups. Some 75 percent of the births in Los Angeles public hospitals are said to be to children of illegal aliens. Contrary to frequent suggestions that few illegal aliens seek welfare benefits—suggestions usually based upon a careless use of an earlier study[32]—there is some evidence that a high proportion of illegal aliens (relative to the general population) actually receive such benefits.[33] A careful analysis by the Los Angeles County Department of Public Social Services found that on 17,684 occasions in 1979, illegal aliens sought welfare benefits but did not get past the initial screen; if they had made it through and been paid at average benefit levels, they would have received over $58 million per year. (No estimate was made of the number who successfully penetrated the screen and got onto the rolls.)[34]

It must be emphasized that these data are inconclusive and quite controversial. They also fail to consider the significant tax revenues generated by this activity.[35] They remind us, however, that the politics of the welfare state is preeminently a politics of group struggle in which needy groups desperately compete with each other for a larger share of an already small pie. (Indeed, in recent years, that pie—the so-called "safety net" programs—has actually shrunk slightly in real terms, and may shrink even more during Reagan's second term.[36]) A bitter political struggle that pits poor blacks against, say, newly-arrived Salvadorans or Laotians can hardly be expected to enhance a sense of community or encourage a warm welcome to newcomers.

Such a struggle is also unlikely to produce a larger pie. This suggests a second risk, related to the first: a communitarian immigration law might reduce the sense of social solidarity that seems politically necessary to sustain the redistributive agenda of an effective welfare state. Suppose that the studies showing high utilization of welfare by aliens were confirmed (or even if false, were nevertheless widely publicized and believed). There is reason to anticipate that political backlash against aliens, poor people, and welfare programs generally would be severe and heavy-handed, perhaps resulting in indiscriminate curtailment of programs that benefit the poor. Such a reaction, for which there is much precedent, might easily produce new and even more objectionable distributional inequities than now exist.

This grim scenario is not at all implausible; it is being played out in some local communities today. Two inescapable realities must be borne in mind. First, a successful redistributive politics must be premised on a pervasive communitarian ethos in which the politically dominant middle class views the poor in some important sense as part of an extended social family sharing a common destiny. Second, most humans find it difficult to conceive of strangers as extended family in this sense unless they are linked to them in some more or less palpable, credible way. As those ties become more attenuated, as our commonalities dwindle and become more theological or abstract ("we are all brothers under the skin"), the extended family analogy begins to lose its mythic, moral power over us, the power to elicit fraternal, altruistic feelings ("there, but for the grace of God, go I").

The point at which diversity erodes that moral sense of community, of course, is ultimately an empirical question. In some African and Asian societies, altruism probably peaks at the level of the tribe or clan. In a liberal, postindustrial society like ours, altruism appears to continue to a somewhat higher level, and in a small ethnically and religiously homogeneous society like Sweden with a strong socialist tradition, those feelings seem to embrace virtually the entire society. The important point, however, is that a limit does exist. That we may be approaching that limit is perhaps suggested by evidence such as the exclusion of aliens from many federal welfare programs and the low numerical ceiling on refugee admissions. A more communitarian immigration could press against, and might even breach, that limit.

A third risk relates to the courts' role in defining the boundaries of this community. As I suggested earlier, the recent movement toward a more communitarian immigration law has been essentially a judicial project. To some extent, this reflects Congress' understandable failure, in enacting the Refugee Act of 1980, to anticipate the flood of asylum claims, often raising difficult constitutional issues, that immediately ensued in the wake of several convulsive developments: the Mariel boatlift from Cuba, increased Haitian migration, and explosive civil wars in Central America. In part, however, it also reflects judicial impatience, even disgust, with the political-administrative process that ordinarily prevails in immigration matters.

Although this judicial reaction is perfectly understandable and in some cases warranted, it raises some troubling questions. First, the judicial tools that are available for improving this process—primarily the Refugee Act, and the Equal Protection and Due Process Clauses—are crude, have a short reach, and may even prove counterproductive. The Equal Protection Clause insists that when government acts, it must treat similarly-situated individuals and groups alike. Except at the extremes (e.g., classifications purely on the basis of race), this principle does not enable a court to tell when they are similarly-situated; it does not indicate which differences between individuals and groups government policy may properly take into account. In some areas, courts have been able to devise "neutral" criteria to answer this question; thus in employment discrimination cases, "job-relatedness" has been used to evaluate tests that produce disparate impacts on different groups. For immigration policy, however, any criteria must be irreducibly political in the best sense of the word, reflecting value choices and policy considerations in which general principles—the courts' stock in trade—usually (and properly) play little part.

The Due Process Clause and the Refugee Act might seem to envision an important role for courts in insisting upon fair procedures for deciding aliens' claims for admission and legal status. This view, however, ignores some serious difficulties that courts cannot readily resolve. Additional procedures (which is what "due process" usually means) entail additional delays in processing aliens; in reality, these delays imply two consequences: protracted imprisonment for some people who, although not entitled to be here, have committed no crime, and protracted freedom for others, also in illegal status, who can then live, work, and "build equities" here, making their eventual deportation very difficult to accomplish. The first consequence means human suffering on a large scale, the second means a breakdown in the immigration enforcement system that not only discredits that system but surely encourages others to try their luck at beating it, thereby exacerbating the problem. Such lamentable results, which accurately describe the current immigration enforcement situation,[37] would write an ironic epilogue to the communitarian project. They would confirm the reality that the courts have only a limited purchase on this complex administrative system. With the best of intentions but the weakest of levers, courts may only succeed in making a bad situation even worse.

A fourth risk is that a more communitarian immigration law, by loosening America's control over her borders, may weaken her control over the evolution of the nation's own character and destiny. When courts wielding some conception of communitarian values empower strangers unilaterally to create and enforce substantial claims against American society, our process of self-definition is seriously impeded. If American society's power to define its common purposes and obligations is hostage to the power of strangers to cross our borders undetected and, by acquiring attachments here, to pre-empt our government's definitional choice, then our capacity to pursue some collective vision—to decide as a society what we wish to be—may be critically impaired. Whether we decide to encourage more immigrants or fewer, to admit aliens with or without regard to their occupational skills, to make asylum easier or more difficult to obtain, or to offer amnesty to illegal aliens, the more fundamental point is not one of policy but of political autonomy and competence: we must retain the power to make such choices collectively and self-consciously, and we must mobilize the will and resources to enable our government to enforce them.

VI

Conclusion

14

NATHAN GLAZER

Conclusion

In 1924 the gates to the United States were in effect closed to all but Europeans from the British Isles and Northwest Europe; in 1965 this preference was lifted, and the gates were widened. Immigration today is far from reaching the volume, as a percentage of the American population, that it attained before World War I. However, in absolute numbers, it is not far short of that peak. In impact on given areas of the country, it rivals the age of mass European immigration. In 1985 the United States continues to debate future policy over immigration, and dissatisfaction with the combination of present law and present reality is almost universal.

Only a few free-market enthusiasts and libertarians insist, "if it isn't broken, don't fix it." They claim there is nothing that should concern us in the present situation. The immigrants clearly come in search of work, not welfare (even if many start on welfare and many others end up on it for longer or shorter periods of time). It is doubtful that, using narrow measures of costs and benefits (charges on public services, contributions to taxes), immigrants cost more than they contribute. The history of America's absorption of vast numbers of immigrants of diverse religion, language, and race suggests it will do the same with the new immigrants. Why worry?

Yet the United States is worried. Enlightened opinion resists some of the reasons for worry as chauvinistic and benighted. There has been a long tradition of antagonism to immigrants in the United States. Yet present concerns draw hardly at all from this tradition. They are not nativistic or prejudiced, do not speak, as Senator Pat McCarran did thirty years ago, of "hard-core, indigestible blocs" in the American mixture. Indeed, those with the greatest concern over immigration are less worried about groups as distant culturally as the Vietnamese or the Asian Indians or the Koreans than they are about groups of Christian religion and European language, such as the Mexicans.

Why then the concern? Why the urgency with which so many feel a policy must be designed and implemented that truly controls immigration in the light of national interests?

I would argue that there are four legitimate sources of concern that make it necessary for us to continue to work towards a new and effective immigration policy.

The first is procedural: here is an area of public policy in which national decisions embodied in law are not working effectively. That immigration laws and enforcement measures no longer control a substantial part of immigration should concern us, whether we believe there should be more or less immigration, of one or another type. It should concern us as much as the failure of the Volstead Act to control the manufacturing and distribution and sale of alcoholic beverages in the 1920s, or the failure of our judicial system to adequately repress burglary and robbery, assault and murder, today. Law should be seen to be just and to be effective. When it fails on either score, disrespect for law spreads and the effectiveness of government declines.

The other reasons are substantive. Even if the present volume of immigration does not raise great and insuperable problems, it is all too easy to see circumstances in which this would change. Law must be in place, enforcement measures must be effective enough, to enable a response to a rise in immigration if it is generally held to be too high and comprised of people we do not want. We have already received the product of a number of mass expulsions.

Some of them, to our distress, have included large numbers of criminals and the mentally disordered. It is unfortunately not the case that every inhabitant who is ejected from a totalitarian or authoritarian country is a worthy and heroic figure. It is not easy to see in general how our immigration policy can deal with expulsions; Michael Teitelbaum in his article in this book has made some suggestions. But expulsions are enough of a possibility to lead us to be doubtful of a purely laissez-faire policy.

Further, immigration is dependent on the creation of channels of information and opportunity. These channels have now been dug deeply to connect us with Mexico and other Latin American countries, and with many countries of Asia. They barely exist as yet to connect us to Africa. There are many countries that do not yet participate in any major way in immigration to the United States. This may change—indeed, it will. It is the nature of channels of immigration to become deeper and wider: the first few immigrants provide information as to difficulties and opportunities, and create in time the legal ability, as resident aliens and as citizens, to bring in larger and larger numbers of relatives. The movement is upward, and both the failures and successes of the non-European world set in motion processes that may lead to immigration to the United States. (Note that South Korea and Taiwan and Hong Kong, despite their incredible economic growth, provide large numbers of immigrants.) At some point the volume of immigration, on the basis of present law, owing to the preferences given to relatives, will raise questions; certainly the level of illegal immigration raises questions already. How a policy is to be devised that brings together a majority of the population and Congress, and how it is to be enforced, are discussed in the preceding essays. But the conclusion must be that a policy must be devised and enforced. In its absence one can envisage, at the extremes, swings of opinion in favor of restriction and expulsion, which would give free rein to the illiberal and xenophobic impulses that once dominated immigration policy, or an incapacity of political processes to devise any policy at all.

A third consideration: immigrants, for the most part, are considered by American laws "minorities," on the basis of the experience of prejudice and discrimination to which earlier members of their group were once subject in the United States. While we add to the number of our minorities by Hispanic and Asian immigration and to some extent black immigration, which may increase, we are still trying to deal with the difficult problems raised by minorities of long standing on the American continent, who suffer from poor education, poor jobs, low income, and a variety of social problems. One of the chief questions that must concern us in considering the volume and socioeconomic character of new immigration is how it affects older minorities. The answer is not a simple one, as the essays by Muller and Briggs demonstrate. Yet at some point it would seem immigration must affect the opportunities of earlier minorities with longer established and more legitimate claims on American polity. To insist that immigration can never affect their interests adversely is the response of a Pollyanna, rather than a sober analyst of American society. We must consider in immigration policy claims of greater or lesser merit. Certainly, a potentially adverse impact on the interests of minorities is an issue we must take seriously, not only because of moral and political obligation, but also because one can envisage a heightening of internal discord and conflict as newer immigrants surpass older minorities in income and the quality of jobs.

Finally, our immigration laws express our values. Our failure to develop and implement an effective immigration policy means that these values, whatever they may be, go by the board. There have been a number of values set forward as a basis for immigration policy. One is that free-market principles, in people as well as goods, should dominate, and the best of all possible worlds will ensue if we exercise the least control. Is that truly so? Do our black and minority populations agree with that? Are those concerned to create a floor of decent labor conditions and reasonable income convinced of that?

Perhaps this is the best policy—but it should be decided upon rather than accepted because we can decide on nothing else. Others argue that the increase of population reduces the quality of our lives and that we have a right to maintain that quality, even if other countries have denser populations and poorer qualities of life. Is this really the impact of population growth? And what are our obligations to those who are worse off? We accept the humanitarian obligation to feed them when their crops fail. What further obligation in spreading the wealth and good fortune of what is still on the whole a well-off and fortunate land do we wish to accept?

Our present immigration laws accept as values the reunification of families—and raise the question of how far the rights of reunification should extend—and a special obligation to refugees. They make a modest bow to persons with occupations in short supply. This seems like a reasonable set of decisions to many. But if they are not enforced, will it not be the case that those who have entered on the basis of no effective enforcement as to whom we shall welcome, but on the basis of their own enterprise, will in effect usurp the places of others we consider worthier and more desirable? It seems unlikely that the American people—taking into account the work of their recent study groups, commissions, the Congress—will feel comfortable with a rate of immigration much beyond the 600,000 a year we now take in. In granting entry as a permanent resident, we grant what is a desirable privilege, one in short supply when compared with those who want it. Do we take our values seriously enough to embody in law to whom we wish to grant this privilege, and to implement that law so it works? Are we capable politically of doing so? If we do not, what consequences may we expect—and fear? These are the questions the current impasse on immigration policy requires us to answer.

Notes
Contributors

NOTES

1. Nathan Glazer: "Introduction"

1. *Statistical Abstract of the United States, 1984,* 104th Edition, (Washington, D.C.: U.S. Department of Commerce, Bureau of the Census, 1983).

2. U.S. Congress, Senate, Committee on the Judiciary, *The Immigration Systems of the United States,* 81st Congress, 2nd session, 1950, S.Rept. 1515, p. 455. Reprinted from David M. Reimers, "Recent Immigration Policy—An Analysis," in Harry R. Chiswick, ed., *The Gateway: U.S. Immigration Issues and Policies* (Washington, D.C.: American Enterprise Institute, 1982).

3. Reimers.

4. (U.S. Congress, House, Subcommittee No. 1 of the Committee on the Judiciary, *Immigration: Hearings,* 88th Congress, 2nd Session, 1964, p. 418. Reprinted from Reimers, p. 35.)

5. Elliott Abrams and Franklin S. Abrams, "Immigration Policy—Who Gets In and Why?," *The Public Interest,* No. 38 (Winter, 1975).

6. "Immigration and the Randomness of Ethnic Mix," *New York Times,* October 3, 1984.

7. *U.S. Immigration Policy and the National Interest.* The Final Report and Recommendations of the Select Commission on Immigration and Refugee Policy to the Congress and President of the United States, March 1, 1981, (Washington, D.C.: U.S. Government Printing Office).

2. Lawrence H. Fuchs: "The Search for a Sound Immigration Policy: A Personal View"

1. Henry Taub in Chemistry, S. Chandras Ekhar in Physics, and Gerard Debreu in Economics.

2. Chapter VI, "Doing Well by Doing Good—The Impact of Legal Immigration on the United States," in *U.S. Immigration Policy and the National Interest,* Staff Report of the Select Commission on Immigration and Refugee Policy, April 30, 1981, Supplement to the *Final Report and Recommendations of the Select Commission on Immigration and Refugee Policy,* pp. 271–278, April 1981.

3. *U.S. Immigration Policy and the National Interest, the Final Report and Recommendations of the Select Commission on Immigration and Refugee Policy to the Congress and the President of the United States,* March 1, 1981.

4. See U.S. Department of State, Agency for International Cooperation/International Development Cooperation Agency, "Impact of Development Assistance, Trade, and Investment Programs on Migration Pressures in Major Sending Countries," Paper prepared for the Select Commission on Immigration and Refugee Policy, Washington, DC, U.S. Department of State, 1980; also see Larry Neal, "Interrelationships of Trade and Migration—Lessons from

Europe," Paper prepared for the Select Commission on Immigration and Refugee Policy, Ur-
bana-Champaign, August 15, 1980; also see Louka T. Katseli Papaefstratiou, "Trade Flows
and Factor Mobility," Paper presented for the Select Commission on Immigration and Refugee
Policy, New Haven, Yale University, August 1980; and Nell W. Temple, "Migration and
Development: A Preliminary Survey of the Available Literature," Paper prepared for the
Select Commission on Immigration and Refugee Policy, Washington DC, Overseas Development Council, July 1980.

5. Jacob S. Seigel, Jeffrey S. Passell, and J. Gregory Robinson, "Preliminary Review of Existing Studies of the Number of Illegal Residents in the United States." Paper prepared as a
working documents for the use of the Select Commission on Immigration and Refugee Policy,
January 1980, pp. 18, 19.

6. John Kenneth Galbraith, Public Hearing before Select Commission on Immigration and
Refugee Policy, Boston, Massachusetts, November 19, 1979.

7. "Staff Report of the Select Commission on Immigration and Refugee Policy, April 30,
1984," *U.S. Immigration Policy and the National Interest,* Supplement to the Final Report and
Recommendations of the Select Commission on Immigration and Refugee Policy, pp. 101–108.

8. Letter from Joyce Reitter, Oakland, California, from the letter file, Select Commission
on Immigration and Refugee Policy papers, National Archives.

9. Testimony of Perry Ellsworth, Executive Vice President, National Council of
Agricultural Employers, at the Baltimore hearing of the Select Commission on Immigration
and Refugee Policy, October 29, 1979.

10. For a history of temporary worker programs, see Congressional Research Service, "Temporary Worker Programs: Background and Issues," prepared for the Senate Judiciary Committee at the request of the Select Commission on Immigration and Refugee Policy, February
1980.

11. For a full discussion of some of this testimony and other material on exclusion, see the
Staff Report of the Select Commission on Immigration and Refugee Policy, April 30, 1981, *U.S.
Immigration Policy and the National Interest,* supplement to the Final Report and Recommen-
dations of the Select Commission on Immigration and Refugee Policy, pp. 754 ff.

12. The INS information, adjudication, and naturalization programs are generally thought
of as service, while the border patrol, anti-smuggling, investigations, and detention and deportation functions are enforcement in nature. The inspections function is in a gray area with
respect to both service and enforcement, because it involves both the admission and denial of
entry by aliens.

3. Harris N. Miller: "The Right Thing to Do": A History of Simpson-Mazzoli

1. In only one campaign in the last few years did immigration become a central issue—the
Democratic Senatorial primary in Texas in the spring of 1984. Congressman Kent Hance (D.-
Texas), considered a long shot in a three person race, came out strongly against legalizing illegal immigrants, and managed to finish second in a very close race. In the runoff election required under Texas law whenever no candidate receives a first ballot majority, Hance was narrowly defeated as he once again attacked legalization. Hance later formed an alliance against
Simpson-Mazzoli with some Hispanic leaders, though the Hispanics strongly supported a very
generous legalization law.

2. *U.S. Select Commission on Immigration and Refugee Policy: U.S. Immigration Policy and
the National Interest* (Washington, D.C.: U.S. Government Printing Office, 1981)—hereinafter
referred to as *Select Commission.*

3. Many argue that because of the disparity between the economic situation in the U.S. and
Mexico and other emigration-prone countries to our south and because of the general ease of

international travel, no legislation can stem the "push factor" which sends people to our country. Also, due to the nature of the U.S. labor market, American employers will always need illegal immigrants, so the "pull factor" which brings people here cannot be ended either. See, for instance, Edwin Harwood, "Can Immigration Laws Be Enforced?" *Public Interest,* No. 72 (Summer, 1983), pp. 107–123, who argues that we should accept the fact that foreigners will come here to work, and hence the issue is how best to regulate the flow, not how to stop it.

4. The lexicon of immigration can be confusing. In this analysis, the focus is on those who enter the country legally to live here permanently—permanent resident aliens—and those who enter the country illegally or who enter legally for a temporary period and then overstay their authorized period of admission—illegal immigrants. I am not talking about those who come here temporarily for business or pleasure and then return home (nonimmigrants); those who are admitted to the country legally having fled persecution in their homeland (refugees); or those who enter the country either legally as nonimmigrants or those who enter illegally and claim they have suffered from persecution (asylees). Also, periodically, the Executive Branch creates classifications that do not exist in the law—such as the Cubans and Haitians who entered in 1980, who are called "Cuban-Haitian entrant/status pending."

5. Some recent analyses, such as that by Thomas Muller, *The Fourth Wave: California's Newest Immigrants* (Washington, D.C.: The Urban Institute Press, 1984) indicate that illegal immigrants have a different impact on the private than on the public sector. They take more from the government in terms of benefits than they give in the form of taxes, but they help the private sector grow and become more profitable, which assists the entire economy.

6. Pleased with their activities in "Operation Wetback," the INS declared in its annual report for 1955, "The so-called 'wetback' problem no longer exists.... The border has been secured." The organization has never repeated that false claim again.

7. For a good analysis of illegal immigrant smuggling, see John Crewdson, *The Tarnished Door* (New York: Times Books, 1983), Ch. 2.

8. Simpson and Mazzoli both emphasize that they have created a "legalization" program, not an "amnesty." The major difference is that "legalization" sets up specific criteria that an applicant must meet to be given legal status, while "amnesty" connotes the mere requirement of application. In popular usage, legalization and amnesty have been interchanged, though I use the term legalization.

9. *Select Commission,* p. 3.

10. Simpson and Mazzoli always tried to negotiate with interest groups, and sometimes they were able to get the support of even strong opponents when certain changes were made in the bill. The Chamber of Commerce supported the House Judiciary Committee—passed bill, but decided to oppose it again when the full House removed a committee amendment it wanted, which limited the record keeping requirements for small businesses as part of the employer sanctions. Some of the large agricultural groups supported the House bill on final passage after the House adopted the temporary worker amendment for which they lobbied so hard. Organized labor was for and against the bill at various times depending on which amendments were included. Some organizations representing large businesses, such as the Business Roundtable, supported the bill because they believed that it was in the public interest and that the employer sanctions would not adversely affect them.

4. Edwin Harwood: "How Should We Enforce Immigration Law?"

1 Bureau of the Census demographers Robert Warren and Jeffrey S. Passel have established a reasonably firm lower bound estimate of two million illegal aliens of all nationalities. See "Estimates of Illegal Aliens From Mexico Counted in the 1980 United States Census," (Paper delivered at the annual meeting of the Population Association of America, Pittsburgh, April 14-16, 1983), p. 12. For a discussion of the many efforts that have been made to count the

illegal population along with the methodological difficulties of arriving at a reliable estimate, see Arthur F. Corwin, "The Numbers Game: Estimates of Illegal Aliens in the United States, 1970–1981," *Law and Contemporary Problems* 45, No. 2 (Spring, 1982), pp. 223–284.

2. See Edwin Harwood, "Alienation: American Attitudes Toward Immigration," *Public Opinion,* June/July, 1983, pp. 49–51.

3. United States Department of Justice, Immigration and Naturalization Service, Report of Deportable Aliens Found in U.S., FY 1983, G-23.18.

4. In FY 1983, about 40,000 aliens with visitors visas and 6,500 with student visas were apprehended. This is very likely only a small percentage of the number of visitors and students who overstay or work without authorization ("visa abusers"). Because of record keeping deficiencies, INS has had difficulty determining the number of visitors who leave at the time their visas expire. See John Crewdson, *The Tarnished Door: The New Immigrants and the Transformation of America* (New York: The New York Times Book Co., Inc., 1983), p. 31 and 136.

5. The notable exception was the study by David S. North and Jennifer R. Wagner, "Enforcing the Immigration Law: A Review of the Options," (Prepared for Select Commission on Immigration and Refugee Policy, Washington, D.C., June, 1980.)

6. See Edwin Harwood, "Arrests Without Warrant: The Legal and Organizational Environment of Immigration Law Enforcement," *U.C. Davis Law Review,* Vol. 17, No. 2 Winter, 1984, pp. 520–525.

7. See Michael S. Teitelbaum, "Political Asylum in Theory and Practice," in *The Public Interest,* No. 76 Summer, 1984, pp. 74–86. Also Edwin Harwood, "The Crisis in Immigration Policy," *Journal of Contemporary Studies,* Vol. VI, No. 4 (Fall, 1983), pp. 47–52.

8. Peter H. Schuck, "The Transformation of Immigration Law," *Columbia Law Review,* Vol. 84, No. 1, January, 1984, pp. 1-90. However, recent Supreme Court decisions as well as some important Circuit Court decisions during 1984 suggest a trimming of the sails and a more conservative tack.

In addition, it is very difficult to assess the *net* impact of many court decisions on INS resources. Thus, decisions which require INS to release political asylum claimants being held for exclusion or deportation hearings may create further incentives to illegal entry among those still abroad. Yet at the same time they also reduce detention costs to INS, at least in the short run.

9. I provide a more extensive discussion of the legal, political and resource constraints affecting INS interior enforcement in my manuscript *In Liberty's Shadow: Illegal Aliens and Immigration Law Enforcement* (forthcoming, Hoover Institution Press).

10. See Harwood, "Arrests Without Warrant," pp. 540–543.

11. U.S. Department of Justice, Immigration and Naturalization Service FY 1985 Authorization and Budget Request for the Congress, January 20, 1984, p. 17.

12. Very few employers have been prosecuted under state laws barring the employment of illegal aliens. When there have been successful prosecutions, the fines have been trivial. Wayne A. Cornelius, "Simpson-Mazzoli vs. The Realities of Mexican Immigration," in *America's New Immigration Law: Origins, Rationales, and Potential Consequences,* ed. Wayne A. Cornelius and Ricardo Anzaldua Montoya, (San Diego, Center for U.S.-Mexican Studies, 1983), Monograph Series, 11, pp. 142–143.

13. As a number of commentators have pointed out, INS would face numerous difficulties in trying to enforce employer sanctions. See Wayne A. Cornelius, pp. 139–149.

A study by the General Accounting Office also found employer sanctions laws in other countries to be ineffective deterrents to illegal immigration. "Information on the Enforcement of Laws Regarding Employment of Aliens in Selected Countries," Report by the U.S. General Accounting Office, August 31, 1982.

14. *Congressional Record—House,* June 20, 1984, pp. H 6166–6170.

15. Nor are these the only problems. I have examined other problems that INS is likely to confront in trying to enforce employer sanctions in another article. Among other things, tough enforcement by INS will not, in sharp contrast to other regulatory agencies that monitor employers, be strongly supported by the public. Without post-passage backing from unions or other watchdog groups, INS' employer sanctions effort could be subject to the same harrassment that has been directed against its Area Control operations. See Edwin Harwood, "Enforcing the Immigration Law: Now and After Simpson-Mazzoli," in *In Defense of the Alien*, Vol. VII, ed. Lydio F. Tomasi (New York: Center for Migration Studies, forthcoming).

16. See Harwood, "Arrests Without Warrant," pp. 536–539.

17. For a brief review of how litigation over amnesty might develop, see Thomas Heller and Robert A. Olson, "Legal Dilemmas in the Amnesty Provisions of the Simpson-Mazzoli Bill," in Cornelius, *America's New Immigration Law: Origins, Rationales and Potential Consequences*, pp. 115–121.

18. The case management system was instituted in mid-1983. It directs the criminal investigators of the Investigations Branch to give higher priority to serious INA violators as well as to other case investigations (for example dual action cases) that are more apt to lead to successful enforcement outcomes. See U.S. Department of Justice, Immigration and Naturalization Service, *Investigations Case Management System*, July 1, 1983.

19. David S. North and Jennifer R. Wagner proposed a slightly different version of this idea several years ago. They suggested that aliens entering on nonimmigrant visas be required to purchase non-refundable round-trip tickets. "Enforcing the Immigration Law: A Review of the Options," (A report prepared for the Selection Commission on Immigration and Refugee Policy, June 1980), p. 32.

5. Rodolfo O. de la Garza: "Mexican Americans, Mexican Immigrants, and Immigration Reform"

1. Octavio Paz, *Labarinto de la Soledad* (Mexico, D.F.: Fonda de cultura Economica, 1959); Oscar Martinez, *Border Boom Town: Ciudad Juarez Since 1848* (Austin: University of Texas Press, 1978), pp. 106-108, discusses Mexican attitudes toward Chicanos. The quotation from the undocumented worker is in Eugene Nelson, Compiler, *Pablo Cruz and the American Dream: The Experience of an Undocumented Immigrant from Mexico* (Salt Lake City: Peregrine Smith, 1975). The definition of "pocho" is from Enrique Hank Lopez is quoted in Arturo Madrid-Barela, "Pochos: The Different Mexicans, An Interpretative Essay," Part I, *Aztlan*, Vol. 7, 1 (Spring, 1976), p. 51.

2. For a discussion of Mexican American reactions to Mexico see Enrique Hank Lopez, "Back to Bachimba," in Edwin Ludwig and James Santibanez, eds. *The Chicano: Mexicano-American Voices* (Baltimore: Penguin, 1971), pp. 261–70; Carlos Morton, "Mexican Diary, 1954–1977;" in *Nuestro* (April 1978), pp. 34–35; Rodolfo O. de la Garza, "A Chicano Perspective of Mexico," paper presented at Border Studies Cultural Institute, University of Texas at El Paso, 1975.

3. Thanks to the efforts of Jorge Bustamante, in recent years Mexicans have slowly become more understanding and accepting of Chicanos. See Carlos Vasquez and Manuel Garcia y Griego, eds. *Mexican-U.S. Relations: Conflict and Consequence* (Los Angeles: Chicano Studies Research Center and Latin American Center, University of California at Los Angeles, 1983) for various perspectives on Chicano-Mexican relations.

4. David J. Weber, ed., *Foreigners in their Native Land: Historical Roots of the Mexican Americans* (Albuquerque: University of New Mexico Press, 1973); Rodolfo Acuna, *Occupied America: A History of Chicanos* (New York: Harper and Row, 1981). Second Edition. Leonard Pitt, *The Decline of the Californios, A Social History of the Spanish-Speaking Californios, 1846–1890* (Berkeley: University of California Press, 1971).

5. This pattern was briefly disrupted during the late 1960s and early 1970s when some militant Chicano organizations took on Spanish labels. Today, while a few groups use Spanish labels, most do not.

6. Clearly, it is very difficult to determine why Mexican traditions, especially language, have survived so well. During the 1960s, a survey in Los Angeles and San Antonio found that Mexican Americans were relatively unconcerned about retaining Mexican values. See Leo Grebler, Joan W. Moore, and Ralph C. Guzman, *The Mexican American People: The Nation's Second Largest Minority* (New York: Free Press, 1978). More recently 77 percent of respondents to the 1984 Texas Survey described in this paper stated that it was very or somewhat important to maintain Mexican traditions. However, when asked to rank how important each of four holidays was to them, 87 percent and 91 percent ranked July 4 and Thanksgiving as very or somewhat important. Cinco de Mayo and 16 de Septiembre, two of Mexico's holidays that are celebrated in most Mexican American communities across the nation, were ranked this high by 46 percent and 47 percent respectively.

7. This question has most recently been raised by Nathan Glazer, "Political Mobilization: Mexican Americans in Comparative Perspective," a paper presented at the conference on "Lessons from Other Societies: Mexican Americans in Comparative Perspective," sponsored by the Urban Institute, Los Angeles, California, March 1984. See also Rodolfo O. de la Garza, "Chicano-Mexican Relations: A Framework for Research," *Social Science Quarterly,* Vol. 63, No. 1 (March 1982), pp. 115–136 and Garcia y Griego and Vasquez.

8. The sources for the attitudinal data are: Rodolfo O. de la Garza, *Public Policy of Chicano Elites,* U.S.-Mexico Project Series Working Paper No. 7 (Washington, D.C.: Overseas Development Council, 1982); Lawrence W. Miller, Jerry L. Polinard, and Robert Wrinkle, "Attitudes Toward Undocumented Workers: The Mexican American Perspective," *Social Science Quarterly,* Vol. 65, No. 2 (June 1984), 484; Rodolfo O. de la Garza and Robert R. Brischetto, *The Mexican American Electorate: Information Sources and Policy Orientations* (San Antonio: Southwest Voter Registration Education Project and The Center for Mexican American Studies, University of Texas at Austin, 1983); SVREP community leader surveys conducted in 1983–84.

9. The quotations included in this section are taken from the testimony provided during 1983 hearings conducted by the Committees on Education and Labor and Committee on Agriculture, U.S. House of Representatives, and the U.S. Senate Subcommittee on Immigration and Refugee Policy.

10. *Los Angeles Times* survey, February, 1983.

11. Richard Salvatierra, "Reaccion Hispana Ante Immigracion," *La Voz,* Semana IV, Julio de 1984.

12. These arguments are discussed in detail in Rodolfo O. de la Garza and Adela Flores, "The Impact of Mexican Immigrants on the Political Behavior of Chicanos: A Clarification of Issues and Some Hypotheses for Future Research," in Harley Browning and Rodolfo O. de la Garza, *Mexican American Community* (Austin: Hispanic Population Studies Program, forthcoming); Thomas Muller, *The Fourth Wave: California's Newest Immigrants: Summary* (Washington, D.C.: The Urban Institute, 1984); Gilberto Cardenas, Rodolfo O. de la Garza, and Niles Hansen, "Mexican Immigrants and the Chicano Ethnic Economy," in Browning and de la Garza.

6. Thomas Muller: "Economic Effects of Immigration"

1. Congressional Record, June 13, 1984, H5711.

2. Congressional Record, June 20, 1984, H6087.

3. Congressional Record, June 19, 1984, H16052.

4. Congressional Record, June 20, 1984, H6116.

5. *Newsweek*, June 16, 1984.

6. Thomas Muller, *The Fourth Wave* (Washington, D.C.: The Urban Institute Press 1985), appendix.

7. Barry R. Chiswick, "Progress of Immigrants: Some Apparently Universal Patterns," in Chiswick, ed., *The Gateway: U.S. Immigration Issues and Policies* (Washington, D.C.: American Enterprise Institute, 1982); and Jean B. Grossman, "The Suitability of Natives and Immigrants in Production," *Review of Economic and Statistics* no. 4 (1982).

8. Francisco Rivera-Batiz, "The Effects of Immigration in a Distorted Two-Section Economy," *Economic Inquiry* 19, no. 4 (1981).

9. Brinley Thomas, *Migration and Economic Growth* (London: Cambridge University Press, 1973).

10. Ibid.

11. Testimony of Althea Simmons, Director, Washington Bureau, NAACP, at Joint Hearing of the Subcommittee on Immigration, Refugees and International Law, April 1, 1982.

12. California Mexican Fact-Finding Committee. *Mexicans in California* (San Francisco: State of California, 1930).

13. Los Angeles County Board of Supervisors, *Cost of Services to Undocumented Aliens*, Mimeo, April, 1982.

14. Julian S. Simon, *What Immigrants Take from and Give to the Public Coffers*, Final Report to the Select Commission on Immigration and Refugee Policy, August 17, 1980 (Washington D.C.: U.S. Govt. Printing Office).

15. Muller, summary.

16. Sidney Weintraub, "Illegal Immigrants in Texas: Impact on Social Service and Other Considerations," Paper presented at Annual Conference of the American Political Science Association, Washington D.C., August, 1984.

17. Hope T. Eldridge and Dorothy S. Thomas, *Population Redistribution and Economic Growth, United States, 1870–1950*, Volume III (Philadelphia: The American Philosophical Society, 1964).

7 Vernon M. Briggs, Jr. "Employment Trends and Contemporary Immigration Policy"

1. John Herbers, "Census Data Show Gains in Housing and in Education; Summary Also Indicates Rise in Foreign-Born Population," *New York Times*, April 20, 1982, p. A-1.

2. Leon F. Bouvier, *The Impact of Immigration on the Size of the U.S. Population* (Washington, D.C.: Population Reference Bureau, 1981), p. 1.

3. Leon F. Bouvier, *Immigration and Its Impact on U.S. Society* (Washington, D.C.: Population Reference Bureau, 1981), p. 23.

4. Vernon M. Briggs, Jr., "Special Labor Market Segments" in *Manpower Research and Labor Economics* edited by Gordon L. Swanson and Jon Michaelson (Beverly Hills, CA: Sage Publications, 1979), pp. 243–276.

5. National Commission on Employment and Unemployment Statistics, *Counting The Labor Force* (Washington, D.C.: U.S. Government Printing Office, 1979), p. 101. (Note: the Commission was only concerned with the lack of data of illegal immigrants. This concern is very important but the lack of good data on legal immigrants, nonimmigrants, and refugees in the labor market also hampers effective evaluation of their respective influences on selected labor markets).

6. U.S. House of Representatives, Select Committee on Population, "Report on Legal and Illegal Immigration to the United States," (Washington, D.C.: U.S. Government Printing Office, 1978), p. 47.

7. *Elkie* v. *United States* 142 US 651 (1892).

8. David North and Allen LeBel, *Manpower and Immigration Policies in the United States* (Washington, D.C.: National Commission for Manpower Policy, 1978), p. 40.

9. Jacob S. Siegal, Jeffrey S. Passel, and J. Gregory Robinson, "Preliminary Review of Existing Studies of the Number of Illegal Residents in the United States," Mimeographed report by the U.S. Bureau of the Census, January, 1980, p. 20.

10. U.S. General Accounting Office, *Problems and Options in Estimating the Size of the Illegal Alien Population*, GAO/IPE 82-9 (Washington, D.C.: U.S. General Accounting Office, 1982), p. 17.

11. Bouvier, *Immigration and Its Impact*, p. i of the inside cover to the volume.

12. David S. North and William G. Weissert, *Immigrants and the American Labor Market Manpower Research, Monograph No. 31* (Washington, D.C.: U.S. Department of Labor, 1974), pp. 18–22.

13. North and LeBel, p. 226.

14. David S. North, *Seven Years Later: The Experiences of the 1970 Cohort of Immigrants in the United States,* R. and D. Monograph No. 71 (Washington, D.C.: U.S. Department of Labor, 1979); Barry R. Chiswick, *An Analysis of the Economic Progress and Impact of Immigrants,* A report to the U.S. Department of Labor prepared under R. and D. Contract No. 21-06-78-20 (June 1980); See also Barry R. Chiswick, "The Effect of Americanization on the Earnings of Foreign Born Men," *Journal of Political Economy* (October, 1978), pp. 897–921, and "Sons of Immigrants: Are They at an Earnings Disadvantage?" *American Economic Review* (February 1977), pp. 376–380 as corrected by an *errata* in the *American Economic Review* (September, 1977), p. 775; see also Barry R. Chiswick, "The Economic Progress of Immigrants: Some Apparently Universal Patterns" edited by Barry Chiswick, *The Gateway: U.S. Immigration and Policies* (Washington, D.C.: American Enterprise Institute, 1982), pp. 119–158.

15. North, *Seven Years Later,* p. 10.

16. *Ibid.*

17. Gregory DeFreitas and Adriana Marshall, "Immigration and Wage Growth In U.S. Manufacturing in the 1970s," Paper presented at the 36th Annual Meetings of the Industrial Relations Research Association, San Francisco, California, (December 29, 1983). The paper will be published in the forthcoming *Proceedings* of that meeting.

18. David S. North and Marion F. Houstoun, *The Characteristics and Role of Illegal Aliens in the U.S. Labor Market: An Exploratory Study* (Washington, D.C.: Linton & Company, 1976).

19. Maurice D. Van Arsdol Jr., Joan Moore, David Heer, Susan P. Haynie, *Non-Apprehended and Apprehended Undocumented Residents in the Los Angeles Labor Market.* Final Draft submitted to the U.S. Department of Labor under Research Contract No. 20-06-77-16, (May, 1979), p. 27.

20. U.S. Senate and U.S. House of Representatives, Subcommittee on Immigration, Refugees, and International Law and Subcommittee on Immigration and Refugee Policy of the Respective Committees on the Judiciary. Joint Hearings, "Statement by Malcolm Lovell, Under Secretary of Labor," (April 20, 1982) (Washington, D.C.: U.S. Government Printing Office, 1982), p. 367.

21. U.S. Department of Commerce, *1980 Census of Population and Housing Provisional Estimates of Social, Economic and Housing Characteristics* (Washington, D.C.: U.S. Government Printing Office, 1982), Table P-2, p. 14–19.

22. North and Weissert, Table 9, p. 67 and also see *1979 Statistical Yearbook of the Immigration and Naturalization Service* (Washington, D.C.: U.S. Government Printing Office, 1982), Table 12A, p. 31.

23. Barry R. Chiswick, *The Employment of Immigrants in the United States,* (Washington D.C.: American Enterprise Institute, 1983).

8. Ivan Light: "Immigrant Entrepreneurs in America: Koreans in Los Angeles"

1. *Los Angeles Times,* April 13, 1980, II, 1.

2. *Los Angeles Times,* February 25, 1979, VIII, 1.

3. Illsoo Kim, *New Urban Immigrants: The Korean Community in New York* (Princeton: Princeton University Press, 1981).

4. Ivan Light, "Immigrant and Ethnic Enterprise in North America," *Ethnic and Racial Studies* 7 (1984): 198.

5. Margo A. Conk, "Immigrant Workers in the City, 1870–1930: Agents of Growth or Threats to Democracy?" *Social Science Quarterly* 62 (1981): 711.

6. U.S. Bureau of the Census, *Census of the Population, 1970. National Origin and Language.* PC2-1A. (Washington, D.C.: U.S. Government Printing Office, 1970), T16.

7. Robert Higgs, "Participation of Blacks and Immigrants in the American Merchant Class, 1890–1910: Some Demographic Relations," *Explorations in Economic History* 13 (1976), T3.

8. Calvin Goldscheider, and Frances Kobrin, "Ethnic Continuity and the Process of Self-Employment," *Ethnicity* 7 (1980): 256–278.

9. Martin T. Katzman, "Urban Racial Minorities and Immigrant Groups: Some Economic Comparisons," *American Journal of Economics and Sociology* 30 (1971): 22.

10. U.S. Bureau of the Census, *1980 Census of Population* Vol. 1. *Characteristics of the Population.* Ch. C. *United States Summary.* PC80-1-C1. Washington, D.C./:U.S. Government Printing Office, p. 72, 99, 119, 263.

11. Sandra Wallman, "The Scope for Ethnicity," pp. 1–14 in Sandra Wallman, ed. *Ethnicity at Work.* (London: Macmillan, 1979).

12. Lovell-Troy, "Ethnic Occupational Structures: Greeks in the Pizza Business," *Ethnicity* 8 (1981): 82–95.

13. Roger Waldinger, "Immigrant Enterprise and Labor Market Structure," Paper presented at the Annual Meeting of the American Sociological Association, San Francisco, Sept. 6th, 1982.

14. Raymond Russell, "Ethnic and Occupational Cultures in the New Taxi Cooperatives of Los Angeles," Paper presented at the Annual Meeting of the American Sociological Association, San Francisco, Sept. 6th, 1982.

15. Kevin B. Blackistone, "Arab Entrepreneurs Take Over Inner City Grocery Stores," *Chicago Reporter* 10 (1982): 1–5.

16. Janet B.L. Chan, and Yuet-Wah Cheung. "Ethnic Resources and Business Enterprise: A Study of Chinese Businesses in Toronto," Paper presented at the Annual Meeting of the American Sociological Association, San Francisco, Sept. 6th, 1982.

17. Walter P. Zenner, "Arabic-Speaking Immigrants in North America as Middleman Minorities," *Ethnic and Racial Studies* 5 (1982): 457–477; and Mary Catherine Sengstock, "Maintenance of Social Interaction Patterns in an Ethnic Group." Ph.D. Diss., Washington University, 1967.

18. Mokkerom Hossain, "South Asians in Southern California: A Sociological Study of Immigrants from India, Pakistan, and Bangladesh," *South Asia Bulletin* 2 (1982): 74–83.

19. Saskia Sassen-Koob, "Recomposition and Peripheralization at the Core," *Contemporary Marxism* 5 (1982): 88–100.

20. Robin Ward, and Richard Jenkins, eds. *Ethnic Communities in Business* (Cambridge: Cambridge University Press, 1984).

21. Howard Aldrich, John C. Cater, Trevor P. Jones, and David McEvoy, "Business Development and Self-Segregation: Asian Enterprise in Three British Cities," pp. 170–190 in Ceri Peach, Vaughan Robinson, and Susan Smith, eds. *Ethnic Segregation in Cities* (Athens, Ga.: University of Georgia, 1981).

22. Kenneth L. Wilson, and Alejandro Portes. "Immigrant Enclaves: An Analysis of the Labor Market Experiences of Cubans in Miami," *American Journal of Sociology* 86 (1980): 303.

23. Alejandro Portes, Juan M. Clark, and Manuel M. Lopez, "Six Years Later: the Process of Incorporation of Cuban Exiles in the United States: 1973–1979," *Cuban Studies* 11–12 (1981–82): 18.

24. Jeffrey Reitz, *The Survival of Ethnic Groups* (Toronto: McGraw Hill, 1980).

25. Ibid., p. 164.

26. C. Wright Mills, *White Collar* (New York: Oxford University Press, 1951).

27. Mitchell Gelfand, "Chutzpah in El Dorado: Social Mobility of Jews in Los Angeles, 1900-1920." Ph.D. Diss., Carnegie-Mellon University, 1981.

28. Ivan Light, "Immigrant and Ethnic Enterprise in North America."

29. Robert V. Robinson, "Reproducing Class Relations in Industrial Capitalism," *American Sociological Review* 49:183.

30. Eui-Young Yu, "Occupations and Work Patterns of Korean Immigrants in Los Angeles." Ch. 3 in Eui-Young Yu, Earl H. Phillips, and Eun Sik Yang, eds. *Koreans in Los Angeles* (Los Angeles: Koryo Research Institute and California State University at Los Angeles, 1982), p. 51.

31. See Chapter 2, Ivan Light *Ethnic Enterprise in America* (Berkeley and Los Angeles: University of California, 1972).

32. Kunae Kim, "Rotating Credit Associations among the Korean Immigrants in Los Angeles: Intracultural Diversity Observed in their Economic Adaptation." M.A. Thesis, Department of Anthropology, University of California at Los Angeles, 1982, p. 21.

33. Kwang Chung Kim, and Won Moo Hurh, "The Formation and Maintenance of Korean Small Business in the Chicago Minority Area." Macomb, Ill. (1984): Department of Sociology and Anthropology of Western Illinois University.

34. Ivan Light, *Cities in World Perspective* (New York: Macmillan, 1983), pp. 322–23, 352.

35. Daniel Bell, *The End of Ideology* (New York: Free Press, 1960), p. 127.

9.   Peter I. Rose: "Asian Americans: From Pariahs to Paragons"

1. A Gallup Poll conducted for *Newsweek* during the time of the debates over the Simpson-Mazzoli immigration reform bill asked a random sample of adults the question, "Do you think the number of immigrants now entering the U.S. from each of the following areas is too many, too few, or just right?" Fifty-three percent thought there were too many coming from Latin America while 49 percent said the same about Asia. Far fewer felt that way about Africans (31 percent) or Europeans (26 percent). See *Newsweek*, June 25, 1984, p. 21.

2. *The Journal and Miscellaneous Notebooks of Ralph Waldo Emerson*, ed. William H. Gilman (Cambrige, Mass.: Belknap Press of Harvard University Press, 1961), p. 244.

3. See, for example, Calvin F. Schmid and Charles E. Noble, "Socioeconomic Differentials among Non-White Races," *American Sociological Review* 30 (1965): 909–922; Stanley Lieberson, *A Piece of the Pie* (Berkeley: University of California Press, 1981); and Thomas Sowell, *Essays and Data on American Ethnic Groups* (Washington, D.C.: The Urban Institute, 1978).

4. The term "model minority" for Asian Americans was popularized by William Petersen in "Success Story: Japanese American Style," *New York Times Magazine,* ed. George DeVos (Berkeley and Los Angeles: University of California Press, 1973).

5. William Petersen, "Chinese Americans and Japanese Americans," in *American Ethnic Groups,* ed. Thomas Sowell (Washington, D.C.: The Urban Institute, 1978), pp. 65–66.

6. Robert Lindsey, "The New Asian Immigrants," *New York Times Magazine,* May 9, 1982, pp. 22–28.

7. "Asian-Americans: The Drive to Excel," *Newsweek,* April, 1984, pp. 4–8, 10–11, and 13.

8. Ibid., p. 13.

9. See Thomas Sowell, *The Economics and Politics of Race* (New York: William Morrow and Company, 1983), especially the chapters entitled "The Overseas Chinese" and "The American Experience," pp. 26–50 and 183–206.

10. Diane Mei Lin Mark and Ginger Chih, *A Place called Chinese America* (Dubuque, Ia.: Kendall/Hunt Publishing Company, 1932), pp. 109–110.

11. Ibid., pp. 155–169. Also see Bok-Lim C. Kim, *The Asian Americans: Changing Patterns, Changing Needs* (Montclair, N.J.: Association of Korean Christian Scholars in North America, 1978).

12. Harry H.L. Kitano, *Japanese Americans,* 2nd edition (Englewood Cliffs, N.J.: Prentice Hall, 1976), pp. 204–205.

13. Ibid.

14. William Petersen, "Chinese Americans and Japanese Americans," in *American Ethnic Groups,* p. 89.

15. George Stewart, *American Ways of Life* (Garden City, N.Y.: Doubleday, 1954), pp. 11–12. See also Tricia Knoll, *Becoming American* (Portland, Ore.: Coast to Coast Books, 1982).

16. See Herbert Hill, "Anti-Oriental Agitation and the Rise of Working-Class Racism," *Transaction/Society* 10(1973): 43–54; and Stanford Lyman, *Chinese Americans* (New York: Random House: 1974), Chapter 4, "The Anti-Chinese Movement in America," pp. 54–85.

17. See Lyman, Chapter 3, "Chinese Community Organization in the United States," pp. 29–53.

18. Norbert Wiley, "The Ethnic Mobility Trap and Stratification Theory," *Social Problems* 15(1967): 146–149.

19. Victor G. and Brett De Bary Nee, *Longtime, Californ'* (New York: Pantheon, 1973).

20. Melford S. Weiss, *Valley City: A Chinese Community in America* (Cambridge, Mass.: Schenkman, 1974).

21. U.S. Bureau of the Census, *Race of the Population by States,* 1980 (PCBO-SI-3).

22. See Stanford Lyman, *The Asian in the West,* Social Science and Humanities Publication No. 4 (Reno: Western Studies Center, Desert Research Institute, University of Nevada, 1970).

23. See Michi Weglyn, *Years of Infamy* (New York: William Morrow and Company, 1976).

24. William Petersen, *Japanese Americans* (New York: Random House, 1971), p. 131.

25. See Sowell, *American Ethnic Groups.*

26. Milton M. Gordin, *Assimilation in American Life* (New York: Oxford University Press, 1964). See especially pp. 60–83.

27. Akemi Kikumura and Harry H.L. Kitano, "Interracial Marriage: A Picture of the Japanese-Americans," *Journal of Social Issues* 20(1973): 67–81.

28. See Harold H. Sunoo and Sonia S. Sunoo, "The Heritage of the First Korean Women Immigrants in the United States: 1903–1924," *Korean Christian Journal* 2(1977): 144, 165.

29. Vincent N. Parrillo, *Strangers on these Shores* (Boston: Houghton Mifflin, 1980) p. 297. See also Lee Houchins and Chang-so Houchins, "The Korean Experience in America, 1903–1924," *Pacific Historical Review* 43(1974): 560.

30. See Illsoo Kim, *The Urban Immigrants: The Korean Community in New York* (Princeton: Princeton University Press, 1981).

31. Lisa Belkin, "For City's Korean Greengrocers, Culture Often Clashes with the Law," *New York Times,* August 11, 1984, pp. 25, 28.

32. Fred Cordova, *Filipinos: The Forgotten Asian Americans* (Seattle: Demonstration Project for Asian Americans, 1983).

33. See Maxine P. Fisher, *The Indians of New York* (New York: South Asian Books, 1980).

34. Ibid., p. 136. See also John Ness, "The South Asians: City's Mysterious Immigrants," *The New York Times,* October 7, 1972, p. 49; and Robert J. Fornaro, "Asian-Indians in America: Acculturation and Minority Status," *Migration Today* 12(1984): 28–32.

35. Lemuel Ignacio, *Asian Americans and Pacific Islanders: Is There Such an Ethnic Group?* (San Jose, Cal.: Pilipino Development Associates, 1976). For another view, see Paul Wong, "The Emergence of the Asian American Movement," *The Bridge* 2(1972): 32–39.

36. Fisher, p. 137.

37. See *Pinoy Know Yourself: An Introduction to the Filipino American Experience* (Santa Cruz: Third World Teaching Resource Center, Merrill College, University of California at Santa Cruz, 1976).

38. Of the relatively few publications dealing with the immigration of people from the Philippines, there is no consistency regarding the spelling of the names of group members. Some, like Cordova, use "Filipino." Others use "Pilipino."

39. Harry H.L. Kitano, "Asian Americans: The Chinese, Japanese, Koreans, Pilipinos, and Southeast Asians," *The Annals of the American Academy of Political and Social Sciences* 454(1981): 135.

40. H. Brett Melendy, "Filipinos," *Harvard Ethnic Encyclopedia of American Ethnic Groups,* ed. S. Thernstrom (Cambridge, Mass.: Harvard University Press, 1980), p. 357.

41. *Statistical Abstract of the United States,* 1984 edition, p. 91 (Source: U.S. Immigration and Naturalization Service, Annual Report of 1980).

42. Lindsey, pp. 22–28.

43. *The Bridge* July (1984): 9.

44. Ibid.

45. W. Stanley Mooneyham, *Sea of Heartbreak* (South Plainfield, N.J.: Logos International, 1980).

46. Once established by precedent, heavy government aid has been used to assist in the resettlement of others fleeing from communist states, including Soviet Jews, Poles, "Marielitos," and some Ethiopians and Afghans. See Peter I. Rose, "The Harbor Masters: American Politics and Refugee Policy," in *Social Problems and Public Policy* (Greenwich, Conn.: JAI Press, 1984). Also see Julia V. Taft et al., *Refugee Resettlement in the U.S.: Time for a New Focus* (Washington, D.C.: New Transcentury Fund, 1979).

47. Recent analyses include Bruce Grant, *The Boat People* (New York: Penguin Books, 1980); Barry Wain, *The Refused* (New York: Simon and Schuster, 1981); Peter I. Rose, "Links in a Chain: Observations of the American Refugee Program in Southeast Asia," *Migration Today* 9, no. 3 (1981): 6–24; and Peter I. Rose, "From Southeast Asia to America," *Migration Today* 9, no. 4 (1981): 22–28.

48. Peter I. Rose, "Some Reflections on Refugee Policy," *Dissent* (Fall 1984): 484–486.

49. John Finck, "The Indochinese in America: Progress Toward Self-Sufficiency," *World Refugee Survey,* 1983, pp. 56–59. There are negative reports, too, especially those that detail the activities of the Vietnamese—and other Asians—involved in organized crime in the U.S. See, for example, "Triads and Yakuza," *Time,* November 5, 1984, p. 30.

50. See "Southeast Asian Refugees in the U.S.A.: Case Studies in Adjustment and Policy Implications," special issue of the *Anthropological Quarterly* 55(July 1982).

51. Han T. Doan, "Vietnamericans: Bending Law or Breaking in the Acculturation Process?", unpublished paper presented at the 92nd annual meeting of the American Sociological Association, 1979. See also Gail Paradise Kelly, *From Vietnam to America* (Boulder, Colo.: Western Press, 1977) and Darrel Montero, *Vietnamese Americans* (Boulder, Colo.: Western Press, 1979).

52. Nathan Glazer, *Ethnic Dilemmas: 1964–1982* (Cambridge, Mass.: Harvard University Press, 1983), p. 315. Glazer is quoting from his and Moynihan's book, *Beyond the Melting Pot,* 2nd edition (Cambridge, Mass.: Harvard-MIT, 1971), p. xxiii.

53. *Ethnic Dilemmas,* pp. 319–323.

54. Ibid., p. 331.

55. See Ignacio.

56. Francis L.K. Hsu discusses the reality of marginality and the positive functions of double identity for Chinese-Americans in *The Challenge of the American Dream* (Belmont, Cal.: Wadsworth, 1971), pp. 129–131. This remains a rather common view among those writing about the various Asian American communities from outside as well as in. It is less well accepted by those concerned with the integration of Hispanics. See, for example, James Fallows' lengthy article, "The New Immigrants," *The Atlantic,* November, 1983.

10.   Nathan Glazer: "Immigrants and Education"

1. Heinz Kloss, *The American Bilingual Tradition* (Rowley, Mass.: Newbury House, 1977).

2. Diane Ravitch, *The Great School Wars; New York City, 1805–1973* (New York: Basic Books, 1974; and Tyack, David, *The One Best System* (Cambridge, Mass.: Harvard University Press, 1974).

3. Joshua A. Fishman, *Language Loyalty in the United States* (The Hague: Mouton, 1966).

4. Nathan Glazer, "Black English and Reluctant Judges," *The Public Interest,* No. 62 (Winter 1981): 40–54.

5. James S. Coleman, and others, *Equality of Educational Opportunity* (Washington, D.C. U.S. Department of Health, Education, and Welfare, 1966); and Frederick Mosteller, and Daniel P. Moynihan, *On Equality of Educational Opportunity* (New York: Random House, 1972).

6. Susan Gilbert Schneider, *Revolution, Reaction or Reform: The 1974 Bilingual Education Act* (New York: Las Americas, 1976).

7. Diane Ravitch, "The 'White Flight' Controversy," *The Public Interest,* Number 51 (Spring 1978): 104–105.

8. Nathan Glazer, *Ethnic Dilemmas, 1964–1982* (Cambridge: Harvard University Press, 1983). Chapter 7.

9. Iris C. Rotberg, "Federal Policy in Bilingual Education," *Harvard Educational Review,* 52, no. 2 (May 1982).

10. American Indians might be considered another exception, but it would be hard to think of them as equivalent to the Welsh or Bretons or other peoples incorporated into European nation-states. They occupied land for the most part as hunter-gatherers rather than agriculturists, and did not have developed state organizations; moreover, European settlers did not acknowledge their rights to occupy the land. They were thus akin to the Australian aborigines in their relation to European settlers rather than constituting small nations absorbed by the expanding European states.

11. U.S. Department of Commerce, The Condition of Hispanics in America Today (Washington, D.C.: Bureau of the Census, 1984).

12. Ibid.

13. U.S. Department of Commerce, *Asian and Pacific Islander Population by State: 1980* (Washington, D.C.: Burea of the Census) PC80-S1-12.

14. U.S. Department of Commerce, *Ancestry of the Population by State: 1980* (Washington, D.C.: Bureau of the Census). Supplementary Report PC80-S1-10, pp. 1–2.

15. *The Condition of Bilingual Education in the Nation, 1984.* A report from the Secretary of Education to the President and the Congress, U.S. Department of Education, pp. 13–14.

16. Thomas Cook, and others, *School Desegregation and Black Achievement* (Washington, D.C.: U.S. Department of Education, Office of Educational Research and Improvement, National Institute of Education, 1984).

17. *The Condition of Education,* National Center for Education Statistics, 1982, 1984. pp. 184–5.

18. *The Condition of Bilingual Education in the Nation, 1984,* pp. 2–3.

19. Barry R. Chiswick, "The Economic Progress of Immigrants: Some Apparently Universal Patterns," in *The Gateway: U.S. Immigration Issues and Policies,* ed. Barry R. Chiswick (American Enterprise Institute: Washington, D.C., 1982). 20.

20. *The Condition of Bilingual Education in the Nation, 1984,* Table 5.1. 21.

21. Leonard Dinerstein, "Education and the Advancement of American Jews," in *American Education and the European Immigrant: 1840-1940,* ed. Bernard J. Weiss (Champaign: University of Illinois Press, 1982), pp. 44–60; and Philip E. Vernon, *The Abilities and Achievements of Orientals in North America* (New York: Academic Press, 1982).

12.   Michael S. Teitelbaum: "Forced Migration: The Tragedy of Mass Expulsions"

1. One example of such a definition of expulsion is "that exercise of state power which ensures the removal, either voluntarily, under threat of forcible removal, or forcibly, of an alien from the territory of a State." Goodwin-Gill, Guy S., *International Law and the Movement of Persons Between States* (Oxford: Clarendon Press, 1978), p. 200.

2. Indeed, it is a surprising fact that the original Latin root of the English verb "to populate" is *populare,* which means "to lay waste, ravage, plunder" (*Oxford English Dictionary,* Vol. VII, p. 1126).

3. *Africa Research Bulletin,* August 1–31, 1972, p. 2568.

4. Fawcett, J.E.S., *World Today,* October 1972, p. 423.

5. Ghai, Yash P., "Expulsion and Expatriation in International Law: The Right to Leave, to Stay, and to Return," *American Journal of International Law* 67, no. 5 (November 1973): 126.

6. Ibid., p. 125.

7. Sacerdoti, Guy, "How Hanoi Cashes In," *Far Eastern Economic Review,* June 15, 1979, p. 24.

8. New economic zones were instituted in 1976. They entailed a massive population relocation from the cities to rural areas in order to cut urban unemployment and stabilize an inadequate agricultural system.

9. As of the late 1970s, there were nearly 10 million overseas Chinese in Southeast Asia (excluding the 2.5 million population of Singapore, which is predominantly Chinese). Most overseas Chinese resided in Vietnam (until the 1978–79 exodus), Thailand, Malaysia, and Indonesia. See, for example, *Encyclopaedia Britannica,* Volume 12, (Chicago: 1978), p. 187.

10. Das, K. "Refugees Rocking ASEAN's Boat," *Far Eastern Economic Review,* June 15, 1979, p. 22.

11. Ibid, p. 22.

12. Sacerdoti, p. 24.

13. Ibid.

14. The *New York Times,* "Vietnamese Blame China for Woes," June 15, 1982.

15. Wain, Barry, "The Indochina Refugee Crisis," *Foreign Affairs,* Fall 1979, p. 173.

16. Chiu, Hungdah, "China's Legal Position on Protecting Chinese Residents in Vietnam," *American Journal of International Law,* 74, No. 3 (July 1980): 686.

17. Winn, Peter, "Is the Cuban Revolution in Trouble?," *The Nation,* June 7, 1980, p. 682.

18. Friendlander, Dov and Goldscheider, Calvin, "Peace and the Demographic Future of Israel," *Journal of Conflict Resolution,* 18, no. 3 (Sept. 1974): 486–501.

19. The *New York Times,* April 4, 1983, page A3. Corroboration of this quotation has been sought from the Israeli Parliament, but this proved impossible since "all Knesset Committee sessions are held in camera and their minutes are not available for publication" (Letter from Shoshanna Kerem, Deputy Secretary General, Knesset, April 25, 1983).

20. *Economist* (London) 285, 13 November 1982, p. 30.

21. Jonathan Kuttab, "West Bank Arabs Foresee Expulsion," The *New York Times,* August 1, 1983, p. A14.

22. Oppenheim, L., *International Law,* 8th Edition, Volume I (London: Longmans, Green and Company, 1955), p. 692.

23. International Covenant on Civil and Political Rights, Article 13.

24. Oppenheim, p. 69; Weis, P., *Nationality and Statelessness in International Law* (London: Stevens and Sons, 1956), p. 51.

25. International Covenant on Civil and Political Rights, Article 12(4).

26. Weis, p. 51.

27. Oppenheim, pp. 645–646.

28. Weis, pp. 123–124.

29. Goodwin-Gill, p. 202–203; Weis, p. 129.

30. Weis, p. 238.

31. U.N. Commission on Human Rights, *Study on Human Rights and Massive Exoduses,* Sadruddin Aga Khan, Special Rapporteur, E/CN.4/1503, 31 December 1981, p. ii.

13. Peter H. Schuck: "Immigration Law and the Problem of Community"

1. C. Friedrich, "The Concept of Community in the History of Political and Legal Philosophy" in *Community (Nomos II)* 20 (1959).

2. See B. Ackerman, *Social Justice in the Liberal State* 89–95 (1980); C. Beitz, *Political Theory and International Relations* (1979): 161–76 and Fishkin, "The Boundaries of Justice," 27 *J. Conflict Resolution* (1983):355, 358–61. ("To the extent one gives independent weight . . . to a special class of persons within the [nation's] boundary, one is departing from the liberal paradigm for theories of justice.");

3. Yick Wo v. Hopkins, 118 U.S. 356, 369 (1886).

4. Prior to the Civil War, of course, all blacks—even those who were free—had been excluded from civic membership, as the *Dred Scott* decision confirmed. *Scott* v *Sanford,* 60 U.S. (19 How.) 393 (1856).

5. This ambiguous legislation died in conference during the closing days of the 98th Congress. Its sponsors intend to reintroduce it in 1985.

6. M. Walzer, "The Distribution of Membership," in *Boundaries: National Autonomy and Its Limits,* eds. P. Brown and H. Shue (Totowa, N.J.: Rowman and Littlefield 1983).

7. See J. Fishkin, *Limits of Obligation* (New Haven: Yale Univ. Press 1982), chap. 5.

8. Walzer, p. 32.

9. Schuck, "The Transformation of Immigration Law," 84 *Columbia Law Review* 1 (1984).

10. Ibid., pp. 10–12.

11. See cases cited ibid., p. 12.

12. See Ng Fung Ho v. White, 259 U.S. 276, 281–85 (1922); *The Japanese Immigrant Case,* 189 U.S. 86, 101 (1903). As a constitutional matter, at least, this is probably still the law.

13. 130 U.S. 581, 606 (1889).

14. For a recent analysis of this question, see Legomsky, "Immigration and the Principle of Plenary Congressional Power," 1984. *Supreme Court Review* (forthcoming).

15. Schuck, p. 15, notes 75 and 76.

16. Nishimura Ekiu v. United States, 142 U.S. 651, 660 (1892). Or in the more pointed formulation: "Whatever the procedure authorized by Congress is, it is due process as far as an alien denied entry is concerned." United States ex rel. Knauff v. Shaughnessy, 338 U.S. 537, 544 (1950).

17. United States ex rel. Knauff v. Shaughnessy, 338 U.S. 537 (1950).

18. Shaughnessy v. United States ex rel. Mezei, 345 U.S. 206 (1953).

19. For a critique of this doctrine, see Schuck and Smith, 'Consent, Community, and the Undocumented Alien: A Reappraisal" (unpublished ms., 1985).

20. Schuck.

21. The Supreme Court's recent decision in *INS* v *Phinpathya*, 104 S. Ct. 584 (1984), which will make it easier for the INS to reject illegal aliens' requests for discretionary relief from deportation, might also be viewed as anti-communitarian. On another reading, the Court did no more than construe the statute literally, leaving it to Congress to modify the policy if it wishes.

22. 457 U.S. 202 (1982).

23. See, for example, the recent decisions of the Eleventh Circuit Court of Appeals in the Jean and Fernandez-Boque cases cited below. 104 S. Ct. 2803 (1984).

24. 403 U.S. 365 (1971).

25. See, e.g., Cabell v. Chavez-Salido, 454 U.S. 432, 447 (1982).

26. See discussion and cases cited in Schuck, pp. 62–65, 68–72.

27. E.g., Jean v. Nelson, 727 F.2d 957 (11th Cir. en banc, 1984); Fernandez-Roque v. Smith, 734 F.2d 576 (11th Cir. 1984).

28. See Select Comm'n on Immigration and Refugee Policy, U.S. Immigration Policy and the National Interest 96 (1982).

29. See Abigail Thernstrom, "Language: Issues and Legislation," in *Harvard Encyclopedia of American Ethnic Groups,* Stephan A. Thernstrom, ed. (Cambridge, Mass.: Harvard University Press, 1980), pp. 619–628.

30. The pending proposal for a Constitutional amendment establishing English as the official language of the U.S., although almost certainly doomed to failure, suggests a growing public concern about the effects of linguistic diversity on community.

31. Placement Policy Task Force, Office of Refugee Resettlement, Department of Health and Human Services, Concept Paper on Refugee Placement Policy (1981). The concentration of Cuban, Haitian, and Salvadoran refugees in south Florida and New York, of course, is especially striking.

32. The earlier study is North and Houstoun, *The Characteristics and Role of Illegal Aliens in the U.S. Labor Market: An Exploratory Study* (1976). The subsequent misuse of that study is discussed by one of its authors in North, *Enforcing the Immigration Law: A Review of the Options* (Washington, D.C.: New TransCentury Foundation, 1980) pp. 73–74.

33. Van Arsdol, *Non-Apprehended and Apprehended Undocumented Residents in the Los Angeles Labor Market: An Exploratory Study* (Los Angeles: USC, 1979) p. 89, discussed in North, note 26 p. 74.

34. Los Angeles County, Dept. of Public Social Services, "Quarterly Report on Alien Status Verification Activity" (Los Angeles, February 6, 1980), also discussed in North, note 26 p. 74. For additional data and discussion bearing on the question of illegal aliens' use of public benefits, see Schuck and Smith, pp. 92–93 and sources there cited.

35. See sources cited at Schuck and Smith, pp. 92–93.

36. See Table 2 in Weicher, "The 'Safety Net' and the 'Fairness' Issue," *AEI Economist,* August 1984, p. 3.

37. Recent developments seem certain to exacerbate the situation. See Schuck, "Immigration Arteriosclerosis," *New York Times,* September 24, 1984.

CONTRIBUTORS

VERNON M. BRIGGS, JR. is professor of human resource economics in the New York State School of Industrial and Labor Relations at Cornell University. He has written numerous articles pertaining to low wage labor markets, minority group employment patterns, immigration policy, and public sector job creation. Among the books he has authored are *Chicanos and Rural Poverty* and *Immigration Policy and the American Labor Force.* He is also a co-author of a textbook entitled *Labor Economics: Wages, Employment, Trade Unionism and Public Policy.*

RODOLFO O. DE LA GARZA is director of the Center for Mexican American Studies and associate professor of government at the University of Texas at Austin. A specialist in Mexican and Chicano politics, his recent research has focused on the role that Mexican Americans play in U.S.-Mexican relations. He is co-author of *The Chicano Political Experience* and has contributed numerous articles on Chicano and Mexican politics to scholarly publications in Mexico and the United States.

LAWRENCE H. FUCHS is the Walter and Meyer Jaffe Professor of American Civilization and Politics at Brandeis University. Author of seven books and dozens of articles, most of which deal with American ethnic politics, Dr. Fuchs served as the executive director of the Select Commission on Immigration and Refugee Policy from May 1979 to May 1981. He has also served in numerous government advisory positions and as director of the Peace Corps in the Philippines between July 1961 and July 1983. A recipient of grants from the Ford, Rockefeller, Sloan, and Exxon Foundations to further his work on ethnicity and public policy, he is currently at work on a new book entitled *The Future of American Pluralism: Immigration, Ethnicity, and Public Policy,* to be published by the Wesleyan University Press.

NATHAN GLAZER, a pioneer in contemporary American sociology, has achieved distinction as an analyst of public policy related to ethnic and marginal groups in an urban context. He is professor of education and sociology at Harvard University, and co-editor of *The Public Interest.* He is the author of numerous influential articles, monographs, and books including *Ethnic Dilemmas: 1964– 82, Affirmative Discrimination: Ethnic*

335

Inequality and Public Policy, and *Beyond the Melting Pot* (with Daniel P. Moynihan). Among his many awards and honors are Guggenheim Fellowships and presidential task force appointments in urban affairs, education, and foreign scholarship.

EDWIN HARWOOD is visiting scholar at the Hoover Institution, Stanford University and a corporate communications consultant. His fields of expertise include criminal justice systems, organizational behavior, and the sociology of entrepreneurship. He has written numerous articles on public policy issues for the *Wall Street Journal, New York Times,* and *The Public Interest,* among other publications. He has just completed a manuscript, *In Liberty's Shadow: Illegal Aliens and Immigration Law Enforcement,* based on his study of the U.S. Immigration and Naturalization Service.

IVAN LIGHT is professor of sociology at the University of California, Los Angeles. He is the author of *Ethnic Enterprise in America, Cities in World Perspective,* and (with Edna Bonacich) *Immigrant Entrepreneurs,* a book-length manuscript nearing completion. *Immigrant Entrepreneurs* deals with Korean entrepreneurship in Los Angeles and is the source from which his contribution to this volume is derived.

HARRIS N. MILLER heads a government relations firm. He has served as a consultant to Congressman Romano L. Mazzoli (D.-Ky.) and on the staff of the U.S. House of Representatives Committee on the Judiciary. Formerly deputy director of congressional relations at the U.S. Office of Personnel Management and legislative director for Senator John A. Durkin (D.-N.H.), he recently ran for Congress. His writings have appeared in several books and scholarly journals, and he lectures on congressional topics.

THOMAS MULLER is principal research associate at The Urban Institute, which he joined in 1970. His work at the Institute has spanned several research areas, including regional growth and decline, economic effects of regulation, and annexation. Dr. Muller's recent work focuses on immigration and the economic effects of federal activities at the regional and local level. He has written extensively on urban economic problems and is co-editor of *Government and Policy.* Dr. Muller frequently testifies before Congress and local legislative bodies on fiscal issues.

PETER I. ROSE, Sophia Smith Professor and Director of the American Studies Diploma Program at Smith College and member of the graduate faculty of the University of Massachusetts, is currently a visiting scholar at Harvard University. He is the author of *They and We, The Subject Is Race, Strangers in Their Midst, Mainstream and Margins,* and editor of a number of volumes on sociology and contemporary society.

PETER H. SCHUCK is professor of law at Yale University. From 1977–79 he was deputy assistant secretary for planning and evaluation at the U.S. Department of Health, Education, and Welfare. His most recent book is *Suing Government: Citizen Remedies for Official Wrongs.* He has also published numerous articles and reviews in scholarly and policy journals and in more popular periodicals. He was awarded a Guggenheim Fellowship for 1984–85.

PETER SKERRY is presently the Robert Hartley Research Fellow at the Brookings Institution in Washington, D.C., where he is working on a book about Mexican American politics. He is the author of articles and reviews on social and political affairs that have appeared in the *Wall Street Journal, The New Republic, The Public Interest,* and other periodicals.

MICHAEL S. TEITELBAUM is program officer at the Alfred P. Sloan Foundation in New York. He has served on the faculties of Oxford University and Princeton University and as staff director of the Select Committee on Population, U.S. House of Representatives. His works include *The British Fertility Decline* and *The Fear of Population Decline.*